D1261158

THE
AMERICAN MALE

THE AMERICAN MALE

by Myron Brenton

London
GEORGE ALLEN AND UNWIN LTD

FIRST PUBLISHED IN 1967

This book is copyright under the Berne Convention. Apart from any fair dealing for the purpose of private study, research, criticism or review, as permitted under the Copyright Act, 1956, no portion may be reproduced by any process without written permission. Enquiries should be addressed to the Publishers.

PRINTED IN GREAT BRITAIN
BY PHOTOLITHOGRAPHY
UNWIN BROTHERS LIMITED
WOKING AND LONDON

TO VICTOR NIELSEN

Who made this book possible

Contents

Acknowledgments

An acknowledgments section in a book of social criticism is usually a paradox. It is here that the writer takes the opportunity of thanking all the people who provided him with information. It is also here that he gets them off the hook by taking full responsibility for the work as a whole. This acknowledgments section is no exception. I plumbed the minds of a great many people, most of them specialists in the various branches of the social sciences. They gave generously of their expertise. I also culled some 300 research publications in the form of books, journals, papers, doctoral dissertations, and the like. And in unstructured interviews I elicited information from several dozen men and women—low, middle, and upper-middle class—in various sections of the country. From them all, I obtained invaluable facts, opinions, and observations. But the way the data is pieced together—the life it takes and the points of view that emerge from it—is totally my own. Knowing the diversity of opinion (to put it mildly) that exists among the various social science disciplines, I'm fairly confident there's something in this book for everyone vehemently to agree with—and something for everyone violently to disagree with. The same, I judge, will hold true for the general reading public.

The fact that this is a book about the American male may in itself raise a fundamental objection. There are in America some half-dozen subcultures, and sub-subcultures galore, and all

9

kinds of ethnic, regional, and religious differentiations and constitutional variations, so who's this American male I'm writing about? Even in this age of ever-increasing specialization it's not possible to write about 88,331,494 men (total male population, 1960 census) on an individual basis. Certain major societal pressures make their impact on everyone, if in varying degree. For that matter there are many psychological reactions—especially in regard to women—that the American male has in common with men everywhere. When a study or other data has particular reference to a specific group, this is made clear. But on the whole the book concerns itself with broad social patterns and major societal trends as they affect the American male generally. Since the United States is by and large middle-class in terms of its values, the greater emphasis is given to middle-class patterns and trends.

The experts I interviewed, whose firsthand observations in clinical situations or in the field helped so much to crystallize my own thinking, belong to several distinct professional fields. Therefore, to facilitate thanking them here for their time, interest, and patience, I have fitted them into several loose-knit categories.

Members of the sociological-anthropological community: Dr. Garda Bowman, of the National Conference of Christians and Jews; Dr. Marvin Bressler, of Princeton University; Dr. Dan W. Dodson, of New York University; Professor Herbert J. Gans, of Teachers College, Columbia University; Dr. Reuben Hill, of the University of Minnesota; Dr. Samuel Jamison, of Valley State College; Dr. Mirra Komarovsky, of Barnard College, Columbia University; Dr. Margaret Mead, of the American Museum of Natural History; Dr. James A. Peterson, of the University of Southern California; Ann Raney, of the New School for Social Research; and Dr. Harold L. Sheppard, of the W. E. Upjohn Institute for Employment Research.

Members of the psychological community: Dr. Louis A.

Acknowledgments

Azorin, of Metropolitan State Hospital, Norwalk, California; Dr. Harvey J. Dain, of the Post Graduate Center for Mental Health; Dr. Ernest Dichter, of the Institute for Motivational Research; Dr. Leonard J. Duhl, of the Professional Services Branch, National Institute of Mental Health; Ruth Fizdale, of the Arthur Lehman Counseling Service; Dr. Harry Gershman, psychiatrist; Dr. Jules Golden, of the Albany Medical College; Dr. Ralph Greenson, psychiatrist; Jay Haley, of the Mental Research Institute, Palo Alto Medical Research Foundation; Dr. Howard Halpern, clinical psychologist; Dr. Raymond A. Katzell, of New York University; Ida Mermelstein, psychotherapist; Dr. Barbara Miller and Dr. Sutherland Miller, Jr., psychotherapists; Dr. Emily Mudd, of the University of Pennsylvania; Dr. Wardell Pomeroy, psychotherapist; Dr. Paul Popenoe, of the American Institute of Family Relations; and Dr. Isidore Portnoy, of the Karen Horney Clinic.

Agencies affiliated with the Family Service Association of America: Dr. Salvatore Ambrosino and Robert Sunley, of the Family Service Association of Nassau County, New York; Dorothy Cohen, of the Family Service Association of Wyoming Valley, Pennsylvania; Ruth Downing, of the Family Service of Memphis, Tennessee; Henry M. Graham, of the Family Service Association of Indianapolis; Dr. Gertrude M. Hengerer and staff, of the Family Service Association of Palo Alto and Los Altos, California; Jeanne Knakal, consultant to the Family Service Agency of Marin County, California; Franklin Parks, Mildred Proske, and Mildred F. Wogan, of the Family Service Society, New Orleans; Dr. Saul Scheidlinger and Thelma Stackhouse, of the Community Service Society of New York; Benjamin Sprafkin, of the Jewish Family Service of Philadelphia; Irwin M. Stein, of the Family Service of Westchester, New York; Nicholas M. Suntzeff, of the Family Service Agency of Marin County, California; John Theban and staff, of the Family and Child Services of Washington, D.C.; Mrs.

11

John H. Trimble, of the Family Service Agency of Princeton, New Jersey; and Clark E. Wooldridge, of the Family Service Association of Lubbock, Texas.

I especially want to mention four individuals whose generous assistance did a great deal to smooth the way in the writing of this book. Not the least of the rewards I count as a result of having called on each of them for help is the warm personal friendship that ensued. They are Oscar Rabinowitz, psychotherapist and staff member of the Child Study Association of America; Susan F. Roberts, Public Information Consultant, Family Service Association of America; Dr. Sophia Robison, professor emeritus of social research, Columbia University School of Social Work; and Dr. Paul Vahanian, psychotherapist and associate professor of education in marriage counseling, Teachers College, Columbia University.

Writers' wives are notoriously long-suffering. I'm grateful to mine not only for doing her duty in that respect, but also for the countless ways she helped in terms of insights, suggestions, and encouragement—and in just being around.

M.B.

I. The Male in Crisis

"He may have been a big hero in high school—president of the student body or a star athlete, that sort of thing. But then he gets out into the world, and he becomes a cog in the organization, and he comes home feeling defeated."—Psychotherapist Jeanne Knakal, during a conversation with the author.

The Active-Passive Man

This is a book about the plight of the contemporary American male. It's about the increasingly difficult choices he is having to make, about the multiplicity of demands he is having to meet, and, most of all, about the invisible straitjacket that still keeps him bound to antiquated patriarchal notions of what he must do or be in order to prove himself a man.

To be sure, the great outpouring of words about the contemporary American woman these past few years has made it seem as though the male either had no problems or didn't count enough to have them aired. An avalanche of books, magazine articles, television documentaries, radio talk shows, and socio-psychological symposiums has been concerned with her troubles. Her psyche—anguished, unfulfilled—has been laid bare for all of us to see. Her basic problem—how to integrate her traditional roles of wife and mother with the wider opportunities now open to her—is being discussed almost without end.

These observations aren't meant to disparage or to deny the reality of the American woman's problems. But when the plight of women is given such intense scrutiny, a curiously distorting effect tends to be created. Suddenly the world is seen only through the feminist prism. Suddenly the woman stands sharply removed from society as a whole, as though her difficulties could really be isolated from the roilings and seethings of societal change that affect both sexes. To the extent that the plight of men is ignored, that of women tends to seem less real.

One of the lady neofeminists, who has written extensively on the trapped-housewife syndrome, has dubbed it the "problem that has no name." The problems besetting men have many names. Call them boredom and restlessness and discontent and frustration. In some men they're intense and consistent. In the majority of men they're much more vague and sporadic. There's a feeling that the job, the wife, the sex, the kids, or the leisure time—in short, the good life—is . . . well . . . good, but not *that* good. Real fulfillment, one senses, is a long way around the corner. According to Dr. Emily Mudd, the famous marriage counselor: "Lots of times you have the feeling they're antagonized and irritated, but they don't know what at and just why." Commenting on his own life—which includes a pretty, charming wife, two bright children, a good income, and the usual split-level with the usual accessories that bespeak the affluent society —a thirty-six-year-old civil engineer told me:

> I don't get it. I've got everything. I really have. All the same, now and then, I get the feeling I'm in a prison or something. Happens when everything's on top of me, closing in, you know? That's when I start wondering if it's all worth it. Sometimes— this is funny because my Dad didn't have much of anything— sometimes I think he might have been better off.

When men—particularly middle-class men—talk honestly about themselves and their lives, the twin themes expressed by this civil engineer frequently crop up: (1) a feeling of somehow being harried, being trapped, and (2) a nostalgia for the old days, at least for an idealized—if inaccurate—version of them.

This is not to suggest that the American male of the mid-1960's is unmindful of what he has. He knows he's in the midst of material plenty—at the very least, plenty more than his father and grandfather had. He knows that his relationship with his wife and kids is more relaxed and easygoing and multifaceted than he recalls his father's or grandfather's being. So, when discontent is expressed, it's often expressed ambiguously—with both puzzlement and regret that this physical and psychical plentitude should create its own problems, exact its own toll. There's a hint of guilt, too, almost as though internally an accusing voice were saying, "You *know* how well off you are, you ungrateful son of a bitch. Why don't you *act* like it?"

Even if the restless, discontented feeling is no more than a faint emotional pinprick most of the time, easy to live with under the palliative effects of the daily routine, there are brief abrupt moments of painful clarity. I remember many men who confessed, when I interviewed them, that their military-service experience was—in restrospect—the time that they felt most "manly," or "rugged, the way a man ought to feel," or "the best time of my life someways, but don't tell my wife." I remember the magazine editor, a hidden corner of his mind illuminated by a couple of drinks, who swept his arms to encompass the concrete-and-glass-faced pillars of civilization that line both sides of Madison Avenue and shouted, "Every so often I feel like making it all disappear—start fresh. Hey, man, wouldn't you have liked to be a pioneer?" I remember the insurance underwriter who, while talking quietly to me, suddenly slapped his desk sharply with the flat of his hand and burst out, "There are times when I want to chuck it all and take a raft down the Amazon!" A week later he called to say that he was starting to take karate lessons.

The insurance underwriter himself provides an object lesson in terms of what is troubling the contemporary American male. He told me that, like everybody else, he has good days and bad ones with his wife, who, he says, is fairly strong-willed. ("Either

15

she tries to boss me around or bitches that I *let* her boss me.")
He loves his two young daughters but becomes impatient after
spending a little time alone with them. His job is somewhat
routine ("I'm a paper shuffler," he says), but he's up for a raise
and can't afford to look around for something better just yet,
because he's inundated by what he euphemistically calls budget
payments. He rarely pays cash for anything he buys.

This is the broad outline of his life, differing not too much
from that of many other men. Now, what lay behind his sudden
impulse to take up a distinctly "masculine" activity? Even without knowing much about him, we can guess that it had to do
with his sense of himself as a man. Actually, the impulse that
drove him to learn karate typifies a common masculine dilemma
these days. It's really two dilemmas, interconnected by their
relationship to the ancient images of maleness. They are:

*1. How to reconcile the sedentary, overrefined present, which
is marked by an extreme lack of physical challenges, with the
age-old image of the male as hunter, builder, hewer of wood,
and drawer of water—a male who, in short, establishes a primitive contact between himself and his surroundings.*

*2. How to reconcile the supposedly democratic present, with
its emphasis on equal rights for women, with the age-old image
of the male as provider, protector, and possessor—a male who,
in short, is given unquestioned sanction to exercise his patriarchal duties and prerogatives.*

It was, I submit, an attempt to resolve these dilemmas that
prompted the insurance underwriter to take up an exotic sport.
Nor is he unique in this respect. Whether they turn to karate or
auto racing or marksmanship or whatever other activity our
society gives a distinctly masculine label to, a great many American men make similar attempts to resolve the contradictions
between the images of the past and the realities of the present.
Does it work? In part, yes; in part, definitely not. Such men are
provided with instant, although momentary, therapy for their
fenced-in feeling. They gain a new outlet for their pent-up feel-

ings of aggression. They have the chance to test their mettle in a more fundamental physical way than the daily routine allows them to. And all this is valuable. But in a broader sense it doesn't make a man more manly. It doesn't give him the guts to stand up to his boss if standing up is needed, or the will to assert himself to a greater extent with an habitually henpecking wife, or the assurance he needs as a lover if he has always had fears about his sexual adequacy. It's fallacious to go in for a so-called masculine activity in order to arrive at a masculine attitude. The two just aren't synonymous, although it's characteristic of men caught in the masculinity trap to confuse activity with attitude.

Not all males whose masculine identity seems pallid to them in comparison with the way males supposedly were in times gone by take up a male-oriented sport or hobby, of course— any more than it can be said that all men who take up such sports or hobbies are motivated by a desire to be more manly. But we may generalize that the more a man looks to the past for some kind of masculine inspiration or confirmation, the more disadvantaged he will feel today. And the more disadvantaged he feels, the more prone he will be to compensate— whether the compensation takes the form of male activity or hostility or both.

We may also draw certain conclusions about activity in general. Although he's as sedentary as any modern male anywhere ("The American, even after subtracting the hours he lies down for sleep, spends most of his twenty-four hours on his rump," observed time and leisure expert Sebastian de Grazia),[1] the contemporary American male is at the same time quite active in all kinds of ways. This isn't as much of a contradiction as it sounds. A man can sit in a score of different places in a relatively short period of time—at work, in his car, in front of the television set, in a bar, at the theater, in a stadium, at a bridge table, or in a movie house. This makes him both sedentary and active at the same time. Furthermore, a relatively small but growing

17

number of men are spending some of their free time in really active pursuits—golfing, fishing, camping, and the like—at least in part as a reaction to their otherwise sedentary lives. Far from unusual is the energized St. Louis attorney who works eight to ten hours a day on his job, devotes six hours a week to his duties as program committee chairman for a social club, plays golf Saturday mornings, does organizational work for a local charity, and goes out of town professionally about a dozen times a year. Nor is the electronics assembler I met in Los Angeles atypical: In addition to his regular job, he moonlights four nights a week as a gas station attendant; he has a home workshop, where he fixes things for the people in the neighborhood; and he goes camping or to the beach with his family when the weather is warm enough.

The quest to fill up every last empty space of free time and the compulsion to have fun are phenomena often remarked upon by scholars, behavioral scientists, and social critics. Several recent popular books have dealt extensively with this aspect of American life. (One of the main themes of Walter Kerr's *The Decline of Pleasure* has to do with the American compulsion to turn free time into useful time. Max Gunther's *The Weekenders* is devoted to middle-class America's frantic round of weekend activities that provide little leisure and less fun and leave one exhausted for the weekday grind.) Even the new dances reflect the feeling that the good life is the exhausted one; it is possible to "frug" one's way into merciful oblivion.

The Protestant ethic with its Calvinistic devotion to toil and the fact that emergent America had no time for idleness and no room for the idle rich are the most common historical factors traditionally cited to explain the mystery of the activity-prone American. These factors are still applicable. And a potent new one has been added—namely, the growth of an outer-directed consumer society constantly being stimulated to want, to buy, to do.

This last factor applies in part most directly to the business

18

of earning a living. Indeed, there are tremendous pressures on the contemporary male to produce, to bring home the bacon in copious quantities. This is particularly true if he's married and has children and subscribes to the prevailing values; his obligations then are considerable. And how many men don't want to give their families as many of the good things in life as they can? For nearly 4,000,000 Americans, moonlighting—either part-time or full-time—is part of the daily pattern. Most moonlighters, surveys show, are married men between twenty-five and forty—precisely the time when they have growing families. Millions more regularly work overtime at their regular jobs. One of my male informants—a man employed in a professional capacity, with earnings in the low five figures, who was married and the father of three children—talked at length and with a bit of chagrin about this feature of modern American life. A resident of a middle-class Long Island, New York, community, he said:

> I can't think of one man I know who's working nine to five and satisfied with that. No matter how high you get, you're always holding on to some part-time work. The guys in my neighborhood—firemen, policemen, accountants—they're all working overtime. They've got something going in every direction. My father worked hard, he put in a good day, and that was it. Now you have a house and mortgage payments and your repairs and all the expenses for the kids. I mean, these are sort of basic; you can't get out of them no matter how you cut things. And then there's college. Even if you're earning fifteen thousand dollars a year, you can't relax, can't count on scholarships. You've got to hustle.

So the American male hustles. We have so often been called a competition-minded, status-seeking, success-oriented society that the point needs little elaboration here. What hasn't been especially emphasized is the connection between work, the fruits of work—like status and material possessions—and manliness. A man may seek any number of supplementary ways of confirming his masculine identity. But work is at the very core of it. I have in my files folders chock-full of case histories of men who broke down completely, whose personality changes were likened to shell shock, when they became suddenly unemployed. Men may suffer terribly from the death of a loved one, the breakup of a marriage, or some other personal tragedy. But what brings them to the point of immobilization most often is the loss of their jobs. Even when the job or career merely goes badly for a time, men often react much more drastically than when they're faced with other crises.

I emphasize the relationship between masculinity and work (*i.e.*, activity) for the contemporary American male because activity is a paradox. It's a way of accomplishing something, of reaching a goal. It may also be an artful way of running away from other, perhaps more fundamental involvements. The busier one is in a group of activities, the more acceptable an excuse one has for avoiding commitments on a deeper level elsewhere—commitments one feels less than adequate to handle. Am I suggesting that this is a trend applicable to the American male of the mid-1960's? When the evidence is sifted, it seems a reasonable conclusion. The men who do this aren't being calculating about it. This is no overt plot to dodge responsibilities in certain given areas. Without being consciously aware of it, they become highly active in some aspects of their functioning as a way of remaining passive—for passivity always denotes inadequacy—in other aspects. Dr. Ralph Greenson, a noted southern California psychiatrist, made these observations about the contemporary active-passive male:

A lot of what the men do doesn't look passive. You know, it's only passive when you look a little harder. I think so very many of the men are quite active, in a very superficial way. They perform all kinds of activities, but these have a warding-off defensive function. It's a characteristic of our society, especially of our big-city organizational society, that there's an agitated boredom that goes through everything. This looks like activity. Men are doing all kinds of things—except when you study what they're doing, they're performing avoidances of all kinds. These look superficially like satisfactions. And then you see that they're taking small satisfactions to avoid bigger ones, because the bigger ones bring in anxiety and danger.

Dr. Greenson was referring to the active-passive modern male generally. But one may apply his remarks to a very specific pattern. For many contemporary American males these are indeed times of anxiety and danger. It is not the danger that immediately springs to mind—the kind faced by a soldier in battle, a mountain climber scaling the heights, or a stunt flier performing his hazardous loops and turns—but a danger of a more subtle type. It is a danger within the context of human relationships.

For a variety of reasons the modern American faces far greater responsibilities than men did 50 or 100 years ago in what sociologist Dr. James A. Peterson of the University of Southern California calls the "affect area of the emotions." He faces far greater responsibilities, too, in exercising his masculine authority. Much more than yesteryear's male, he's expected to involve himself in the lives of his family members. But the same society that sets up these new expectations does little in the way of readying him to assume these added dimensions of human involvement. Thus, it's hardly a coincidence that, in my conversations with psychiatrists and caseworkers, I was repeatedly given case histories of men who displayed strength and vigor and assertiveness in the breadwinning role and possibly were quite active in the weekend round, but were undynamic, passive, or completely dependent in other aspects of life.

Irwin M. Stein, executive director of the Family Service of Westchester, New York, commented, "We get an amazing picture of the husband who is very active in the business world and maybe quite successful in some corporation and yet at home is a very passive or disinterested individual. We're getting quite a few of those." Repeatedly I was told, not only in the context of the clinical situation, but from a community-wide frame of reference, of men leading a "polygamous existence," as one sociologist aptly put it, "married to their jobs, as well as to their wives, and through a series of alienations living practically in name only with the latter." Several of the experts mentioned this phenomenon as being particularly applicable to many of the men who specialize in a narrow scientific area. There is an ever-growing number of such specialists, of course, and the pattern that emerges is one of males who place great emphasis on the material aspects of life, on intellect, and on achievement, but who have great difficulty involving themselves in family life on any other level. For them, as well as for similar men in other fields of endeavor, work becomes synonymous with love; by working, by achieving, they believe they are giving a full measure of love. It's by no means unusual, however, for such an individual to become embittered later on, when he realizes that achievement really hasn't brought him the love he thought would accompany it.

It should be noted that the syndrome of active men evading real family life is no respecter of class or status. When University of Michigan psychologists studied night-shift workers, they found that for a number of married men the night shift provides a refuge from the home.[2] When author Vance Packard explored the nation's pyramid-climbing executives, who put in more hours at work than any other occupational group, one of the things he found was that the executive often learns to use the office to avoid the home "and on weekends retreats to his golf club where everything is well ordered and his status confirmed at every turn."[3]

Of course, a considerable number of men in the larger corporations *seem* to be more assertive in their jobs than they really are. Fence-sitting is often developed into a specialty that sees a man through many long years of steady advancement. Decision

making by committee or computer or both can take the edge off
individual responsibility. In what is perhaps a sweeping judgment but one that has a measure of truth, sociologist C. Wright
Mills once wrote that "a bureaucracy is no testing field for
heroes." The corporation man sometimes emerges as much less
than heroic to the one person in a real position to know—his
secretary, on whom he often becomes markedly dependent. He
may rely on her completely. She stalls people he doesn't want
to see. She fields for him when his superiors are pressing him
for a decision he'd rather avoid making. She buys his wife's
birthday or wedding anniversary gift for him. In extreme cases
she presses his clothes in the office and makes sure that his tie
is on straight. A secretary to a major corporation executive who
went through this routine for five long but well-paid years told
me afterward, "Honestly, sometimes I got the feeling it was a
wonder he could even blow his nose alone."

The New Demands

Many of the enormous new demands being made on the
American male—demands he'd just as soon forget by losing
himself in his job, on the golf course, in the home workshop, or
elsewhere—find their wellspring in the female's more direct
assumption of power and greater expectation of having her own
needs gratified. Then too, women are proving their competency
in all the intellectual and occupational fields that were formerly
tagged "For Men Only." While they still have a long way to go
before they can claim equal pay for equal work, women are able
to maintain themselves quite nicely without male financial support, although in most states alimony laws are still based on the
unfair and unrealistic assumption that women are close to helpless. The old-fashioned diaphragm and the new-fashioned pill
allow women to have more freedom of decision in regard to
their sexual relations. Add to this the fact that an increasing

number of women are entering recreational and social domains heretofore exclusively reserved for men. What it adds up to is that masculinity is no longer assured solely by virtue of female dependency. For a significant number of men this is still an overwhelming fact. It renders them hostile and resentful toward women. Needless to say, hostile and resentful men create women similarly disposed toward them. The result is increased competition—not cooperation—between the sexes.

Beyond Surface Togetherness—Within the family itself the dislocations caused by the equalitarian trend have been considerably aggravated by another overwhelming change in family patterns over the past 100 years or so. Yesteryear's family was sizable. It included—in addition to parents and children—uncles, aunts, grandparents, siblings, and other members of the extended family. By contrast, today's family constellation has shrunk. It has largely become what the sociologists call nuclear, meaning that it consists only of father, mother, and offspring living together under one roof. This may seem an academic fact, something primarily of interest to social scientists. Actually, it's of tremendous importance to the male who is a husband and father. He's put in a position quite distinct from that of family men in earlier times.

This is so because, as Dr. Peterson pointed out, he's the single source of both male affection and male authority within this modern family. In times past, if a man was harsh or if he couldn't show affection, his wife would turn to other men in her family—her father, grandfather, brothers, or uncles—for succor, for nurture. They were right there, living in the same house or fairly close by. Now she must rely almost exclusively on her husband. If he doesn't live up to this added dimension of responsibility, she may channel all her affections toward her children or may plunge into extramarital affairs. Overmothered children are a common phenomenon in the United States, and infidelity on the part of wives is growing.

The same set of circumstances applies to the male's role as father. If in the past he failed to meet his paternal responsibilities, there were always other male family members around to act as surrogate fathers. Today it's all up to the father alone. If he ducks out on these responsibilities, the entire child-rearing job falls on his wife. This, again, may cause her to do more smothering than mothering. To be sure, working—that is, earning a living—is one aspect of fathering. It's one means that the father has of extending protection to his family. But it's *just* one. If he concentrates on this to the exclusion of other aspects, it becomes not a form of fathering, but an escape.

I am not suggesting that all—or even that the majority—of American men are never to be seen around their houses, that all wives are grass widows; all children, pitiful little half-orphans. It's true that many American men are occupied in ways that keep them physically out of the house a good deal of the time. It's also true that for a great many American men the home itself is a fulcrum of activity, even if much of it is concentrated on the weekend. They help their wives with the housework; they help the kids with the homework; they fix, repair, paint, and putter. Does this contradict my theme of uninvolvement on the part of the American male? I think not, unless involvement is made synonymous with activity. Surface togetherness—the family-that-plays-together-stays-together kind of thing—serves a desirable end when it isn't carried to absurd extremes. But when it becomes an end in itself, it definitely turns into a specious form of personal communication.

Thus, a man may dry the dinner dishes night after night, help diaper the baby, cook up a barbecue on Sunday afternoon, and regularly take his family for drives or to the movies. However, this doesn't necessarily demonstrate involvement. It doesn't serve as an index of his ability to be—or his adequacy as—a figure of strength and purpose for his family. It doesn't provide proof of his readiness to make decisions. It says nothing about his competence in communicating on the deepest emotional or,

25

for that matter, sexual level. You may serve barbecued steaks in the backyard because you like doing it. You may serve them because your wife likes barbecues and you want to please her. You may serve them, too, because your wife insists on it, and you find it easier to acquiesce than to put up your back, even if you can no longer stand the sight of charcoal and easy-flame solvent. Doing things around the house or with the family is by itself no proof of psychic involvement. In too many cases, doing things seems to be a substitute for such involvement.

This also holds true for a man's relationship with his growing children, particularly his sons. He may be a "pal" to them —something quite common these days—and thereby nourish the illusion that he's fulfilling his paternal responsibilities. He may be a compulsive kind of parent who pushes his boys to demonstrate masculinity either in terms of scholastic achievement—something that middle-class fathers are especially prone to do—or of excellence in a wide range of traditionally masculine activities. But such patterns of fathering don't imply involvement. They bespeak the father's inability to handle the paternal role, his failure to see his children as individuals with unique personalities.

The Man in the Kitchen—That men are increasingly performing tasks traditionally demarked female and that women are participating in areas formerly reserved for men are themselves causing a considerable amount of tension. There's a great deal of talk these days about the blurring of the roles, as if only through a rigid division of labor between the sexes people can retain their sexual identities. *Why the hell can't she act like a woman? Why on earth doesn't he act like a man? What's she trying to do, make a woman out of me? Why won't he let me be a person?* Questions like these, spoken and unspoken, hover in the air, poisoning the marital atmosphere.

When the situation is viewed with a modicum of perspective, it seems rather ludicrous that a man could be emasculated or exploited by sticking his paw into the dishwater or by sliding a spoonful of food into his baby's mouth. To be sure, there *are* men for whom such functions have a demasculinizing effect, who do them with the feeling that they're being turned into a second wife or mother. (Perhaps they are made to feel this way by other people, including their own wives.) But these henpecked men show their male inadequacy in a variety of ways, and their reaction of being demasculinized when they do traditionally female tasks is less a cause of unmanliness than a symptom of it. Yet indiscriminately, the cry of "Mama's helper" resounds from the lips of psychiatrists and nonprofessionals alike. Social observer Russell Lynes' melancholy observations are a case in point. Presenting his views—actually the views of a substantial number of American men—in a book called *A Surfeit of Honey,* Lynes calls today's husbands "the new servant class." Citing a few statistics—vague ones in the sense that they confirm only that men are helping around the house, not how often and to what extent—he writes:

> Man, once known as "the head of the family," is now partner in the family firm, part-time man, part-time mother and part-time maid. He is the chief cook and bottle washer; the chauffeur, the gardener and the houseboy; the maid, the laundress and the charwoman. [As for the man who doesn't help out at home, he's the] vestigial remnant of another age in which a man's position in the community was measured by the number of people who contributed to his creature comforts rather than by what he contributed to the community.[4]

The implication, probably unintended, is that the only way the male feels like a real man is if he's treated in the manner of a grand pasha. Actually, what's all the fuss about? Comprehensive sociological studies of American marriage patterns show the following: (1) The traditional division of labor in the home —husbands doing the repairs and other heavy work; wives occupied with kitchen, cleaning, and child-rearing chores—is

27

breaking down in favor of more sharing and (2) the breakdown of the old divisions isn't at all as extreme as popularly supposed.

When sociologist Mirra Komarovsky did an in-depth study of blue-collar marriages in 1964, she found that in four-fifths of the families under investigation, cooking, laundry, and cleaning were duties exclusively handled by the wives. Nearly two-thirds of the husbands hardly ever gave a hand with the dishes. As for child care, one-third of the husbands surveyed rarely helped, another third helped occasionally, and the rest helped on a regular basis.[5]

When sociologists Robert O. Blood, Jr., and Donald M. Wolfe surveyed 731 urban and suburban families of *all* classes in the metropolitan Detroit area, they found that the more income a husband makes, the more the *wife's* mean-task performance in the home rises. She may not necessarily do the actual work— very likely she can afford to hire help—but the responsibility is much more hers than it is in families on descending income levels. The authors suggest that the reason that the husband in a high-income family participates less in household chores is that he's "so absorbed in his career." In the Blood and Wolfe study, too, the vast majority of wives—70 percent—always did the most common shared household activity, washing the dishes, all by themselves. Although the two investigators believe that the majority of American families are no longer adhering to the old patriarchal values, even they are forced to admit that the "traditional sex roles in the home" will not "be abandoned in the foreseeable future. At least they are still very much in evidence." Cited as factors are the advantages of role specialization, individual preferences, and the biological differences between the sexes "which continue to influence the division of labor."[6]

What does it all mean? It means that unless one's point of reference is complete nonparticipation, the fact that contemporary husbands do some "woman's work" around the house isn't at all as striking a phenomenon as the worry about it indicates.

But the worry itself is illuminating. It shows how much relevance the patriarchal patterns still have. It discounts the fact that some men genuinely enjoy doing traditionally female household chores of one kind or another and that more men would own up to this if it weren't still thought of as somehow unmanly. It shows, too, the profound sense of insecurity with which many men face the equalitarian trend in the relationship between the sexes—an insecurity that goes far deeper than the surface question of doing chores at home. I was constantly astounded by the number of men who, when the topic of equality in marriage was introduced into our discussion, spontaneously—and bitterly —responded, "I don't see why a man has to wash the dishes at night after working hard all day." Their image of equality apparently was the lopsided one of the woman leading the man by the nose. Washing the dishes somehow represented the ultimate in subjugation. It never occurred to these men that they had the option of saying no, as well as yes, when they felt the pressure becoming too much for them, of talking things out with their wives, of retaining their autonomy.

Cornered in the Bedroom—The contemporary male faces sexual responsibilities far exceeding those of men in earlier times. He must gratify himself *and* his sexual partner. He has to make sure he's a better lover—or at least no worse—than other men. He has to cope with the sexually liberated woman, something that can require a considerable amount of coping. He has to put up with the bittersweet fact that while sex is fortunately no longer hidden away in the Victorian darkness, it has been pushed all the way to the other extreme, where every aspect is spotlighted for detailed examination—and himself along with it. Psychoanalyst Dr. Milton R. Sapirstein noted:

> Modern man literally lives in a sexual goldfish bowl, where he is constantly up for reappraisal. His girlfriend has usually read the latest psychiatric book on sexual behavior, in which practically anything he does is called "infantile"; his friends

29

openly discuss frequency and duration of sexual act; his family ridicules him if he escorts an unattractive female; and for years he has heard the older females mocking the sexual prowess of their husbands. There is a constant aura of jokes about male sexual *in*adequacy in the atmosphere.[7]

Also clouding the atmosphere is an aura of constant worry about the subject. Sexual inadequacy is a frequent preoccupation of males who seek psychiatric counseling. Paperback books and popular magazines dwell on the subject at length. A case in point is *True,* a hairy-chested outdoorsy magazine for men that promotes all the masculine stereotypes and sells more than a couple of million copies a month. In 1956 its editorial director told a gathering of males that the magazine was so popular with men because it "stimulates his masculine ego at a time when man wants to fight back against women's efforts to usurp his traditional role as head of the family." [8] During the intervening nine years the editors must have seen a disheartening number of male casualties resulting from this fight. In 1965 *True* ran an article titled "Impotence, the Secret Fear that Haunts Men." It was the first time that the magazine came even close to admitting that the American male isn't a caveman Romeo. Even "gutsy" *True,* it seems, has had to buckle to the times.

And the times are unkind to the American male in terms of his reputation, as well as in the preponderance of problems facing him. His reputation for both sexual and social assertiveness is really in a sad state of disrepair. Talk about "she-men" abounds, the implication always being that women rule him out of the bedroom and lead him by the hand into it. There is, as Dr. Sapirstein suggested, a distinct lack of pride in America—in both men and women—about the American male. Later on, we shall examine some of the reasons that this is so. We shall come to see that there are, in the United States, historical, cultural, and culturally induced psychological factors that tend to create an imbalance in the relationship between the sexes, with the greater weight on the side of the women—a direct, if ironic, result of our patriarchal heritage.

If sexual adequacy is a growing worry, the fear of being a homosexual—latent or otherwise—gives every appearance of being an even greater source of sexual anxiety for the contemporary male. In the privacy of a psychotherapist's office more and more heterosexual men are articulating fears about themselves or about their sons in connection with possible homosexual inclinations. New York psychotherapist Oscar Rabinowitz, whose practice is three-fourths male, describes the increase in concern about homosexuality among his patients as "phenomenal." He's far from alone in making this assessment. Many of the other clinicians I interviewed also indicated a substantial increase in the number of male patients who voice fears about homosexuality.

There's no way of knowing whether the incidence of homosexuality has risen in comparison with times past. Quite a few authorities insist it has, and it seems a reasonable assumption in view of the threat posed by the shifting relationship between the sexes, the increased economic and psychological demands made on family men, the heightened sexual competitiveness existing in our culture, and the other anxiety-provoking aspects of modern life—all of which act to precipitate a flight from women by men so predisposed.

Furthermore, these threatening aspects having been taken into account, it's reasonable to assume that there has been a distinct qualitative, if not also quantitative, change in homosexuality in America. Homosexuality was by no means unknown among the Indian fighters and the cowboys of frontier America, but for the most part these men engaged in the practice not because they rejected women but because they needed a sexual outlet and there were few women around. Today there are estimated to be at least 2,000,000 to 4,000,000 homosexuals in America,[9] and while a host of causative factors is generally regarded as responsible for their existence—prominent among these being brutal rejecting fathers and "castrating" possessive mothers—a simple sociological phenomenon, like a shortage of women, is hardly one of them. There are plenty of women around today.

Despite the fact that homosexuality in the present-day United States has been widely discussed, few contemporary cultures are as hostile to homosexuality as America's is. That there should be intense hostility is understandable both from the viewpoint of the Puritanical roots from which this nation's sexual attitudes have emanated and from the threat that the mere existence of homosexuality poses to men concerned about their adequacy. It's significant that society is much more tolerant of female than of male homosexuality.

The hostility referred to here shows up in the fact that homosexuality, even among consenting adults, is a legal offense almost everywhere in the United States. It may also be inferred from extant discriminatory practices. For example, during World War II, homosexuals were subject to a special medical discharge that barred them from all G.I. benefits, although no other medically discharged group was so barred. It is also seen in the denial by the Civil Service Commission of employment to homosexuals, even for nonsensitive jobs.

Such animosity creates a vicious circle in which both homosexual and heterosexual males become victims: The heterosexual-male world feels threatened by the homosexual world and shows marked hostility and discrimination. This hostility produces a defensive reaction in homosexuals, who now feel free enough to become militant, forming their own social and political action groups, seeking publicity within the framework of their organizations, putting out their own homosexual magazines, and the like. Furthermore, the homosexuals find natural allies in the growing number of women who, for one reason or another, are hostile to heterosexual men. The homosexual influence becomes stronger and more pervasive, and the result is that the heterosexual male feels even more threatened than before. It's noteworthy that homosexuality is a greater problem in the countries that proscribe it in any circumstances—like the United States and Great Britain—than in those that don't—as, for instance, Denmark, Sweden, France, Italy, and Switzerland, where consenting adults are free to engage in the practice.

Mechanization and Complexity—To examine the contemporary male outside the framework of his particular and peculiar environment would be to view him myopically at best. Yet to take into account all the nuances and ramifications of his culture as it compares with Grandpa's time is to bridge the gap between the horse and buggy and the guided missile. It can be done, but the task boggles the mind. In effect, mid-twentieth-century life boggles the mind and involves tremendous new pressures brought on not only by the shifting relationship between the sexes, but by the technological age as well.

The modern American male lives in a world of unprecedented change and choice. Change itself is nothing new. Cultures are always shifting; people are always discarding old ways, trying new ones. But the pace and intensity of change in today's society are unprecedented, making tremendous demands on the individual's ability to adjust. As philosopher Charles Frankel has noted, it always takes time for individuals to "learn new skills and habits, and to get over the nostalgia and resentments that come when old and familiar things are destroyed." Today values and ways and skills and habits become outmoded or obsolete before they've even been fully integrated. "There is a conservative in every man" is Frankel's conclusion, "and, in the world into which we are moving, he is going to get a harder workout than ever before." [10]

The day looms when it will be the norm for every American male to have three or four different careers, when he and his family will move to a dozen or more localities in his lifetime. Some men are already approaching these patterns, and already

33

a whole new set of psychological problems is forming in terms of the rootlessness and the superficial relatedness to others that result.

The remarkable strides made in the field of communications add to the burdens of complexity which the American male, along with men and women in other highly advanced technological nations, must face. A man in Idaho sitting in front of his television set and watching film clips of a riot in Ceylon, an uprising in Algeria, or a new flare-up over West Berlin may not understand all the implications. But he knows that his nation—therefore, he and his family and friends—is somehow affected by this new turn of events. The broad view of world events seen through the misty screen of half or quarter knowledge brings on uneasiness or outright anxiety and fear.

Touching on this facet of contemporary life, Dr. Leonard S. Duhl, a psychiatrist with the National Institute of Mental Health, has noted the impact that it has on the individual. He contends that:

> As man has extended his ability to receive information via a variety of electronic devices . . . he is faced with a paradoxical situation. He has extended his consciousness so that the whole world is now sending information to him. Thus, on the one hand it is easier to communicate with his fellow men and to find out what is happening elsewhere on the globe, which might possibly affect him. On the other hand, this tremendous increase of information is now being received in an overwhelming and, in many cases, a confused way, leading to the difficulty for the individual of sorting out a position of identity for himself.[11]

The knowledge that a riot in Ceylon, a flare-up in West Berlin, or, for that matter, a debate on Medicare in Congress may have a profound effect on him also leaves the modern man with a profound sense of helplessness. The world grows smaller all the time, he is told, yet he sees it growing constantly bigger

34

and more bureaucratized. He wends his tortuous red-tape-marked way through a maze of Big Government, Big Business, Big Unions, Big Education, and even Big Charitable Enterprises, and he may be pardoned for sometimes feeling like the proverbial mouse in a maze. What can he do? How can he change the course of events? That some people are trying—college students picket against the depersonalization of their schools; there has been a reawakening of political enthusiasm on all sides of the political spectrum; the civil rights movement has caused a coalescing of conscience—is a heartening spectacle, the flowering of individualism in organizational soil. But the spectacle must be kept in perspective. The participants are vocal—but well in the minority. For most people the gloomy words of Yale professor Kenneth Keniston might be more applicable: "Never before have men experienced such mass resignation before the forces of society, such a sense of distance from the sources of power. . . ."

So, despite the heightened political activity, despite the fact that each new generation has more formal schooling than its predecessor, and despite the so-called ferment of the young which has taken place over the past few years—despite all this, individuals in the twenty-one to twenty-nine age category are typically the *least* politically active age category in the electorate. So concerned has the American Heritage Foundation of New York become about the political apathy of America's young that in the fall of 1964 it announced its sponsorship of a two-year $1,000,000 program designed to modernize civic education programs in the nation's schools.

Competition Versus Security

Added to the growing complexity and mechanization of life are two mutually contradictory pressures whose impact takes a terrific toll of the American male: (1) the heightened competitiveness and (2) the heightened quest for security. American civilization has always been highly competitive, of course. But there's a big difference between competition that has the invigorating effect of a mild electric shock, spurring a man to give the very best he has, and the frantic paralyzing kind. Owing to pressures rooted in the economic life of the nation, to an emphasis on consumption as the hallmark of the good life, and to the population explosion—which brings on many more people to compete against—it's the latter type of competitiveness that has gained preeminence. It's the latter kind that, for many contemporary American men, acts as a crushing force.

Time and again, when I explored the problems of the midcentury American in my talks with the behavioral scientists, they brought the intense drive to succeed, to compete, to make it, to triumph, into the discussion. "I think everyone in our culture feels terribly threatened because of the competition," said Dr. Emily Mudd, reflecting the consensus.

Dr. Isidore Portnoy, attending psychoanalyst of the Karen Horney Clinic, was even more emphatic than Dr. Mudd. "Neurotic competitiveness is not the spice added to the dish," he said. "It has displaced the whole dish and become an aim in itself. It is a thing that poisons human relationships."

But this is only half the story. Intense competition is no isolated phenomenon. A parallel development exists: a quest for security, both financial and emotional, that is fully as intense as the drive to compete. In part this quest results from the extremely insecure state of a world growing ever more complicated and mechanical, and existing in the unremitting shadow of a nuclear war that makes possible total annihilation. In such circumstances, a feeling of self-worth becomes extremely difficult to achieve and an overriding need to adjust, to belong, to quash a feeling of inner hollowness via superficial relatedness to others, takes its place. In part, the security quest results from some of the same economic factors that bring on the heightened competitiveness. Finally, this competitiveness itself, so threatening to one's emotional equilibrium, does its share to engender an intense craving for security—for being safe, being liked.

Superficially, security has never been easier to come by, at least in economic terms for the highly skilled and the well educated. For years, college campuses have been besieged by corporation recruiters, fat contracts in hand, looking for trainees. Pointing to this fact, Dr. Peterson observed, "There is a feeling of overrichness of opportunity for everybody. How are you going to worry about security when you get bombarded with job offers?"

The answer is that the conditions surrounding the quest for security aren't amenable to it. The more one has, the better off one is—but the more one can lose if things go wrong. More than 100,000,000 Americans purchase consumer products on the buy-now-pay-later plan, and personal indebtedness—as well as personal bankruptcies—are at an all-time high. Automation and the threat of human obsolescence affect everyone. More important, in terms of his psychological state, the contemporary male is trapped by two utterly conflicting needs: he has to be highly competitive, and he has to be very secure and well-liked regardless of how much this may affront his innermost self. As Dr. Portnoy puts it, "People are caught between the compulsive need to triumph and the compulsive need to submit or surrender."

When people are caught between these two compelling but quite opposed compulsive philosophies there is a pulling in both directions, a feeling of being thrown off balance psychologically. There is conflict and anxiety. Thus psychotherapist Oscar Rabinowitz stated:

The big thing as far as men are concerned today is that they don't know how to handle the competition they're exposed to all day long. They're both afraid and eager for it. How does one engage in competition without being under constant threat, under constant fear of, "I'm not going to succeed"?

Some men resolve the conflict by dodging it—in effect, by hiding. It's far from uncommon these days for a man in a large organization or government agency *not* to blow his own horn so that he won't be observed and won't be advanced. Caught on the horns of the competitiveness-security dilemma, pulled in two opposing directions, he suffers from a kind of psychic impotence disguised by surface activity. He is, when all is said and done, an underachiever.

Since adult symptoms are invariably reflected in the juvenile population, which does a much less able job of camouflaging them, it's not surprising that underachieving boys are a serious and rapidly growing problem in the nation's schools. Dr. Howard Halpern, a clinical psychologist who made a special study of the youthful underachievers, considered this problem more serious than juvenile delinquency. The "child who won't" (Dr. Halpern's term) rarely does his homework or always turns it in late. In school, as at home, he tries to get away with a minimum of effort. He doesn't help out around the house, and he either spends all his time with his friends or, conversely, isolates himself in his room, engaged in solitary pursuits, like watching television and building models. Although he won't gratify his curiosity or develop his competence, the "child who won't" often frenetically and single-mindedly follows just one pursuit —be it a passionate devotion to cars, rock 'n' roll records, a natural science like astronomy, or a particular girl. "His drive for accomplishment in these areas may be very high," stated Dr. Halpern, "while other areas remain singularly barren of incentive." [12] Needless to say, "boys who won't" often turn into "men who won't" with similar characteristics.

The tensions caused by the constant pressure to succeed and to be secure are creating a unique and truly ironic situation. In any poll ever taken in which each sex answered the question *Would you rather have been born a member of the opposite sex?* far more women wanted to be men than men wanted to be women. One famous Gallup poll, for instance, showed that 31 percent of the queried women wished that they were males, whereas only 4 percent of the men could recall ever having had the impulse to be women.[13] The women's discontent lies in their foreshortened opportunities, in their being restricted both biologically and socially—a feature of the eternal woman's problem. Yet several of the psychotherapists I spoke to were beginning to see an increasing number of men who look with real envy at the housewife and the roles she plays.

These men aren't suffering from a specifically sexual disorder. They have no tendency to be transvestites. They are not homosexuals. Nor are they particularly nurturing men, whose psyche would be more gratified by taking care of children than by working. These males are simply envious of the fact that housewives don't have to enter the competitive arena, don't have to fight for their security. For instance, the Family Service Agency of well-to-do Marin County, in northern California, in recent years has had a number of male clients who actually want to reverse roles with their wives. What they want to do is to stay home while their mates go out to work. Nicholas M. Suntzeff, the agency's executive director, observed that this isn't a one-class thing: these men come from various socioeconomic levels.

Dr. Paul Vahanian, a psychotherapist and an associate professor of education in marriage counseling at Teachers College, Columbia University, noted in this connection:

> Not infrequently you'll find a kind of undercurrent of resentment and jealousy among the men. "Here's the gal," they think. "What does she have to prove? All she has to do is keep the damn house clean, and that's only for me or for the people we invite into our home. Sexually, what does she have to prove?" Whereas the man goes out into the cold cruel world; he has to

39

be good on his job; he has to be competitive; he has to bring home the bacon; he has to be a good lover; he has to be potent; he has to live up to his kids' expectations of him.

Dr. Vahanian began his practice about twelve years ago. At the time very few men complained to him about having a tough life or conveyed the idea that women have it much easier. But the number of such men has been increasing steadily in recent years. "More and more men are in effect lamenting, 'If I'd only been born a woman!' " he concluded. "If we were living in a society where you could admit this openly, without any kind of onus, I'm sure you'd find a fair number of men who would say they'd prefer to be women."

The fundamental purpose of this book is not to encourage men to be women. It is to encourage men to be men. To this end it has a thesis, a point of view. At the present time in his history, the American male is subject to an unprecedented number of pressures and tensions. Their effect is needlessly deleterious, because he's still trapped by the beliefs and value systems of the past. To be sure, there are outward manifestations of equalitarianism, of role flexibility, of a relaxation of the rigid sexual double standard. But the American male hasn't really integrated these new ways into his personality. He nurses a fairly potent patriarchal hangover. In effect, he's juggling the forms of the present against the substance of the past. But it won't work.

It won't work because his vantage point inside the masculinity trap allows him a very limited view of what masculinity is and how he can express it. He's forced to behave in stereotyped ways that have little relevance in contemporary times. His choices of what to be and do and think are considerably narrowed. His scope as an individual is lessened. Frustrations and anxieties are heightened, and distorted compensatory behavior increases, when the outmoded masculine stereotypes clash with his real temperament. Paradoxically, adherence to stereotypes that aren't relevant to his unique personality cause him to become hostile to or overdependent on the female sex.

One thing is self-evident. Both masculine and feminine stereotypes have hampered the development of personality irrespective of sex. It's not possible to discard the old stereotypes of masculinity without doing away with the antiquated feminine stereotypes that are the other side of the patriarchal mirror. To these purposes this book will largely devote itself.

What I will attempt to demonstrate, then, is that the patriarchal system, with all its presumed advantages for men, has proved to be fairly costly to men—a cost that is considerably higher in today's shifting, complex society. Equality of the sexes in this context becomes equality not only for the female, but for the male as well.

II.   The Masculinity Trap

"There's an overconcern with the definition and differentiation of sex roles."—Dr. Raymond A. Katzell, during a conversation with the author.

"The guy in the neat suit, with no dirt under his fingernails, drinks to prove he's as much of a man as his father. The old-timers didn't have to prove anything. And while they swore, they didn't talk dirty. The crew-cut, manicured string beans who come in today often have filthy mouths."—A New York City bartender.[1]

A Human Look at Human Beings

What's the essential nature of the male? Of the female? People have been puzzling over this particular conundrum for a good many centuries. Their efforts have produced everything from ecclesiastical pronouncements to lengthy philosophical treatises to psychoanalytic dictums to arbitrary lists (parlor-game fashion) of the ways in which men and women supposedly differ. The trouble with the pronouncements, the treatises, the dictums, and the lists is that life keeps on confounding them. Let us look—but briefly, since the game has been played so often—at some of the myths and some of the facts.

A common notion, attested to by men from Aristotelian times to ours, is that males are more intelligent than females—well, if not *generally* of greater intelligence, at least superior in mathematics, analytical perception, spatial aptitude, and the like.

Psychological tests show that on the average boys do somewhat better than girls in mathematics and related fields. But they also show that the largest number of boys and girls in any given group tested do about equally well.

Moreover, some of the newer studies strongly suggest that the differences in the way men and women use their intelligence do not arise out of inborn factors. Studying a group of twenty boys who had been badly overprotected by their mothers, psychiatrist David M. Levy found that they did very well in language work at school (something that girls are supposed to be good at) but were terrible in something that men are supposed to be good at—namely, mathematics.[2] A recent Stanford study shows that girls who are highly competent in mathematics and spatial tasks typically have mothers who leave them alone to solve problems by themselves—in other words, mothers who promote independence. Another recent study indicates that children superior in analytical perception have parents who started early to promote their independence and initiative.[3] Does the fact that girls are, generally speaking, far more sheltered than boys have anything to do with their differences in aptitude? From the point of view of research, it's too early to make a categorical statement. But it's a demonstrable fact that girls are *less* sheltered today than in the past, and many *more* of them are excelling in the mathematical and analytical fields.

Another venerable notion has it that in their essential natures men are more logical and intellectual than women and that women are more emotional and intuitive than men. Not only the average man ("I'll never understand the way a woman thinks!") but also a great many thoughtful toilers in the psychoanalytic vineyards are utterly convinced that this is true. To be sure, a nose count would probably show more men operating logically and intellectually and more women responding emotionally and intuitively. But studies show that: (1) the cultural encouragement of logical thinking in men and of intuitive response in women has an exceedingly strong effect on their development; (2) the split between the sexes in terms of these traits just isn't as great as commonly supposed; and (3) the innate capacity for logical thought is roughly the same for most males and females.

Psychiatrists might say that a woman who operates primarily on a highly logical, intellectual plane is neurotic, and they would be correct on two counts: First, anyone of *either sex* who operates on just one plane is blocking off a large chunk of his psyche; second, since intellectuality *is* equated with masculinity in our culture, the intellectual woman may come to have strong doubts about her femininity. But none of this proves that the essential natures of men and women are different in this respect. The evidence so far would strongly suggest that both men and women possess the capacity to be logical, intellectual, emotional, and intuitive, although they do not use their capacities equally. The fact that in successful psychiatric treatment the highly intellectual male permits himself to use his emotions far more than he did before and the highly emotional female becomes more ordered in her thinking than she was previously would tend to demonstrate this. So would the fact that in an extremely patriarchal country, like Iran, the culture nevertheless expects the men to be much more emotional, sensitive, and intuitive than women. Never having been told that it goes against their "essential natures," this is exactly what Iranian men are.[4]

A couple of widely accepted but hoary chestnuts about the differences between men and women may be swiftly disposed of. Males are supposedly less vain than females. But in adolescence, at least, this is hardly the case. "Boys . . . seem to me usually more concerned with their appearance than girls and also to have more idea what they actually look like and how other people will respond to the way they look," noted Edgar Z. Friedenberg, one of the more perceptive American observers of adolescent life.[5] The fact that grown men now are such heavy users of cosmetics that the cosmetics industry has had a 10 percent growth rate every year doesn't necessarily show that men are becoming more feminine. What it shows is that vanity is sexless. Then there's the supposed fact that men are by nature less devious and more direct than women. Yet politics—historically a male-dominated and masculine activity—turns deviousness and indirectness into an art form. Business methods, in both buyer-seller and employer-employee relationships, have become increasingly manipulative—a sharp change from the entrepreneur's style of straightforward aggressiveness, although the businessman's image in our present-day society is definitely masculine.

Even the belief and value systems of the two sexes, which often appear so different as to seem irrefutably innate, contradict the way the two sexes actually behave in real life. Several years ago three social scientists spent a full half decade interviewing the inhabitants and observing the daily life of a typical North American middle-class suburban community that they christened Crestwood Heights. One of the things that struck them was this contradiction between belief and action. Each of the sexes held beliefs and values opposite to the other's; but in carrying them out, the men acted the way the women might be expected to, and the women acted in a fashion more consistent with "masculine" values.

The authors of the study used several pages to give a variety of fascinating examples, merely a few of which will serve to illustrate the Alice-in-Wonderland quality that comes to any rational examination of the "real" differences between the sexes. Men think in terms of organization, club, activity, group, and law, but men perfect the art of interpersonal manipulation and learn the chinks in a person's armor to handle him better as an individual. For women, the supreme value is happiness of the individual, but instead of taking individual-to-individual action, women work in context and use group pressure. Men believe in free will, but they think that they can determine good results by their actions. Women believe that human nature and social life can be perfected, but they are more apt than men to reconcile themselves to the unchangeableness of human nature. Men are concerned with immediacies, but in action they are the makers of long-range plans. Women think from a long-range point of view, but in action they work on short-range projects.[6]

One last major assumption about the differences between the sexes needs to be explored. It's the most fundamental one, for it's the peg on which rests a good bit of the patriarchal structure. This assumption holds that way down, at the core of their psychological beings, there's an irrevocable split between men and women—a split in their natures that nevertheless allows them to complement each other beautifully. Men, so goes the belief, are aggressive and independent; women are passive and dependent.

There's no question but that practically all the various patriarchal societies throughout history have acted as if this were indeed the case. In a purely pragmatic way it often *was* the case when hostile environments required superior male strength. But the value of this superiority decreased in direct ratio to the rising power of the machine. We're now at the point where unskilled male labor, the portion of the work force which offers only brawn, is rapidly becoming obsolescent. In an automated age the notion of male aggression-independence and female passivity-dependence has a curiously hollow ring. Nevertheless, it persists, if it is not always voiced so bluntly as it is here. It persists in the pages of the women's magazines and the men's magazines and in the grumblings of men and women discomfited by the challenges which a less rigid definition of the sexes imposes. It also persists in the viewpoint of Freudian psychoanalysts, who have strongly influenced the mass media and popular thought.

Working with very neurotic female patients in the highly restrictive Victorian era, Freud evolved his famed penis envy theory, ascribing to all women an innate sense of inferiority and incompleteness because they lack the male sexual organ.

47

According to Freud, some women compensate for this lack by becoming "masculine"—embracing careers and the like. The "normal" woman embraces true femininity—that is to say, resignation (to her lack), charm and vanity (as positive compensatory mechanisms), passivity, dependence, and the will to be dominated.

Freud never really felt at ease about women, either in his personal or in his clinical life, and he offered his penis envy theory somewhat tentatively. It has since been vehemently defended and attacked. The defenders claim to see it time and again in their work with female patients. The detractors are convinced that insofar as it exists, it has a cultural—not biological —basis: the fewer chances the society offers a woman to expand her personality, the more envious she becomes of the male sex. Thus, the penis comes to represent power and opportunity. We have already seen how cultural pressures can create envy of the opposite sex; the men who envy women their relative freedom from competitive pressures could be said to have a kind of vagina envy.

But some of Freud's earnest and dedicated followers have rejected all cultural modifications of the penis envy theory. Men, they insist, are aggressive, independent—and sadistic. Women are passive, dependent—and masochistic. It's man's role to do, to achieve, and to conquer both the world and, during his sadistic act of sexual intercourse, the woman. It's the woman's role to be passive, to nurture, to receive, and, during intercourse, to accept her masochistic subjugation. Man is the provider; woman, the homemaker and child rearer. For either the man or the woman to deny any of these prescribed roles or to cross sexual lines is to deny his or her respective masculinity or femininity. If these were obscure notions adhered to by a handful of cultists, they could be viewed as curiosities; in fact, both professional and popular literature has been consistently shot through with them, and they are, to a greater or lesser degree, part of popular thinking.

Justification for this inflexible differentiation of both psyche and role, say the devout believers, is to be found in the sexual and other biological functionings: Woman—not man—conceives, is parturient, lactates, and menstruates. Even more significant to the believers is the fact that the male *thrusts* his penis into the vagina and that the sperm *fertilizes* the egg. Hence, men are the penetrators and women the receptors, and this holds true on a narrow sexual level and more broadly as well.

To extrapolate a whole array of inborn psychosexual sociosexual patterns from the simple fact that the man enters the woman during the sex act seems a dubious enterprise, especially since anthropological data just doesn't support it. After reviewing about 200 cultures, for instance, professors Clellan S. Ford and Frank A. Beach found that sexual aggression is encouraged as a part of love play in a great many societies. Such love play is not unilateral: *both* sexes inflict little acts of sadism, like biting or hair pulling, on each other. They also found that in cultures permitting it, women are as prone to initiate sex—to be the intruders, the penetrators, in that sense—as the men are.[7]

Other anthropological studies also refute the notion that men are per se aggressive and sadistic and that women are per se passive and masochistic. They show that in some cultures the men are fully as nurturing as—or more so than—the women. They show that in some cultures the women are the ones who do the heavy work. Indeed, in primitive agricultural societies the women generally worked out in the fields, a clear-cut reversal of our traditional roles. Are we to say of such cultures and societies that the men aren't really men and that the women aren't really women? What are we, for instance, to make of Tasmanian women, whose job it was to clamber the rocks, stalk the seals, and club them to death? Tasmanian women presumably were *women;* they conceived, gave birth, lactated, and menstruated. If the male is innately aggressive, what are we to say of Arapesh men, made famous by Dr. Margaret Mead, who are as fully inclined as Arapesh women to be cooperative and

49

maternal. The majority of Arapesh men presumably are *men;* they possess all the male sexual apparatus, use it heterosexually, and have no apparent problems in terms of sex identity.[8]

This is not to suggest that no differences between men and women exist other than those culturally determined. The physical differences are gloriously and unchangingly apparent. The differences in biological functioning are not to be denied. To say that the biological differences create no psychological differences would be absurd; every woman knows how different she feels at various stages in her life—during pregnancy, for instance, or after her baby has been born. She's acutely aware, before she becomes a mother, of the potentialities for creation of human life inside her body. She knows the changes in mood and feeling that she goes through before and during menstruation (although some women claim to go through none at all). But how much of this is innate and how much is the result of cultural conditioning remain questions. As Morton M. Hunt, who has written extensively on the problems of the modern woman, astutely phrases it, the question is really "whether woman's unique experiences must make her radically unlike man in temperament, or merely create tendencies which some societies radically exaggerate and others do not." [9] The same observation would apply to man's greater musculature, his greater expenditure of energy, and other such developmental differences.

To date, no one has been able to isolate an essential core peculiar to each sex, a basic indivisible something, an immutable organic quality peculiarly different in the male and in the female. No one has been able to do this and say, "See? It's here, glimmering in my hand!" as the chemists can extract a speck of gleaming radium from a mass of pitchblende. No one can say precisely where biology leaves off and culture begins. Some apparently innately different sex-linked patterns can be divined from observation of the play of very young children, before the culture has had much chance to do things with them.

But even here the cultural impact is already at work: studies show that—unconsciously—many mothers react to boy and girl babies quite differently, even in the way they hold them.

There are still geneticists who see all human life as genetically determined and environmentalists who insist that human beings are something of a blank slate until culture draws its imprint on them. However, the heredity-environment debate has lessened in recent years, as behavioral scientists are coming to realize that it's a fruitless quest to determine which trait is the result of which factor, or to what exact proportion heredity and environment contribute to a particular type of behavior pattern. The human being doesn't exist independently of his culture; by the same token, the culture can only react on a living organism with a specific genetic structure. Nor can the problem of which characteristics are peculiarly male and which are peculiarly female be fully answered by observing the behavior of animals, for human beings, far more than animals, are subject to the learning process that enculturation implies. Notes Judd Marmor, clinical professor of psychiatry at U.C.L.A.:

> The lower an animal is on the scale of evolution, the more complex are its inherited instinctual patterns and the less modifiable they are by environmental conditions. As one moves up the evolutionary scale, however, one finds that inherited instinctual patterns become less complex but more subject to modification by learning. This development reaches its apogee in human beings who are born, not with complex instinctual adaptive patterns, but with relatively unfocused basic biological drives. The direction these drives take in human beings and the objects to which they become attached are subject to enormous modifications by learning. It is precisely this fact that gives human beings their remarkable adaptability.[10]

Whatever the biological components, then, culture plays an extremely important part in psychosexually differentiating men and women. Quite possibly, as social scientist John Paul Scott concluded from studies of aggression, there's an *"average* difference between the sexes in traits related to aggressiveness." But this doesn't mean that women are passive; what it means is that *on the average* they're aggressive to a lesser degree than men are. In this sense, women's passivity is really a man-made phenomenon, rather than a phenomenon rooted in nature. Furthermore, biology itself isn't constant, unvarying. Quite the contrary. Human beings—whether male or female—show enormous constitutional variation in the range of their sex-linked differences. Scott stated that "evidence from the science of heredity is strongly against the conventional 'stereotypes' that all men are strong and aggressive and all women are mild-mannered and peaceable. Both men and women are highly variable in physique and behavior." He added that this variability is a "common deficiency of cultural codes" so that "one of the things which we need to do in our own society is to make better provision for the unusually aggressive woman and the unusually peaceful man." [11]

It would be incumbent on society to make this provision if the people who didn't conform to the average constituted a small, relatively insignificant minority. Actually, it may well be that human beings vary to a greater degree within their own sexual group than they do in terms of the opposite sex. In any event, overlapping is far more extensive, and applies to a much greater number of people, than to just a few deviant stragglers at either end of the scale. And it must be remembered that the stereotypes of masculinity and femininity—what's appropriate to men and women—refer to a very wide and very complicated range of acts, gestures, thought processes, and behavior patterns. This being the case, deviation to some degree touches almost everyone, a vital point stressed by social psychologist Roger Brown:

> Where the sex roles are very elaborate, including occupational preferences and every sort of taste and attitude, there

are likely to be many people whose personalities will not exactly fit their sex roles. There will be few who do not have something "sissified" or "tomboyish" about them and so, few who do not experience some of that personality role conflict which is called confusion of sexual identity.[12]

The most important consideration is not whether most men are and do one thing and most women are and do another thing, but whether each person of either sex is recognized to be— and encouraged to be—unique unto himself. Society sets up its rules for what constitutes masculinity and femininity, but masculinity and femininity are after all just words, whereas human beings are not. Too, human beings have an enormous range of possibilities in terms of traits and in the ability to play roles of all kinds. These possibilities are severely foreshortened by the process of sex differentiation too rigidly applied and by masculinity and femininity too narrowly defined.

Badges of Manliness

One can begin to see the foreshortening, imprisoning effects of the masculine stereotypes by digging a little more deeply into the concepts of the aggressive-sadistic male and the passive-masochistic female. For many a man, even if he's untutored in the subtleties of psychological thinking, this kind of division of the sexes has a good solid sound to it. "Why do women have to fight their natures all the time?" a married civil engineer, working in Newark, New Jersey, asked me rhetorically. "Why can't they just relax and let us take care of them, like the good Lord intended?" He might well subscribe to the theories of femininity espoused by Dr. Helene Deutsch and Dr. Marynia Farnham, the two psychiatrists most closely identified with the back-to-the-*Kinder-Küche-Kirche* school of femininity.

Their vision of femininity has women fulfilling themselves

solely through the achievements of men. The normal married woman, an acquiescent being, derives her sense of self in terms of her roles as housewife and mother; the single woman, in terms of helping her male superior or taking care of her father. And so on, through all the levels of the passivity-receptivity pattern—the kind of vision many a male, hard put to handle a seemingly aggressive and demanding wife, might think of as an ideal situation.

But is it really that ideal? Let's look at the situation not from the point of view of women but from that of men. If a woman can achieve herself solely through the male, what it amounts to is that she's living her life through him. This may be great for the male ego; it's also a fairly awesome responsibility. Many a marriage has broken up when a man who in his younger years delighted in taking care of a highly dependent wife, eventually grew to resent her dependency and buckled under the strain in middle-age. Furthermore, since a woman who in the slightest denies her passive-masochistic polarity does violence to her essential femininity, it must follow that—to be consistent—a man who isn't right there with his manliness, being as aggressive-sadistic as he can, isn't being as masculine as he might be. Dr. Helene Deutsch is indeed consistent:

> Our hypothesis is that with the final differentiation of the human species, with the displacement of the body's formation of powerful prehensile appendages, the male could free himself from his dependence upon the female rhythm and take sexual possession of the female even without her consent. It is no exaggeration to say that among all living creatures only man, because of his prehensile appendages, is capable of rape in the full meaning of the term—that is, sexual possession of the female against her will.[13]

Dr. Deutsch doesn't suggest rape as the proper sexual course for a man, of course, but she does view the sex act as a "sadistic act of taking possession" by the man and as a "masochistic sub-jugation" by the woman. By implication, the entire relationship between a man and a woman becomes bathed in this harsh light. If he lessens his aggressive guard, or if he doesn't have the compulsion to be some kind of mid-century caveman, there apparently goes his masculinity.

There it goes, too, if as a husband and a father he so much as extends a toe beyond the line of activities traditionally demarked male. Any help he gives his wife automatically puts him in the category of the female-dominated and renders his heterosexuality suspect:

> Many women solve . . . difficulties by drawing their husbands into the field of their motherly activities. Naturally, the husband must have a large amount of feminine readiness in order to agree to this emotional proposal of his wife's.[14]

Nor, if one follows these rules, is the really manly man permitted to enjoy his children by helping to take care of them. The aggressive-sadistic stereotype requires him, furthermore, to stifle his intuition and to choose only the occupations that preclude a deeper level of human contact. Otherwise, he leaves himself open once again to the charge of "feminine readiness":

> While ascribing a greater degree of intuition to women, we do not deny its existence in men. In men too the experiences of adolescence can have a fruitful and lasting effect. But a sensitive, intuitive man probably has a strong feminine component in his entire personality. This seems particularly true of artistically-gifted men and of those whose professions require psychologic understanding of other people. It has been rightly stressed that literary works written by men often reveal deep psychologic understanding of the feminine soul. These men obviously used the sublimated forces of their own femininity for a successful identification with women.[15]

55

It's one thing to state that every person contains both masculine and feminine components. This is just a different way of asserting that every person has the potential to express all the traits we now ascribe separately to each sex, with society stressing some characteristics at the expense of others. It's quite another thing to say in effect, "You're a sensitive intuitive man? Brother, there must be a lot of woman in you. You're an artist? A writer? A minister? A psychologist? Brother, the female is showing!"

To label as feminine traits like sensitivity, intuition, and the capacity to understand people is to fit the male into a masculine straitjacket. Unless a man is so insulated against this kind of pressure that he can disregard it totally—and not too many men are—one of three major results takes place, all of them destructive: (1) he's never encouraged to develop these expressive, cooperative traits; (2) he feels their presence and defensively squashes them, overcompensating by adopting a highly aggressive, "masculine" manner; or (3) he displays them but, understandably, has attendant doubts about himself, which also cause personality distortion.

With the masculine straitjacket operative, small wonder that a large number of American men are still ill at ease about or are afraid of giving or receiving tenderness under any circumstances. They're afraid to show warmth. Their motto is: "Treat 'em rough. Then you're a man."

Small wonder, too, that with artistically gifted men labeled feminine, many sensitive men who possess such a gift still shy away from occupations that would make full use of their capacities. There is, on the part of the larger society, growing concern these days over the fact that homosexual males are gaining preeminence in a whole gamut of fields requiring sensitivity and artistic feeling—fields like the theater, the dance, antiques, and fashion design. But this concern is ironic, for these are the very fields that heterosexual males for the most part avoid, leaving a vacuum of sorts, which homosexual men who possess the qualities of sensitivity and artistic feeling gladly fill.

Small wonder that with the "psychologic understanding of other people" also labeled feminine, most middle-class fathers don't want their sons to go into the academic field. Here's another irony. Often such middle-class fathers are concerned that their sons display an appropriate amount of masculinity, know their offspring need more exposure to adult men during their younger years, but help to perpetuate a situation that keeps the lower school grades predominantly filled with women teachers. Because of what educational sociologist Patricia C. Sexton calls the "female character of the school," boys are poorer than girls in scholastic achievement and they form a much higher percentage of dropouts and present far more behavior and discipline problems than girls do. The hypothesis is that boys show a resistance to school because: (1) the teachers are women; (2) learning is "sissy," and poor school adjustment is a proof of masculinity; and (3) boys are less socialized than girls at younger ages but are graded for deportment on a value scale identical for boys and girls. In any event, school could be a place to offset what's often a heavily feminine home atmosphere. It isn't, because men are reluctant to enter the teaching profession at a low level (those who do soon opt for an administrative position).

At the highest level, within the ivy-covered walls of academia, the masculine straitjacket creates defensive teachers and distorts teaching, frightening off the very students who might get the most out of the courses. Thus, in a field not viewed as masculine, masculinity itself becomes a virtue ranked above effective communication of the subject. According to David Riesman, this is particularly true of coeducational colleges and universities:

> Every curriculum contains many implicit statements about ideas as "feminine" or "masculine"—statements which are carried in the language or the texture of the discipline, and in the

57

tone and attitudes of its professors. For instance, there are many teachers of psychology in college who resent the fact that women "who are interested in people" come into their courses, and these teachers react by turning their subject into a branch of engineering—an aggressively "male" subject from which all concrete and human concerns of both men and women are excluded in the name of rigor. . . .[16]

Riesman goes on to say that in many colleges the more sensitive students of both sexes find themselves alienated from "mathematics, physics, chemistry and technology generally." He then points out:

> This may, in a few cases, be because they associate these fields, understandably enough in our time, with missiles and war maneuvers, with all that they find oppressive and intractable in the modern world. But it is also because these subjects are often taught in such a way that the subtlety of their ideas is not conveyed, but only the "hardware." As I think of the great physicists and mathematicians of recent times, it seems to me that their ideas (consider Einstein, Oppenheimer, Bohr) have a quality which should not alienate sensitive and very feminine women or sensitive and very intraceptive men. But both in high school and college, these fields are often taught, mainly by men, for whom the text is a kind of cookbook—an old-style cookbook at that. Conversely, English and art are taught in many secondary schools and some colleges as very much prissy, traditionally female and snob-tainted subjects.[17]

Of course, there are men who are intuitive or tender, who teach grade-school youngsters, or who do whatever else it is that goes against the stereotypes without having doubts or being defensive about themselves. But in a society that sexualizes so much, the dice are loaded against such a man.

They're loaded against him not only because of the way he may feel himself, but also because of the attitude others around him may take. It goes without saying that having been conditioned by the patriarchal system, lo, these many centuries, women are as caught up by the stereotypes as men are, and it's far from unusual for a woman's concepts of masculinity to be even more rigid than a man's.

One day I discussed this subject with a psychologist who is a college professor. We agreed that on the surface many of the old stereotypes seem far less virulent now than they did in the past. ("Look at all the men collecting art," he said. "Look at all the Sunday painters.") We also agreed that underneath the surface the stereotypes still hang on tenaciously.

He told me an anecdote to illustrate this point. Not long ago a group of businessmen, among them a friend of his, were attending a series of sensitivity-training programs. These programs were designed to give executives a heightened awareness of their effects on other people, a greater sensitivity to interpersonal relationships. At the close of the series there was a family day, and the executives' wives were invited to visit them at the resort where the program had been given. The executive in question arranged for his wife to attend the family day. When she arrived, she asked him to tell her about the program. After he did, he asserted that he could now be more considerate of other people, more sensitive to their feelings.

Only half-facetiously, she exclaimed, "Oh, they're taking away your virility!"

Her concept of virility was that of a dominating man not too concerned about other people's feelings. Although accommodating behavior is increasingly becoming the norm, her rigid concepts of what it is to be a man wouldn't allow her to see her husband change without viewing the result as a demasculinization. She might have been at home in the ruthless nineteenth-century entrepreneur days.

Of course, maybe her husband doesn't feel wholly at ease about his change, either. The more the who-you-know-and-how-you-handle-him manipulative pattern of doing business becomes institutionalized, the more management men seem to relish seeing themselves as hard-driving, power-loving types belonging to the only truly omnipotent force in the United States today. For instance, see "The Drivers," a series of clever articles about the middle-management man as virile, aggressive nonorganization-man hero in *Fortune,* September to November, 1964.

Quite likely a woman of the kind described above would be horrified to have her husband share his business or financial problems with her. Another nineteenth-century legacy for men, actually dating much farther back, is the image of the masculine male as a man who keeps his troubles as guarded as his poker hand—the strong silent leave-it-all-down-in-the-guts type that Gary Cooper used to play in the movies.

To be sure, men are much less stoic than they ever were in the past. There has been a considerable loosening up. The American male is much more able today to talk about his insecurities than he was before. But to acknowledge this is not to contradict the fact that the image of the strong silent male even now has a great deal of relevance among all classes and all age groups of American men. When Dr. Mirra Komarovsky asked the husbands in her blue-collar study what subjects they would be most reluctant to discuss with their wives, their answers included the following: anything having to do with the job; financial worries; hurt feelings and aggravations having to do with friends or relatives; hopes, dreams, and dissatisfactions (anything having to do with the man's inner core); any gripes the men had about their wives; and things they were told confidentially.

Dr. Komarovsky concluded: "Talk about the job carries the connotation, for the husband, of 'griping,' which is thought to be unmanly." [18]

But the image of the strong silent type is hardly restricted to the blue-collar males. Many of the family service counselors I interviewed commented on the reluctance of the middle-class males in their areas to open up with their wives, the result being only partial communication between husbands and wives. Perhaps representative of the middle-class men who feel that it's somehow wrong to be too open with their wives (or any woman) is the thirty-eight-year-old director of a public service organization in a New York City suburb who told me:

> I have a feeling that it's not very masculine to come home at night and to—if not complain—to kind of share your burdens with your wife. I feel that, Why involve her? If you're a real man, you'll carry these things. The point is, you're imposing your needs on your wife. I think there are so many more important things to share. For example, family decisions of all kinds—when the hell you're going to paint the house, or where you're going on vacation, and what the kids are up to in school. There's all this to work out. . . .

A pretty good case could be made for encouraging men to unburden themselves at times—both from the standpoint of the deepening communication that would result between themselves and their spouses and from the standpoint of mental health, for what he holds back may eventually erupt in the form of psychosomatic and other disorders. But that isn't the purpose here. The purpose is simply to suggest that the masculinity trap is a needless constriction, that a male is neither a superior man for always keeping silent about his troubles nor an inferior man for candidly discussing them with his wife. The "strong silent" stereotype has as its source not an impulse to protect women but male vanity—vanity that says, "You can't see me hurt or distraught, for that would destroy the image of my invincible self, which I must always present to you"; vanity that says, in the pathetically honest (and wistful) words of a Harvard student quoted in *Sex and the College Girl*, "Women tell men how women feel. It just pours out. But men have to go out and get drunk before they open up. Otherwise it isn't manly." Nor can the manly American male ever find release in tears, though men in many other nations are not so constrained.

The unconscious hypocrisy that substitutes the motive of protectiveness for the motive of vanity may be seen in the way that money is handled by many families, even some so-called equalitarian families. When the authors of the Crestwood Heights suburban study examined the attitude that the upper-middle-class men in their community had toward their earnings, they were in for a surprise. These families were supposedly run along democratic lines, which called for a cooperative approach to spending. Nevertheless, many of the wives and most of the children had no idea how much money was being earned. In fact, the men created an "air of secrecy" around their incomes.

The sociologists observed that "this secrecy in regard to income seems strangely inconsistent with the norms which require responsibility in the spending of money by all members of the family." They suggested that the father withholds the facts concerning his income because he has the conviction that financial responsibilities are his alone and the little woman must be spared worries and problems about money.[19] We may surmise, however, that there's more to it than this. In a world of ever-shrinking male prerogatives even the exclusive knowledge of how much money he makes becomes for some men a way of affirming their masculinity and independence.

The masculine stereotypes keep men bound to a belief that it's a sign of maleness to know their way around the tool shed. Despite the fact that countless women are mechanically adept, as both their performance on some mechanical aptitude tests and their achievements in factories indicate, and despite the fact that a fair number of men are all thumbs in grasping a tool handle, proficiency with hammer and related items is still a *sine qua non* of masculinity. In fact, the masculinity motivation may in large measure be responsible for the tremendous growth of the power tool industry, which services avid do-it-yourselfers. Analyzing the results of a motivational research study for the power tool industry, Dr. Ernest Dichter observed:

Men tend to rate themselves and be rated by their families as handy or not handy. Handiness is, to a certain extent, a badge of manliness. Power tools permit the man to show his skill and competence. The rational reason given for buying a power tool is that it helps a person save money by permitting him to do things himself. In reality, the tool itself often is the object rather than the product made with it.[20]

It's a case of confusing a "masculine" activity with a "masculine" attitude. This accounts for the fact that many men are disturbed to discover that women are as mechanically adept as— or more adept than—they are. Dr. Dichter made a pertinent comment about this reaction during a *Playboy* symposium on "The Womanization of America." He alluded to a scene in the film *The African Queen*. A nearly exhausted Humphrey Bogart tries to repair the broken screw of an old-fashioned fishing boat in Africa. He can't do it. Katharine Hepburn offers to do the repair job. Bogart refuses. She offers again. "A woman just can't do that," he tells her. She replies, "Why not?" A few seconds go by before Bogart says, "I really don't know." Then Katharine Hepburn goes down and does the repairing. Dr. Dichter mused, "So when approached logically the man has no explanation. Why *can't* the woman dive down and repair a propeller shaft as well as he, particularly if he's tired out?" [21]

For that matter, why shouldn't a wife fix the faucet or repair the refrigerator, either because her husband is too tired when he comes home in the evening or because she can do the job better than he can? But in many American homes either the husband or the wife finds this kind of flexibility denigrating to his or her sexual identity. Dr. Salvatore Ambrosino, executive director of the Family Service Association of Nassau County, New York, has observed that many women complain about having to do "masculine" things like gardening or painting, even though in the same breath they admit that they are better at them than their husbands are. When women do a task that's traditionally male, "they do it self-consciously, as though they're doing the man's work."

The masculine stereotypes keep men bound to the notions that athletic prowess when they are young and at least a vicarious enjoyment of sports when they are older are a necessary ingredient of true maleness and that the man who doesn't indulge is less the man for it. A few years ago professors David F. Aberle and Kaspar D. Naegele set about finding out the relationship between middle-class fathers' occupational roles and the fathers' aims for their kids. Most of the men in the sample were either in the professions or in business on a managerial level. These fathers as a group wanted their sons to show responsibility, initiative, stability, the guts to stand up for themselves—and athletic ability. Just one father in the entire representative group of middle-class fathers didn't have his heart set on his boy's being particularly athletic. The researchers point out that these athletically minded fathers didn't envisage their sons' becoming professional athletes. No, they viewed athletics symbolically: A boy who doesn't do well in this area, they felt, might grow into a man who isn't aggressive or competitive enough.[22]

The intimate relationship between athletics and masculinity makes men and women take extremely different attitudes even when they're engaging in an identical sport. For a woman the sport is simply a leisure-time activity, something she engages in for fun. Fundamentally, it can't be fun for the man. His masculinity goes on the line.

Joan Salvato, the champion lady flycaster of the world, has always noticed this big difference in the men and women to whom she teaches fly casting. She told an interviewer:

> When a man sets about learning a new sport, he feels he has to prove himself. He feels he has to be, if not the greatest, at least very good. If he doesn't pick it up right away, he's impatient and insecure. When a woman takes up a sport, she

doesn't have to prove herself. She's proved herself with children and a house—or, if not married, by just being a woman who isn't expected to be a great sportsman. She is surprised and delighted when she finds she can learn—and in that frame of mind she learns more quickly than a man.[23]

None of this should be taken to suggest that athletics in itself is subversive of masculinity. On the contrary, it's fun, and it serves several useful purposes, not the least of them being the physical well-being that results from physical exercise and the mental well-being that results from physical testing. As I have already suggested, a paper-shuffling age doesn't provide enough purely physical challenges for its men. The straitjacketing effect of athletics occurs when so much emphasis is placed on it as a masculine value that it has, as Joan Salvato implied, a distorting effect on the men who participate in it and a distorting effect on society's view of men who do not; when, to put it another way, the emphasis placed on athletics as a masculine value has a skewing effect on other values. "The number of adolescent boys who would like to be Mickey Mantle is beyond calculation," sportswriter Roger Kahn has stated. "Compare it with the number who would like to be Robert Frost." [24] In sum, we're back to a familiar theme: In terms of the stereotype, athletics becomes not a choice but a compulsion.

The masculine stereotypes insist that the very fact of innate male aggressiveness makes it impossible for war ever to be eliminated. The idea that basically every true man is drawn to the battlefield because it gives him an outlet for his innately violent nature has been around a long time. There are plenty of signs to tell us how strongly it still persists.

One such sign in the United States is the appellation "hawks" to designate the members of Congress and the presidential advisers who favor escalating the cold war and the name "doves" for their colleagues who prefer a more conciliatory approach. The labels were first used during the Cuban missile crisis of

1962. What red-blooded American boy wouldn't rather be a
hawk than a dove? Early in 1965, during a television debate on
the Vietnam issue, a U.S. Congressman, who made it clear that
he favored negotiating with the Communists, nevertheless felt
constrained to begin his initial remarks by declaring that he
wasn't really a dove, for he had been a fighter pilot during
World War II.

To the people who have embraced the a-real-man-is-a-warrior
stereotype, anybody who campaigns for peace seems to pose a
threat that goes beyond genuine difference in ideology or political approach. To them, no matter how much individual courage a peacemaker may show, he's never seen as courageous. Just
the opposite. He's equated with cowards or women, because
everybody knows what a fearful lot the females are. Thus, in a
mass-circulation men's magazine article picturesquely titled
"The Female Fears That Bind a Man" bravery and cowardice
are neatly polarized between the sexes:

> The female's blind fear of injury expands on a larger scale
> to a fear of violence in general. Women don't seem ready to
> accept the hard facts of life. Life of any kind, from human life
> all the way down to the life of one-celled creatures wriggling in
> the ooze at the bottom of the sea, is violent and has always
> been violent.[25]

By implication, love of violence becomes associated with male
patriotism, and hate of violence is made to seem at least vaguely
subversive:

> Like their other fears, women's fear of violence represents
> a dangerous softening in the national character. Women would
> have us junk all our nuclear weaponry, for example. Every time
> the United Nations holds an important session in New York,
> delegates coming and going from meetings are badgered by
> pickets urging them to Ban the Bomb. At least 75 percent of
> these pickets are women.[26]

66

However, since the subject under discussion is the kind of violence that could easily become nuclear, it's acknowledged that even brave men tremble at the thought—slightly:

> Everybody fears nuclear war, of course. Nobody finds it pleasant to contemplate the idea of being vaporized. But . . . Marching Mothers and other panicky pickets have failed to see a truth that almost every schoolboy knows by the time he's 10 years old. The best way to prevent a bully from picking on you is to let him know, let him understand beyond doubt, that you're ready to fight.[27]

Whether the "Marching Mothers" are politically right or wrong is totally immaterial to the question of masculine stereotypes. They're taking a distinctly unpopular position, taking it boldly and openly. Only from the constricted viewpoint of narrow masculinity could it be seen as even remotely fearful or cowardly. Only from this constricted viewpoint, too, is it possible to equate the fantastically complex power struggle taking place these postwar years with the simplistic notion of a schoolboy fight.

Schoolboys, by the way, are hardly exempt from the traditional concepts of what it means to be a man. No, the pressures to conform to what an Air Force sociologist called the "narrow, rigid sex-typing pattern" of males begin early in life and are much greater than the corresponding pressures on girls to conform to a feminine ideal. Exploring "Sex Role Development in a Changing Culture," the behavioral scientist Daniel G. Brown noted some of the ways in which this development differs between boys and girls. Girls may wear boy's clothing, but boys don't wear skirts or dresses. Girls are often given boys' names—for instance, Jackie, Roberta, and Pauline—but it's a rare boy who acquires a feminized name. Girls may play with all the "masculine" toys—trains, guns, cars, and science sets—but few parents react calmly to a son who starts playing with dolls and

67

dishes. Girls often play at being a cowboy or a spaceman, but any boy who wanted to play at being a movie goddess would be jeered at by his playmates and would likely be hustled off to a child psychiatrist by his parents.[28]

Few social scientists would argue in favor of no childhood sex differentiation. It's difficult to conceive of a boy who is given a girl's name, consistently dressed in girls' clothing, and encouraged to play with dolls and such growing into a man at ease with his own sexuality. Many psychiatrists can point to cases of male patients who have had childhood patterns similar to the one I have just outlined; these patients are possessed of an enormous fund of personality problems. The danger lies not in making it clear to the boy that he's of the male sex, but in making it so inflexibly clear that the boy, father to the man, will grow up to assume the many adult stereotypes of masculinity that have such an imprisoning effect on personality.

Thus, psychologist Ruth E. Hartley, in a paper titled "Sex-Role Pressures and the Socialization of the Male Child," points out that boys are already pressured to restrict their activities exclusively to what is "masculine" while they're only in kindergarten, whereas girls "amble gradually in the direction of 'feminine' patterns for five more years." The demands on the boy are made before he has had a chance to understand the reasons behind them. They are harshly enforced and are usually defined not positively but negatively "as something he should *not* do or be—anything, that is, that the parent or other people regard as 'sissy.'" Consequently, a great many boys are "in virtual panic at being caught doing anything traditionally defined as feminine, and in hostility toward anything even hinting at 'femininity,' including females themselves." [29]

Another scientist studied a group of middle-class children in the upper elementary grades and found that the boys who scored high in sex-appropriate behavior—that is, the ones who were the most masculine in their outlook and behavior—were also the ones who scored highest in anxiety. The scientist speculated that "striving to maintain a masculine role is for the boy of this age group stressful enough to be associated with manifest anxiety." [30]

Needless to say, if adhering to strict male patterns is this stressful for a grammar-school boy, it becomes apparent that a considerable amount of anxiety is generated in the adult male for whom the masculine stereotypes are an ever-present reminder of his own need to measure up and, quite possibly, a reminder of his failure to do so.

The very insecure male may actually become compulsive in his attempts to make a man out of his boy. What he's asking the youngster to do essentially is to display overtly the manliness that he feels he himself lacks. Significantly, a number of family service counselors and psychotherapists have told me that they see an increasing number of fathers whose complaint is: "My son is too passive. My son is too effeminate. My son is running around with a bunch of boys who don't seem masculine enough. I hope my son isn't turning into a homosexual. Is there anything I can do?"

Sometimes a deeper look shows that there's nothing at all the matter with the boy; only the father's exaggerated notions of masculinity have made him think there is. Sometimes the father's worry is realistic: The boy is indeed effeminate or showing signs of homosexuality or drawn to homosexual boys. Realistic or not, says Oscar Rabinowitz, who has observed many such cases in his work with the Child Study Association of America, "I would want to see what kind of a man the father is." Usually, Rabinowitz says, the father turns out to be either overaggressive or very passive. Correspondingly, the mother is either cowed and ineffectual or dominating and overprotective.

Dr. Gertrude M. Hengerer, executive director of the Family Service Association of Palo Alto and Los Altos, California, states that when too much stress is placed on a boy's being masculine, when he's made to feel that he must live up to an image of masculinity harking back to the rugged pioneer, then he tends to wind up "disorganized and helpless." The push to exaggerated masculinity breeds anxiety; anxiety breeds passivity. Dr. Hengerer observes:

> We see many children who have literally been sacrificed to Papa's expectations of them because they can't make it. Papa's expectations are unrealistic because they don't involve anything he can do, either. They're always in relationship to things he was deprived of doing, and who knows whether he could have done them were he given the opportunity? This is where the child gets lost.

A psychiatric counseling service located in the Midwest, outlined a case of this kind. It involved a family with three children, a boy and two girls. The father was a technician, always moving up from one job to another better job. The mother, who suffered from headaches and depressions, usually had to stay behind, close up the house, get everything sold, and make arrangements for a new home in the new community.

The one with the greatest personality problems was the boy, who was in his teens. His father wouldn't "get off his back." I was told, "That father started out on him right from the beginning to teach him to be a man." This meant that the boy had to mow the lawn expertly, to throw a baseball just right, to do all the things the father equated with exclusively masculine skills—and there were many such things. Finally, the boy reacted to the constant pressure by turning into a delinquent.

During the course of treatment what came out about the father? First, his parents were divorced when he was very young and his mother shunted him from relative to relative; second, he had barely managed to eke out a high school education but had had no schooling beyond that point, resulting in a profound feeling of inferiority; third, in essence he had *lost* every one of the jobs that had forced him to move to a better one; fourth, he was terribly afraid that his wife would find out how inadequate he really was; fifth, although he insisted that only the lack of a Ph.D. prevented him from joining the top rank of his profession, on a deeper level he was very unsure about how well he would really have made out had he been able to get his doctorate.

This father was genuinely upset by the fact that his boy had been displaying destructive tendencies. But some fathers of delinquent boys—fathers who feel inadequate in terms of their own masculinity—actually display feelings of pride about sons who commit acts of delinquency. The pride isn't often displayed openly; but it filters through, and the boy is quick to pick up the cues. Abiding by the terms of the masculine stereotypes, such a father sees delinquent acts and destructive acts as proof of his offspring's manliness.

I was told, for instance, of a Southern psychiatrist's experience with a father whose son had been arrested for stealing a car and driving it across the state line. During the psychiatric session, in which both the father and the boy participated, the boy described in great detail how he'd stolen the vehicle. The father's immediate, spontaneous reaction was: "It must have taken a lot of guts to do that—swipe the car and drive it all the way to Nevada." A moment later, oblivious of the pride he had just expressed, the father told the psychiatrist feelingly, "What my son did is terrible, just terrible."

When the father was reminded of what his immediate reaction had been, he absolutely refused to believe it. Only when the tape of the session was played back to him would he acknowledge making that comment about his son's courage, and he was genuinely appalled by it.

Police departments throughout the United States notice a growing number of cases in which fathers (and mothers) of sons arrested for vandalism, fighting, and stealing refuse to cooperate with law enforcement officials. Such parents are actually outraged that their boys were "picked on" by the police. We may surmise that at least in part a parental reaction of this kind is motivated by unconscious pride in Junior's masculinity. Nor is this surprising—not when toughness and acts of hostile aggression are still so closely identified with manliness.[31]

III.   Notes on the "Feminization" of Society

"In our society, success, generally equated with love, is for men specifically equated with masculinity. Many a male feels genuinely alarmed by a woman who can match wits with him, beat him in a debate, more quickly solve a problem in calculus, or write a better piece of advertising copy. He uneasily tells himself she is 'cold' and 'unfeminine,' but at the unconscious level he feels a threat to his traditional male superiority and hence to his very potency."—Morton M. Hunt, *The Natural History of Love*.[1]

"Men today are becoming economic serfs whose strenuous efforts provide their wives with comforts and conveniences that the men themselves have little prospect of enjoying. The higher standard of living toward which the American family is ever striving consists of machines and labor-saving devices, household comforts and services, vacations, new clothes—most of which chiefly benefit women."—A professor of sociology's comments in *Coronet*.[2]

Our So-Called Matriarchy

Man has always felt uneasy about Woman, whose body he enters for his pleasure, whose womb creates new life, whose

73

breasts swell with milk, whose embrace either comforts or maddens. He has never quite known how to take her, so he hasn't taken her—at least not simply as a person, like himself. His tendency has always been to exaggerate either her faults or her virtues, to make her an object of play or of veneration.

The Judeo-Christian ethic—which is perhaps best exemplified by St. Paul—holds the female to be morally inferior to the male, with the Biblical references to the Fall offered as proof of her perfidious nature. This view eventually lost its direct impact but was taken over by the Freudian ethic and in transmuted form was given "scientific" justification. Because the girl doesn't have castration fears, for she considers herself already castrated by having been born without a penis—said Freud—she doesn't have as much of a chance to develop the kind of self-controlling conscience that boys develop for possessing the castration fear. Hence, she's deficient in matters of principle, in a sense of justice, in morality. For this reason and others, it's up to men to lead women and to act as the family's ultimate disciplinarian, ultimate authority, and ultimate conscience. That the male should arbitrarily be *the* authority figure in the family is a concept still very much with us and is, in fact, being given new impetus these days as the effects of the imbalance in the relationship between the sexes become increasingly apparent.

The Victorian ethic, on the other hand, offers an extreme idealization of women. The Victorian lady's virtues were magnified to the point of absurdity. She was—in her sexless form—made the embodiment of moral excellence, particularly as she assumed the roles of wife and mother. She was expected to be the essence of purity because, it was believed, her innate nature meant her to be thus.

Here, then, are two diametrically opposed viewpoints of the human female within the context of morality—one highly condemnatory, the other highly laudatory. They're just two sides of the same coin, one suspects. And the coin is what? Disquietude? Suspicion? Fear, because her body is so different or because of the gifts it offers or the demands it makes? We may puzzle about the answer, as people have always tried to puzzle out and piece together the male's contradictory reaction to the female.

However, no puzzle—simply observable fact—is the effect of the two conflicting attitudes in the United States, where their influence has been particularly strong. How do you reconcile such seemingly irreconcilable points of view? You do it, as it must be done, in a somewhat schizoid manner. You accept the moral superiority of women but reject the implications. Compared with the contemporary male, the Victorian had a relatively easy time of it. The Victorian made sure never to confuse strength of soul with strength of body or mind. With society decreeing his superiority, he could worship the female while retaining the status quo—*i.e.,* her legal inferiority and his masculine prerogatives.

Today it's not that simple. Most of the prerogatives are going, if they are not already gone. The male's status is no longer assured. Many contemporary American men vaguely accept the female's moral superiority and prove it by leaving the job of socializing the children, of teaching them to adjust to society, almost entirely to women. At the same time, though, they view emancipation as a force subversive of masculinity and see the dangers of feminization lurking behind every bush. The plight in which such men find themselves as women expand their roles and the antagonism this fosters between the sexes were summed up by Dr. Paul Vahanian:

> It seems to me that the very preoccupation with sexual difference fosters competitive antagonism. In other words, the sexes in certain respects become almost like enemies. Each has to watch out for the other: If you don't, she or he will take advantage of you. This is more the male attitude. If you let a woman get too close, you open the door to who knows what? There's an attitude that women aren't to be trusted, that you can't understand them, that they're a species quite apart from

75

men. This kind of thing has been fostered for so many years that today a lot of men can't admit to themselves that maybe they can understand a lot more than they think they can. That women aren't that different. That a man can get close to a woman and still hang on to his precious masculinity.

In effect, such men, viewing the contemporary scene, say, "The mark of the female is everywhere." They say, "The women are wearing the pants—figuratively, as well as literally. We're living in a matriarchy." And in a sudden uncharacteristic moment of overt rage they rip off, at least symbolically, their handsome "His" aprons which they donned to do the after-dinner dishes.

The degree to which a man subscribes to the traditional masculine stereotypes dictates in part the attitude he has regarding women and the world he must share with them. The more trapped he is by a rigid view of masculinity, the more dismayed he finds himself. He may be pardoned for coming to the unrealistic and unscientific conclusion that we are indeed living in a twentieth-century matriarchy, for from his orientation it surely seems that we do. He can bring in all kinds of statistics to prove his contention.

There are now, for instance, approximately 3,500,000 more women than men in the United States. At first blush this may seem quite advantageous to males, especially if they're swinging bachelors or in the marriage market. But the beleaguered male will point out that this surplus of women casts a feminine "pall" over everything (as one disgruntled stockbroker in his fifties put it to me) and provides him with additional competition in other respects.

Life expectancy rates in this country sharply favor women. The life expectancy of newborn girls is roughly 6.3 years longer than that of boys. "We work like hell all our lives to provide for them and wind up wearing ourselves out years ahead of our time," asserted a dapper married businessman in his fifties who looked exceedingly unworn-out. "What's the percentage?" Such a man chooses to disregard, among other things, the ego gratification he gets from making it as a provider in a success-oriented culture that gauges his masculinity largely by his achievements as a breadwinner.

American women own approximately 70 percent of the nation's wealth. They own two-thirds of all privately owned bonds. They hold $100,000,000,000 worth of stocks (housewives are the largest occupational group among shareholders). They hold about 70 percent of the financial estates, 50 percent of the railway and utility holdings, 45 percent of all real estate mortgages and bonds—and, for some reason, most of the country's thoroughbred racehorses. Such figures seem overwhelming. But to go on from these statistics to say—as is so often said—that American women control the wealth of the nation is to stretch the facts to force a point. In some instances husbands who fear possible legal entanglements prudently put all their assets in their wives' names. As for the widows and divorcees who hold most of this wealth, usually they turn it over to banks, investment houses, and law firms—in other words, institutions controlled by men—to control for them.

The beleaguered male certainly can't look to politics to back up his contention that a matriarchy has descended on us. Enfranchised in 1920, women have since then hardly provided a shining example of voter enthusiasm. The Commission on the Status of Women stated in its 1963 report: "Women outnumber men by some 3.75 millions but in terms of registration and election-day turnout their failure to use the vote converts them into a minority." Nor do women seem a very strong and forceful lobby in Washington; it took them more than four decades after they first got the vote to push through Congress a bill providing equal pay for equal work for both sexes (although only for jobs covered under the federal minimum wage law). As for women in political life, in 1964 just 2 U.S. Senators and 11 Representatives out of 435 Congressmen were women. The dismal showing has prompted some of the severe critics of the female sex to say, in sum, "See what happened after all that fuss they made? What was the point in giving them the vote?" This attitude betrays a certain naïveté both about the prejudice facing women in political life and about the assumption that women would somehow fix the mess and make everything come out all right.

But the beleaguered male struggling inside the masculinity trap can point to all kinds of other signs to support his matriarchal fears. There's advertising, for example. Between 60 percent and 80 percent is female-directed—and often for products that don't even fall within the woman's traditional purview. Doesn't this prove that women wield the purchasing power in consumer products, with men merely in attendance to provide the wherewithal? What it proves is that women have a substantial amount of influence within the family unit, not that this should come as a surprise. What it also proves is that women have—or take— more time than men to shop for things. As the advertisers well know, the one who does the shopping more often than not is the one who picks out the specific product. But it does not prove a matriarchy, at least not if we are to use the proper definition of the word—namely, autocratic rule by females. Women have a great deal of leverage in the United States, as we shall see, and dominate in certain areas, but they're far from being at the center of national power.

For the male concerned about the feminization of his environment, any softening of line or form and any attempt to add a little grace or color to coldly functional objects can somehow become a threat to his masculinity. Thus, Philip Wylie, the iconoclastic, freewheeling social critic, has long been concerned about the "wanton womanization" of our "national life." He looks glumly at this mid-century American world and offers his melancholy vision of a feminized future:

> On some not very distant day I expect to see a farmer riding
> a pastel tractor and wearing a matching playsuit. And as he

ploughs, I'll realize with horror it's not a contour job; he'll be fixing his fields so the crops will match an "over-all design-feeling" incorporated in his home by the little woman. . . . Functional reality is so softened and maleness so subdued that the only inanimate object I can think of offhand which still has masculine integrity is the freight car, and even some of these are being glamorized. I would have added the steamroller, but today on the way to my office I passed one which our local Department of Streets—doubtless bowing to some women's club—had transformed from factory yellow to chartreuse and beige.[3]

To the beleaguered male, all his traditional avenues of escape, one by one, seem to be closing. Increasingly, wives are accompanying husbands on hunting and fishing trips. Many—not all —sportsmen resent this but apparently can't find a way of telling their wives that they don't want them along.

Dr. Ernest Dichter pointed out that with a true fisherman fishing becomes devalued when his wife is with him, because one of the main reasons he goes away to fish is to get away from women. Why does he need to go away from them? Fishing alone or with the boys, Dr. Dichter speculated, may be a way the man can relax, can perform under his own control, whereas with his wife along he may have much more of an urge to prove himself because of the biological relationship between the two. Another psychiatrist suggested to me that it's perfectly natural for a married man to want to spend an evening with his male buddies occasionally, just as his wife may enjoy a few evening hours alone with her girl friends every once in a while. On the other hand, he said, when such a man has a really compulsive need to hunt or fish with the boys on a very frequent basis or when several times each week he insists on spending a night out on the town with the guys, he may be acting out an unconscious homosexual need.

Wives are increasingly accompanying their husbands to conventions and, to a lesser extent, on business trips. Some men

79

like and encourage this. To the beleaguered male, however, it's unsettling. He already sees the time when the typical convention fun—getting "loaded," watching stag movies, pinching girls' fannies, and finding some congenial feminine companionship for the night; that is, having a lot of *manly* fun—may become as rare as the stately old brothels on the edge of town.

Very nearly a thing of the past as well are the all-male bars and clubs, where, as Philip Wylie stated in a *Playboy* article, a man could "talk and think of himself as a sportsman, a lover, an adventurer, a being of intellect, passion, erudition, philosophical wisdom, valor and sensitivity"; where he could, we are told, discuss women in other than idealized terms and, if his wife was sex-terrified, obtain the telephone numbers of "ladies who were especially joyous over their femininity when aided in its proper celebration by male ardor." [4]

Mr. Wylie's concern about womanization notwithstanding, if the primary function of the all-male redoubts was to provide a place for a man to pretend to be something he wasn't, a retreat where he could obtain hot telephone numbers after being unable to make it with a wife whose own sexuality was repressed by sex mores that men have had a very great share in promulgating, then the passing of the all-male clubs indicates less womanization than maturation.

Playboy itself could in a way pass as the bible of the beleaguered male. Its philosophy, as well as its choice of articles on the male-female relationship, reflects for the most part the attitude that unless the two sexes are pigeonholed in well-defined, clearly differentiated slots in life, soon nobody will be able to tell the girls from the boys. The *Playboy* prescription is apparently the old one of the female as man's plaything. In fact, it's not unfair to say that the *Playboy* heroine is the perfect definition of the contemporary woman as a play object. For millions of American men, it seems, the girl of their dreams isn't the girl next door but the centerfold caricature of womanhood —small brain, large breasts, and magnificent navel. For these same millions of men, it would appear, their symbol is the rabbit—that wonderful little real-life "make-out" artist, hero of the juvenile joke "Wham, bam, thank you, ma'am."

But if prolifigacy is one side of the rabbit coin, timidity is the other. The rabbit, it ought to be remembered from Zoology I, runs, and as for the bushy-tailed buxom *Playboy* "bunny," she provides the rabbity male with a perfect foil. In her presence he can seem like the most intelligent of men, for no intelligence is needed; like the most human of persons, for no qualities of humanity or even of companionship are needed; like the most virile of lovers, for the invisible sign hanging over her proud breasts reads: "Look, but do not touch." This is indeed separation of the sexes—and of an extreme form, guaranteed for life to ward off role blurring. But surely the problems that beset the sexes in their interaction today and the admirable intent to preserve some of the differences between men and women deserve a better answer than turning people into rabbits.

Woman in Man's Workplace

One of the important changes the American male has been facing is the dearth of possibilities for all-male achievement. This is, I daresay, more serious than the dearth of all-male clubs and bars. Not only in American society but also in cultures the world over, tasks have traditionally been differentiated in terms of masculine and feminine. Traditionally, too, men have valued their accomplishments at least in part because they took place on the male side of the sex-differentiated fence. Dr. Margaret Mead has elaborated on this point:

> In every known human society, the male's need for achievement can be recognized. Men may cook, or weave or dress dolls or hunt humming-birds, but if such activities are appropriate occupations for men, then the whole society, men and women alike, votes them as important. When the same occupations

81

F

are performed by women, they are regarded as less important. In a great number of human societies men's sureness of their sex roles is tied up with their right, or ability, to practice some activity that women are not allowed to practice. Their maleness, in fact, has to be underwritten by preventing women from entering some field or performing some feat. Here may be found the relationship between maleness and pride; that is, a need for prestige that will outstrip the prestige which is accorded any woman. There seems to be no evidence that it is necessary for men to surpass women in any specific way, but rather that men do need to find reassurance in achievement, and because of this connection cultures frequently phrase achievement as something that women do not or cannot do, rather than directly as something which men do well.[5]

To the undying astonishment and regret of many men, there are few things in the United States today that American women do not or cannot do. They have invaded nearly all the formerly all-male occupational strongholds. As far back as 1950 the census already showed women to be employed in all the 446 reported occupations. There are female sailors, tractor drivers, and carpenters; female pilots, telephone linemen, and lumbermen; female fishermen and locomotive engineers; even stevedores and longshoremen. Words that indicate occupations in terms of the male sex are, it seems, an anachronism.

Why do I list the "manly" job categories which the ladies have infiltrated? Not to cause astonishment; not to mourn the passing of the all-male job world. I list them to emphasize that in America today it is no longer possible for men to affirm their maleness simply in terms of the tasks reserved for their side of the fence. The fence itself is splintering and buckling all up and down the line, although at a much slower rate than the fiery feminists of the 1920's anticipated. In 1964 a *Time* survey on women and work offered some startling statistics. The number of women in the "more rewarding professions" rose 41 percent since 1950. There were 1,800 women brokers on Wall Street,

10 times as many as in 1946. There were more than 600 women advertising executives on Madison Avenue, two-thirds of whom earned more than $10,000 annually. On the other hand, there has been much greater resistance to women doctors; the rate went up only 1 percent in a 5-year period.[6]

During the last quarter of 1965 there occurred an event that could, in beleaguered eyes, be termed catastrophic: Title VII of the Civil Rights Act of 1964 went into effect. Slipped in almost as a joke, the section in question forbids employment discrimination because of sex. Because unfortunately the sex section of the Civil Rights Act hadn't been thought through, it's hardly surprising that in its earliest days, as this chapter was being written, it spawned little more than panic and confusion. Not only unequal hiring practices but also unequal seniority lists, pay scales, and fringe benefits; state protective regulations favoring women; and company policies that dictate the automatic firing of a woman employee once she gets married—all are theoretically to go by the boards.

It's not difficult to see that compliance will in the initial stages create tremendous headaches. Nor can the law be applied on a mass basis without regard to the demands of particular jobs that are intrinsically geared to one sex or the other. As financial columnist Sylvia Porter has observed, it's not going to be easy to translate the sex antidiscrimination law into "significantly broadened opportunities for women."

It's going to be even more difficult to eliminate the prejudice facing women in high-level positions. Not only medicine but also the academic and business worlds show an enormous resistance to the entry of women into their traditionally all-male fields. Arousing the most resistance, it seems, is the entry of women into supervisory positions. According to Dr. Garda Bowman, director of the Merit Promotion Program of the National Conference of Christians and Jews, who researched promotion practices in the New York area, "Amazing as it may seem, the prejudice against women in a position of authority appears to

83

be even more deeply rooted in our culture than the concept of white supremacy." [7]

The businessmen in the study unburdened their hearts to Dr. Bowman—and it is apparent that these were quaking hearts indeed, at least insofar as the subject of career women is concerned. To hear an executive's reasons for not wanting women in supervisory positions in his shop is to gain insight into his inner workings. Here, then, are four of the main reasons why American managers of the mid-1960's can't abide the notion of female counterparts, together with Dr. Bowman's interpretations as she related them to me:

1. "Women belong in the home." The executive who says this seems to be indicating a desire to make the home the only meaningful aspect of a woman's life. Why should he have this desire? Because he identifies himself with that brother male, the woman's husband, who feels the need to be the one and only focus of interest for his wife. A woman who leads a balanced life in which she also partakes of the wider world appears threatening to some husbands.

2. "Women are too emotional." "Their whole value system is different." "They're too personal." "They don't have the stamina to react well against pressure." "They aren't management-oriented in outlook." Reactions such as these show that the men who have them operate from a stereotyped view of women. They see only those women who conform to the stereotypes, are totally unable to accept the fact that there are also numerous exceptions.

3. "Women by and large don't want to work for other women." Dr. Bowman agrees that there's a bit of truth to this statement. There can be tensions on both sides when women boss women. Women, like any other disadvantaged group, sometimes tend to push too hard. On the other hand, there are numerous instances in which such relationships among women work out exceedingly well.

4. "Women have babies; they only work temporarily." A

generality with a high degree of truth. However, Dr. Bowman feels, it too is being far too broadly applied, denying far too many women a chance to show how they will work out as individuals.

Dr. Bowman, whose study uncovered a variety of discriminatory attitudes directed against the various disadvantaged and minority groups, noted several distinctive conditions applying to employer prejudice against women: Although most of the employers felt guilty about discriminatory practices based on race or national origin, they felt no qualms at all about discriminating against women; the tendency to lump together all members of an underutilized group, disregarding individual differences, was especially marked with respect to women; and "there seemed to be more resentment toward those few women who did get ahead in business than against supervisors in other disadvantaged groups." [8]

Men in the academic and scientific worlds show a not much greater tendency to welcome women with open arms (as colleagues, that is). Not long ago sociologist Jessie Bernard scrutinized women in academia to see how they fare. They don't, on the whole, fare too well. Merely because a man is a college professor doesn't mean, of course, that he can show objectivity toward such a subjective subject as the female sex, particularly if a member of this sex is teaching right alongside him. Compounding the difficulties facing women in academic life is the fact that they themselves can't quite get rid of the standard stereotyped view of themselves.

In effect, the academic woman can't win. If she tries to be inoffensive, instead of acting like a pushy, driving female, her male colleagues find her "withdrawn." If she teaches part time, she's neglecting her family. If she has a warm relationship with her students, she becomes the overpossessive Mom.

The beleaguered male, trapped by his notions of what men and women are, finds it exceedingly difficult to adapt to the idea that a woman can be as competent as he is in what's just about

85

the most meaningful aspect of his life. As Margaret Mead has pointed out, he's taught, when he's young, not to hurt little girls because he's stronger than they are. He's taught not to cry like little girls because he's stronger. He's taught not to tease little girls because he's stronger. Small wonder that later he gets his back up when she tries to take a place alongside him in the work arena. Even smaller wonder that his self-esteem suffers— in both his and her eyes—if her position is superior to his and he must work under her.[9]

Other factors also come into play to account for male resistance to career women. The sexual element is important. Several businessmen complained to me that—as one aggressive New York City merchant put it—"when it comes to a tight situation businesswise, she's apt to try to take unfair advantage by using her body." That career women have them sexually disadvantaged is a genuine fear on the part of many men in business. At the same time these men often assert that career women are masculinized, that they ape men. If career women are indeed masculinized, generally speaking, it's difficult to see how the same women can be using sexual wiles with any great effect. Furthermore, men in business can hardly expect businesswomen to eschew the same techniques they themselves use. In some sectors of business the use of sex to gain competitive advantage is rather well institutionalized, as the employment of call girls and amenable secretaries to promote business deals makes perfectly clear.

One former middle-management executive who had worked in a Kansas City plant recalled the virulence with which the men around him directed their antagonism toward women executives:

It was a very clubby, one hundred percent men kind of place, and except for their secretaries and other female office personnel they were determined to keep things that way. It reminded me of a frat house atmosphere. Don't get me wrong.

86

This was a hard-working bunch of men. But they were so chummy with each other, the jokes and everything, there was no room for women. Actually, there was a vague undercurrent of something—I wouldn't say exactly homosexual—but something.

In any event, the continuing resistance to career women is a losing game for the very men putting up the most resistance. They deprive themselves of so much talent that otherwise goes to waste. Moreover, prejudice has deleterious effects on everyone, especially on the prejudiced individual. Also, when only the women with abilities far superior to those of the men they compete with have much chance of being hired for the top jobs—something very much the case at present—then a growing number of such high-caliber women will prove themselves even more frightening and intimidating to the men around them than is true at present.

The career woman finds herself under another serious handicap. Sharp, intelligent women do not—at least for the American male—have an aura of romance about them. The stereotype of the somewhat dependent girl who in most respects looks up adoringly at her big, strong, and intellectually superior man is still very potent. In fact, the more intelligent a girl is, the more difficult she often finds it to attract men. The less intelligent women have a much easier time getting married. Even well-educated males often seem to prefer them. This was vividly illustrated by the results of an informal study of underachieving boys by a family service agency located in northern California. All the fathers of these boys were men of science, holding jobs in what might be called brain functions. These fathers didn't communicate well with their families, lacked to a marked degree the capacity for emotional involvement, placed a very high premium on intellectuality—and uniformly chose to marry women who were beneath them intellectually.

Well aware that a girl of above-average intellectual gifts can easily have a demasculinizing effect, many young college and career women did—and to an extent still do—hide these gifts under a bushel of calculated reticence. In other words, when they are out on a date, they pretend to be much dumber than they really are in order not to frighten off their escorts. It's difficult to understand what they gain, for in the long run they can't help losing respect both for themselves and for the men they feel need such merciful treatment. On a short-term basis, of course, it beats facing dateless evenings. For that matter, many a talented girl, mindful of the statistics, has rejected a serious career for herself. The statistics show that only half of all career women get married.

One must be optimistic, however, and assume that in time the old stereotypes will break down, that men will allow women with excellent minds to achieve positions commensurate with their abilities, and that in personal relationships men will not feel desexed by such women. The stereotypes have been breaking down to a considerable extent, after all, insofar as women's acceptance in the workplace generally is concerned. Of course, sheer economics has had a great deal to do with it, for women are an abundant source of cheap labor. In a notable shift few American husbands still feel emasculated by the fact that their wives are working at some outside job.

Wives have always worked, of course, in capacities having nothing to do with their domestic duties. In the self-sustaining farm families that produced their own food, as well as in the factory families that produced cloth, furniture, and a host of other products at home, a wife toiled alongside her husband— under his control. When industrialization progressed and outside factories required workers, low-class wives often went to meet the demand and to supplement the family income. This movement became accelerated as factory-produced clothing, prepared foods, commercial laundries, and the like did away with many of the woman's traditional tasks in the home (and gave impetus to the feminist movement). By and large, however, middle-class husbands could still exercise their masculine prerogative of being the family's sole breadwinner. Two world wars changed all that; especially in the present postwar decades, middle-class women's entry into the labor force has been unprecedented. Nearly 25,000,000 women—one-third of the female population of the United States—are now working. Three out of every five are married. The largest number fall into the forty-five to fifty-one age group. This is in accord with the typical pattern of the middle-class working wife: working until the children are born; quitting until they're grown; then reentering the labor market.

What makes today's husband take a more relaxed attitude about his wife having a job? Finances, for one thing. The second income affords the family the opportunity of maintaining a considerably higher standard of living—up to 40 percent higher, in fact. His masculinity isn't threatened because, after all, her job has a lower status than his and he makes more money than she does. But this shouldn't detract from the very meaningful fact that he is, generally speaking, secure enough to accept his wife's working without having it reflect on his own breadwinning abilities. As a subsidiary compensation, many husbands have been delighted to discover that their wives have become more interesting and alive companions after getting a job.

A lot of men these days actually *encourage* their wives to go out and find a job after the children are in school or grown. "I could understand what she was doing at home when the kids were there," they say, "but I don't understand what she's doing there now."

This is not to suggest that working wives create no marital problems. In the overall picture, middle-class husbands have adjusted to the situation and in some cases are even more enthusiastic than their wives about it. Yet there are still husbands who protest vehemently if their wives even suggest going to work. And in specific circumstances even a man who doesn't mind having his wife take a job may find the results unsettling. This is sometimes true if her working makes it incumbent on him to help out around the house to a degree that he isn't used to. Trouble may also come if she proves herself the more competent breadwinner.

I was told about one such case, in which the husband kept going into business and failing. At last the wife became so exasperated that she went out and got a job. At this point the husband collapsed. He took to his bed; he started drinking and taking drugs. Intermittently, he tried to find himself a job but never succeeded in getting one. This prompted him into terrific temper tantrums. None of it fazed his wife, who kept right on working, even though it became very clear after a while that he was trying to get her to quit her job so that he could at least seem to be taking care of the family again.

There may be conflicts on the wife's side as well when she supplements the family income with her income. Friction sometimes occurs if she insists on setting up a special bank account of her own, to use as she pleases, while the husband's income keeps on going into a joint account. Friction occurs if she wants to have it both ways without relinquishing any of her prerogatives—if, for instance, she wants to be idealized and protected as wife and mother, while at the same time she wants to enjoy all the advantages of the more emancipated working woman. And there are, not infrequently, conflicts about timing—when, during the initial years of marriage, the wife decides to quit her job and have children long before her husband is ready for her to do so.

On the whole, American husbands react most emotionally to the prospect of their wives working while the children are very young. A great many women too feel that a mother shouldn't work when her children are in their preschool years and should work only part time, if at all, in the years they're going to school. But men often seem more vehement about it. In 1964, Dr. Alice S. Rossi made an intensive study of career choice and implementation, using as subjects men and women who had been graduated from American colleges and universities in 1961. Among other items, the graduates were asked to react to the statement that "even if a woman has the ability and interest she should not choose a career field that will be difficult to combine with child-rearing." Two-thirds of the men but only half of the women respondents agreed to this proposition. They were also asked to register approval or disapproval of a statement that it is appropriate for a woman to work part time while her child is a preschooler. One-half of the women but only one-third of the men gave their approval. They were also asked to react to the statement that a woman shouldn't take up a full-time job until the children are completely grown up. One-fourth of the men okayed this view, while only 14 percent of the women did.[10]

One reason that men may be more conservative in this respect is that not being around the youngsters as much as women are, they have an exaggerated sense of protectiveness about them. Unresolved dependency needs of their own may also play a part. And, of course, there's the old blurring-of-roles bugaboo: "If I work and my wife works, if she does the household chores and I do the household chores, how are the children going to know who is the man and who is the woman?" They know. Ruth E. Hartley, a social scientist, studied 157 children of working mothers to determine how such children perceive their mothers and fathers. All the youngsters were U.S.-born; in the five-, eight-, and eleven-year age groups; and without significant emotional problems. Despite the fact that their mothers, as well as their fathers, went off to work each morning, the youngsters retained the traditional concept of male and female roles:

> Our subjects clearly tell us that the basic homemaking duties are still the woman's; the money-getting role is still primarily the man's. Whenever women are perceived to have assumed the work-role, they are generally perceived to do so as "help-

ing" persons within the family group. . . . Similarly, fathers occupied with domestic activities are seen as "helping" the mother in her myriad home-centered responsibilities, not supplanting her.[11]

As for how the mother's holding a job affects the children, men are inclined to see a deleterious effect; the neofeminists, who spot a potential career woman in every female, see no ill effects at all; the reverse feminists, who insist that a woman's place is in the home, are inclined to prophesy all kinds of crises. All such unidimensional views are simplistic. Psychologist Lois M. Stolz surveyed the studies that have been made on maternal employment and on how it affects the family. She learned that some of the children of working mothers become delinquents, and others turn out fine; some are well adjusted, and others are maladjusted; some learn to stand on their own two feet, and others become overdependent. She concluded that a mother's employment—or lack of it—is not the most important factor in determining the child's behavior:

> It might be more profitable to focus attention on the psychological conditions within the family, especially on the personal characteristics of the mother and father and the kind of supervision and guidance which they provide, not only when the parents are at work but when they are at home as well.[12]

A husband may not feel at all threatened by a working wife so long as she has a lower status and less pay than he does. But what happens if she moves ahead more rapidly than he does? Dr. Bowman told me she knows women who "suffer tremendously" under such circumstances. Yet one may assume that the man, trapped by the masculine stereotypes, unable to handle the situation realistically, suffers just as much. The man who can accept the fact that his wife has a larger salary and higher status than he does is rare indeed. Often one of the following occurs: (1) The woman has to give up her career; (2) she keeps her career but slides back a little; (3) she refuses to do either, and the man falls to pieces, often becoming an alcoholic; or (4) she leaves her husband, choosing to discard him for the career.

Even when both husband and wife have professional careers, something that is happening with increasing frequency, the husband often finds it difficult to accept the situation, because the demands each makes—and has a right to make—on the other are now equal. This is especially true if he can look back with nostalgia on the way that things were in his parents' home. Thus, a professional man married to a professional woman confessed:

> I used to be a militant feminist, but now, I envy my father his conventional marriage. I remember that when Father returned home in the evening, Mother would make us children tiptoe out of his way to allow him to rest. When I come home, no matter how tense and weary, I have to play with the children because I know that their mother and I were both away during the day. My mother could protect my father's rest, and surround him with comfort, and adjust herself to his needs. I cannot count on such services from my wife, whose career is just as exacting as mine. She may need to relax when I am in a creative fury, and I may need a "backer-upper" just when she wants to tell me some news rather than do all the listening.[18]

One may reflect that it's easy to be a "militant feminist" when there's nothing to lose. And while the picture of Mother tenderly ministering to Father, tiptoeing gently around him, has its appeal, it does leave one with the impression that he has to be treated as gingerly and extravagantly as a hothouse flower or he might just curl up and wilt away.

Dr. Isidore Portnoy feels that the American male enjoys having a wife who achieves something in her own right and reflects glory on him—but only up to a point. This point is reached when she becomes important enough in her own right to make him feel small. Equally sensitive is the point at which she's investing enough of herself in her own pursuit to threaten his displacement from the kind of "favorite child" role that he might formerly have played in her life or that he might have seen his father play in his mother's life. What happens when she oversteps the line is that the male becomes forced for the first time to acknowledge to himself the dependency needs he has always had. Many of the experts I talked to, including Dr. Portnoy, feel that it's extremely difficult for the American male to acknowledge his dependency needs either to himself or to others. Of course, how a professional couple gets along depends as much on her as on him—whether she pursues her career because of its intrinsic rewards or because she needs to be competitive with her husband.

Husbands and Wives: The Mechanical Touch

Many a beleaguered male whose wife doesn't have an outside job finds himself in exactly the same position as the discomfited professional man. It's a common scene, remarked on both in the marriage counselors' offices and out of them. "I work hard all day. Get fed up to the teeth with all kinds of people constantly complaining about this and that," a supermarket manager in his thirties told me. "When I come home, all I want to do is relax. Just dump myself in the easy chair and forget the nagging housewives. So what happens? My wife greets me at the door with a long list of everything that went wrong in her life that day. And the kids are right there, too, with their beefs. That's about the time I'm ready to run—right out to the nearest bar somewhere." Succinctly summing up such male complaints, Dr. Gertrude Hengerer observed: "Men are looked on as people to come and fill in . . . to mow the lawn and fix the refrigerator. Men are looked on as functional."

In point of fact, both sexes look at each other from the narrow viewpoint of functionalism, one of the inevitable results of the rigid sex role differentiation that's part of the patriarchal heritage. The husband expects his wife to bring him pipe and slippers and make him a cooling drink while he eases off the day's tensions. The wife expects him to listen to her troubles, to fix the things that need fixing. He can't understand what kind of tensions *she* could have gone through in the cozy nest that for him represents—or, he feels, ought to represent—a retreat from the day's cares and worries. She can't understand how he could have had it so tough because at least he got to meet new people, talk about interesting things, and face the kinds of challenges she feels such a dearth of in her own intellectually barren life. He insists that she doesn't appreciate how hard he works, how much he's knocking himself out for her and the kids. She insists that he doesn't appreciate how hard *she* works, how much she's knocking herself out for him and the kids. Neither relates to the other, partly because neither is there to watch the other's activities, but mostly because they have a whole series of the old sex-role stereotypes so firmly fixed in their minds that they can't see each other as flesh-and-blood human beings and therefore can't communicate meaningfully. The relationship between them becomes a matter of "principles," and "duties," and "you're supposed to because you're a man," and "you're supposed to because you're a woman" patterns of response. To top it off, each of the marital partners takes it for granted that the other should—and will—meet needs and desires not actually articulated.

This mechanical quality in the relationship between husbands and wives is nothing very new, of course, but it becomes exacerbated when wives take equalitarianism seriously enough to want their own psychic needs met and when husbands find it difficult to adjust to the prospect of not being catered to the way their fathers or grandfathers perhaps were. This is not to say that his needs aren't as legitimate as hers, nor is it to say that one partner's needs should be favored over the other's. There are dozens of ways for marriage partners to work out accommodations that satisfy both his and her requirements. But no accommodation can possibly work out satisfactorily so long as they see each other in the old male-fostered patriarchal ways that inhibit communication, nor can it work out when the husband insists, because that's the way it has always been, "I come first," and then feels either cheated or humiliated when he discovers that he doesn't. On my desk is an issue of the *Saturday Evening Post* with one of its familiar husband-wife cartoons. This one is a bit different. The house has just burned down, everything is in ruins, and the bedraggled wife is standing in the smoking front doorframe, clutching a passel of screaming kids, when her perspiring husband comes rushing home from work, oblivious of everything around him. His first words are: "Before you say a word, let me tell you about the day I had." The joke has a point.

It's one of the ironic by-products of the patriarchal heritage that something which has always been to the advantage of men now boomerangs to their obvious disadvantage. This is true generally in the case of functionalism and true specifically in the case of the male's emphasis on work and the fruits of work as the primary measure of his masculinity. In effect, a great many American women seem to be saying, "You want to feel like a man, Buster? All right, produce." The epithet generally applied to them is "pushing wives."

To be sure, there have always been wives who pushed their husbands to increase their earnings or earning potential. Sometimes they've done this to motivate a shiftless man; other times their motivation has been pure and simple greed. But it's reasonable to suppose that more of this is going on now than ever before, as the competitive quest for financial security and status grows increasingly intense. Women aren't exempt from the cultural pressures. Time and again in my interviews with both authorities and husbands in middle- and working-class milieus the pushing-wives syndrome was presented to me as a very common problem. In fact, motivational researcher Dr. Ernest Dichter advises companies to use the wives of employees to get more production out of the employees themselves: "It is the wife of the salesman who can often be used to stimulate him and urge him to make more money." [14] (Some wives know just how to use the masculine stereotypes to twist the knife. One mother of six, chiding her husband for not showing more get-up-and-go, shoved his paycheck under his nose and said, "This looks like a receipt for a woman's paycheck instead of a man's.")

We can speculate that when a woman pushes her husband to make more money, even though his earnings are reasonable, she places more importance on things than on relationships, or she is dissatisfied with her own role and tries to live his life vicariously, or she has a compulsion to control him, or she gets him to work longer hours as a device to keep him out of the house even more than he is. But from the husband's point of view—if he gives in to her demands, why does he? That it's easier than having constant arguments is the obvious answer. Yet it's too simple—and too unfair to him—to say merely that he doesn't have the gumption to stand up to her. He may not have it, but if she feels the competitive pressures of the times, he feels them even more than she does. By producing, he's not made to seem less productive than the other men on the block or his relatives or his circle of friends. He's not giving the impression that he's slowing down in comparison with the go-getters. As Dr. Dichter described his reasoning, when I queried him about it, "Such a man is really thinking, 'I don't want my wife to think another man is more potent than I am.'" He may feel beleaguered, but in another way his male pride is nurtured.

The beleaguered American male—beset by the problems and pressures of a transitional period in the relationship between the sexes, a period in which many women are testing their relatively newfound power and men haven't yet reconciled themselves to their having it, a period in which some of the age-old tensions between men and women are being magnified—may come to feel something he hasn't consciously given much

97

thought to before. He may come to feel that marriage itself is a social invention totally alien to his innate self, that he's basically a wild creature who should be free to roam at will.

This point of view was, curiously enough, expressed by a male contributor to a symposium on "The Family's Search for Survival," held at the University of California's San Francisco Medical Center in 1964:

> First of all, considering man as he is, as a mammal, monogamous marriage is a bizarre and unnatural state. In a state of nature a normal buck, stallion or primate collects, dominates, protects and impregnates as many females as he possibly can. This has had beneficial genetic results in assuring that the species will be bred from the strongest and most aggressive males. . . . To circumvent this tremendously powerful natural instinct is indeed a traumatizing experience, and does entail a certain agony of conformity.[15]

It may be proper to compare the human male to the buck, stallion, or primate. If so, it's also proper to point out that the human male has certain physical and psychological characteristics that these animals do not—characteristics that give him his complex nature and allow him to erect bridges, build cities, and send his own kind into space; characteristics that also cause him to have needs peculiar to his particular species.

However, if the unnaturalness of marriage for the male is to be proved, primitive man may just as well serve as a reference point:

> There are other sources of agony, partly instinctual and partly psychological, that particularly affect the male rather than the female. One of these is the strong drive for freedom from restraint. The primitive man roamed far and wide and freely as a hunter; the woman cowered in the protection of the cave. The home is usually the world to the woman; often it is a cage to the freedom loving male. The English club and the

98

old-time (no women allowed) saloon represent attempts in the modern world to achieve this freedom. The nagging female's "Where have you been all this time?" is part of the agony of lost freedom.[16]

There's no doubt about the fact that many men do feel agony and do feel imprisoned in their marriages today. One of the main reasons is precisely the fact that women are no longer content to—or need to—remain huddled meekly in their caves. The woman who demands to know where her husband spent every last hour may really be expressing her own feeling of being stifled. The well-educated housewife who simply can't find enough self-fulfillment during the difficult years when her children are very young and who perhaps becomes a bit shrewish as a result does so not so much to trap her husband inside as to vent her frustrations at being somewhat trapped herself. Then, too, if it's the wife who has absented herself from the house or is unduly late in returning home, it's far from unusual for the harried husband to be the one who demands, "Where have you been all this time?"

But if the woman is to bear exclusive blame for the confinement that the contemporary male feels within his psychic self, she may as well also be blamed for the fact that he no longer feels like a hero, for he was apparently a hero only at her expense:

> The loss of the hero role in modern marriage does violence to another deep-seated male psychological drive, i.e., the desire to be a hero. Again, when the primitive male dragged the game home to the family, he was a hero; when he killed his rival and stole his rival's women, he was a hero; when he, one male, dominated a harem of females, he was a hero. Now, with equality established, the male as a hero, except perhaps in the prize ring, is no more. And he misses it. A few smart wives still use the "Aren't you wonderful?" technique, but this is a pale substitute for the pedestal of the hero.[17]

There's nothing amiss, of course, in a wife's telling her husband he's wonderful—*if* it's a heartfelt sentiment, not a stage prop to bolster his ego. For that matter, there's everything to recommend a husband's telling his wife how wonderful *she* is, under similar circumstances. If modern marriage needs a hero role, it needs a heroine role equally as much. What it really needs, of course, is two people who love and appreciate and know how to give to and how to take from each other. There's plenty of room for heroism under these conditions.

Insofar as the male and monogamous marriage as an institution are concerned, it ought to be remembered that this institution has proved amazingly durable, so durable that it has persisted in practically unaltered form through countless generations and despite the vicissitudes of the civilizations in which it has been functioning. If marriage were indeed so alien to the male temperament, might its structure not have long ago broken down or at least undergone some very radical changes? The very fact that the father-mother-child constellation remains the basic family unit—even with the disappearance of the family's religious, economic, and educational functions—shows how strong is male concurrence in the maintenance of such a unit. This concurrence would hardly be forthcoming if the male were not deriving some fairly potent gratifications from his participation in the family venture.

However, some of the deeper psychological gratifications that marriage offers the civilized male are not so readily acknowledged by him. Typically, the American male has ambiguous feelings about matrimony. On the one hand, he's an incurable romantic. When the right girl comes along, something "clicks" —he can't pin it down much more definitively than that—and he falls head over heels in love with her. He knows that he wants her to live with him for the rest of his life, and he knows that he wants her to be the mother of his children. If he's honest with himself, he also admits that this is the girl he wants as his permanent sexual partner (although he may be less apt to realize that part of his motivation for marrying her is to gain exclusive sexual rights).

On the other hand, he has the feeling—if it is only vague—that the institution of matrimony is of much greater benefit to the female than to the male. His viewpoint isn't as extreme as that of the symposium participant whose speech I have excerpted, but he's convinced that—dependent creature that she is—she has infinitely more need than he does for the emotional security that marriage ideally brings. He's convinced that, much as he's looking forward to having a family, her urges in this direction are much more basic than his. Weighing marriage so defensively, he's also apt to gloss over the gratifications that come to him from providing for and protecting his family.

I talked one afternoon with a man, now married, who was a young bachelor when he served with the U.S. Army Air Force during World War II. He was a tail gunner then, and he was acutely conscious of the dangers facing him in his service-connected tasks. What worried him most, he recalls, wasn't the fact that he might be killed on one of the bombing missions he flew, but the fact that he might die without knowing the rewards and fulfillments of marriage and fatherhood. However, he was a rather sensitive person—or a person placed in a position in life that brings out sensitivity of this kind. In his book on the U.S. Special Forces in Vietnam, *The Green Berets,* author Robin Moore mentions being struck by the fact that the rugged men doing their precarious jobs in Southeast Asia are really quite dependent on their wives and families.

When a man feels that marriage is of far greater benefit to females than to males, then no matter how much he urges a girl to marry him, he harbors an unconscious resentment against her—against all women, in fact—for putting him in this unfair position. Indicative is the kidding remark that men often make when they announce their forthcoming marriage: "I chased her 'til she caught me." On the surface it's a joking recognition of her pursuit—albeit a circuitous one—of him. But it's also an apology. It gives him an out for deserting the glamorous state of bachelorhood: She, not he, was the one really responsible, and he, victimized creature, was trapped. This attitude, that marriage is a trap set by women to snare men, is fraught with implications of hostility. A man trapped is a man whose freedom—in effect, his virility—is being taken from him.

This attitude also shows up when a man has to deny his dependence on a woman, to insist, "It is she who needs me, not I who need her." As I have pointed out, on the whole the American male is apt to deny—or at least to minimize drastically—his own security and dependency needs. The fact is that everyone—man, woman, and child—has dependency needs. They're residual, carried over from the earliest stages of human development, when the newborn being is completely helpless and dependent. In mature people these feelings don't interfere with the ability to function independently. In a psychological context, denial of dependency needs lies rooted in child-parent patterns—in feelings of rejection or the experience of the sudden loss of a loved one on the child's part. But American culture itself contributes greatly to the denial of dependency needs in the male sex. Independence, insofar as men are concerned, is not so much stressed as overstressed. To acknowledge the need to lean on someone else is somehow cause for shame and fear—shame because it seems weak to have such a need; fear because there's always the possibility of becoming overdependent and therefore under somebody else's control. Nevertheless, the need is there and fundamentally cannot be denied. This often shows up most vividly in the self-made man, the one who professes to be completely self-sufficient. He'll deny dependency to his dying day, but he is outraged if his mate fails to anticipate and meet his psychic needs.

Of course, if a man reaches the age of thirty-five or forty without having been married, he may paint fond word pictures about the wonderful psychic rewards that marriage brings to the male fortunate enough to have a loving and feminine wife. He may say that he'd like nothing better than to be a bit dependent on a good woman. But he doesn't necessarily believe what he says; it may be a way of calling attention to himself, of gaining sympathy. Nicholas Suntzeff, who has given special attention to the problems of middle-aged bachelors in his work with the Family Service Agency of Marin County, points out that many "appear to act as if they were still adolescents. And in many ways they really haven't achieved a higher maturity. They're dating on a very superficial level." Such men seem to be looking for marriageable women. But they really aren't. They make sure to date safe girls—the ones who clearly aren't the right type for them, the ones who themselves have problems in forming relationships, the ones who indicate that they won't make any demands, the ones who also deny dependency needs or are clearly overdependent types.

As for married men of thirty-five or forty or so, the ones who have a number of years of marriage behind them, should the early romantic bloom wither, their feelings that matrimony is of much greater benefit to women than to men may well intensify. If this happens, the feeling of being trapped grows stronger. The result, not infrequently, is alcoholism or infidelity or both—and finally divorce. Finding himself in this position, a man may come to have a pretty good hunch that marriage—at least modern monogamous marriage in an equalitarian society—is essentially unnatural for the male sex. It often comes as a great surprise for him to learn that his wife too feels a bit trapped.

Turning Back the Clock

The beleaguered American male may be inclined to blame his predicament—and the predicament of the modern dissatisfied woman—on the fact that she's getting a man-style education. Education, like advertising, is often trotted out to explain whatever flaws there may be in the American character or way of life. In this case, education is not infrequently blamed for two unhappy sets of circumstances. The first is the spectacle of college-trained women determined to use their education to fullest advantage even in the traditionally male fields. The second is the equally grim spectacle of educated stay-at-home house-wives sitting bored, nervous, frustrated, and maybe slightly alco-holic in their gingerbread houses, watching their brainpower ooze away amid a welter of dirty diapers and dirty dishes.

There are some grown men (and women, too), themselves well educated and practicing in the professions, in science, and even in education, who still question whether women ought to receive the kind of education men do. To the beleaguered male and to the woman's-only-place-is-in-the-home women who are fully in accord with him, the rationale for this viewpoint goes something like this: Since most women marry and have chil-dren, higher education of the kind that men get is wasted on them. Once they get it, it creates false ambitions, makes them discontented when these ambitions aren't fulfilled, leaves them less eager to play their exalted roles of housewife and mother, and sets them off to compete with men. They wind up making their husbands (and themselves) unhappy, crushing their boys' identities, and creating all kinds of mischief in society generally. No, the rationale goes, much better for women to get their own special kind of education, the kind that redefines them in terms of their traditional homemaking and mothering roles. Then won't everybody be happy?

The rationale not only blithely assumes that women are wives, mothers, and homemakers first and people second, but also conveniently overlooks a few facts, to wit: (1) Having a longer life expectancy, women may have to work when they're widows; (2) if another war comes and men are conscripted, it will be up to the women to assume some vital and complex positions in industry; (3) many divorced women must work be-cause their former husbands' alimony is insufficient (and what woman realistically can assume that her marriage will never end in divorce?); and (4) one out of every ten women never marries and has to be self-supporting her entire life.

The rationale also blithely assumes that the women who do marry will rush headlong into matrimony right after matriculating from the school for brides without finding it necessary to earn their keep for a while first. That many women do marry right away hardly negates the fact that many do not. Overlooked, too, are some of the long-range effects of foreshortening women's education. If women are expected to embrace intellectual mediocrity as a sop to men—if this is the standard set up for one half of the human race—eventually the intellect of both women *and* men will suffer.

This is not to deny that the present educational setup creates many problems for women. As schoolgirls, they are expected to compete with boys for grades and to develop their own minds. As wives, they are expected to drop all semblance of competition—at least with their husbands—and to relegate their intellectual development to a distinctly minor place. Then, too, educational institutions by and large still do not provide for the discontinuities in most women's lives. But the solutions lie in enlarging women's chances educationally, as well as occupationally, not in turning back the clock to narrow their opportunities and, in the process, their personalities.

The beleaguered male's attempts to turn back the clock in one way or another not only shows the extent of his discomfiture but also indicates to what degree he has invested the "good old days" with his special brand of nostalgia. *Those were the days, all right. A man was a man, and a woman was a woman, and each of them knew what that meant. Father was the head of the family in the real sense of the term. Mother respected him for it and received all the gratifications she needed or wanted at home, doing her well-defined jobs. There were not many neurotic, complaining women then. They loved to take care of their men, and their men did everything to protect them. Man was*

105

strong, woman was feminine—and there was little loose talk about phony equality. Or, to quote Philip Wylie on womanization:

> This calamity has befallen us in a mere quarter century. Before that the male aura dominated a society dreamed up by males, by males pioneered, made free and kept united by males —a culture still sustained by males in the main, but men whose sweating effort nowadays lops a decade off their lives that the damsels do not sacrifice.[18]

It would be instructive to take a hard look at those good old days, when the "male aura" permeated the societal atmosphere and Father was king of his domain. For that matter, a walking tour through some of the contemporary culture groups still labeled patriarchal might prove insightful and full of surprises, for it would show to what extent the beleaguered male has duped himself about the past.

IV. Back to the Good Old Days: The Patriarchal Myth

"I'm not sure why they want to be back in the good old days. Do they want to be back there as the father, or do they want to be back there as the child?"—Ruth Fizdale, of the Arthur Lehman Counseling Service, during a discussion with the author.

"They got up and gave him the softest seat in the house, but my grandmother was the one who saw to it, in 1910, that five kids got off to college. What did he do? He played pinochle." —A doctor, in Washington, D.C., discussing his grandfather.

Power Is Power Is Power

The woman sitting in the Los Angeles psychiatrist's office was in her sixties. Like Freud, she had been born in Vienna and had spent her childhood there; like the brilliant father of psychoanalysis, she lived in strongly patriarchal times. Indeed, she told the L.A. psychiatrist that her father was regarded as the boss in the family; her mother, as a very compliant woman. She said, "We couldn't even sit in Father's chair."

"And how," the psychiatrist wondered, "did your father manage that?"

"Oh, he had nothing to do with it," the lady replied. "Mother told us that if we sat in Father's chair, we'd get pimples on our bottoms!"

Like so many other people firmly anchored to our so-called equalitarian times, I had an unidimensional black-and-white view of Pop the Patriarch. He was the authority figure, I believed, the towering strength of the family. He didn't abuse his authority, but his word was law, sanctioned by society, respected by his loving spouse and children. He was, in short, powerful.

Then, beginning the research for this book, I spoke at length with the psychiatrist who told me this revelatory little anecdote about life with Viennese Father. It was good for a laugh. It was also good for a bit of thought. Here was no picture of a powerful father; it was the picture of a powerful mother holding up a supposedly powerful father. The psychiatrist told me, "I keep seeing a lot of things like that from patients who had a patriarchal upbringing."

It makes sense. It makes sense from a variety of different angles, although all of them lead back to a single base—the inherent flaw, in terms of male superiority, of the patriarchal system. Within this system male superiority depends much less on what the male *is* than on what the female *isn't*. He's strong because she's weak. His judgment is more reliable than hers because her judgment is more emotional than his. His intelligence is of a higher sort than hers because hers is so much more "personal" than his. His supremacy is assured by her subordinacy.

But the argument is circular. Under patriarchy, women have often been treated abominably enough to delight the heart of the most rabid modern-day misogynist. For centuries—with few periods of relief—the woman was her husband's (or her father's) property; she was denied most or all of the legal rights possessed by men; she was subject to be raped, whipped, sentenced to death if her husband thought her transgression grave enough. Even when the more oppressive strictures were removed her roles and rights were still severely limited. The fact that she was often shrewd or resourceful enough to acquire considerable power despite her handicaps doesn't alter the reality of these conditions.

This, then, is the crux of male "superiority": society arbitrarily stated that there were things the woman was permitted to do and other things she was forbidden to do; then it proclaimed the male superior and the woman inferior precisely because she couldn't do the things she'd been forbidden to do in the first place! If this indeed is superiority, one must marvel at the male's capacity for self-delusion and shudder at the sight of his awesome insecurity.

By and large the Victorian male—often viewed as the prototype of the strong family head—was no brutal martinet, ruthlessly subjugating his family. Nor is the mid-century man who is—or perhaps might like to be—his family's patriarch. Yet there's a striking similarity between their attitudes and that of the pathologically authoritarian male, the compulsive he-man type who frightens everyone around him because of his bullying, domineering ways, who can't help playing at being the strong man of life's circus. This may be seen by the way that the he-man—who's really only the absurd end product of the patriarchal system—conceptualizes masculinity. As Irwin M. Stein, of the Family Service of Westchester, put it, "He does it by minimizing the female structure, her assets. There's a taking for granted what a wonderful thing masculinity is, because he thinks it's so terrible—so weak—to be female. . . . Partly, he holds an image of strength or effectiveness simply by virtue of being nonfemale."

However, as Dr. Hengerer observed, the controlling, domineering man is at bottom very weak. What the caseworkers invariably find when dealing with him is how "vulnerable and soft he feels about himself inside." He displays a firm-looking shell to conceal his tacky insides.

Authoritarians have many different ways of acting out their compulsive need to dominate. In extreme, but far from unusual, cases they resort to wife beating. In 1964 three psychiatrists released some data reflecting the results of the first detailed psychiatric study of wife beaters. Probing the psyches of thirty-seven wife beaters referred to them by Massachusetts courts, the psychiatrists determined that the husbands were really "shy, sexually ineffectual mother's boys" married to women who were "aggressive, efficient, masculine and sexually frigid." [1]

According to Dr. Paul Vahanian, one trait common to the majority of domineering men, the indicator of their basic weakness, is unquestioned obedience:

> They insist that those whom they consider their responsibility respect and obey them unquestioningly. They are, in effect, the unquestioned masters of their households. They don't brook any kind of questioning of that self-conceived role.

Whenever such men *are* questioned about anything that they want or do or think, they become highly upset, even enraged. Their whole system of functioning is based on an absolute adherence to their self-image. "Any questioning of this is tantamount to questioning their potency as the authority," explained Dr. Vahanian. "I think such a personality is on very tenuous ground."

In a monumental study of the authoritarian personality (conducted jointly by the Berkeley Public Opinion Study and the Institute of Social Research), the same insecure tendencies were noted. Men who scored high on authoritarianism saw themselves as ideals of masculinity. But they were unable to accept any failures or shortcomings in their roles as men. They were experts at rationalizing everything that might be even remotely construed as weakness, softness, or passivity on their part. The study, which was undertaken to determine the psychological bases of prejudice, saw these men in terms of "pseudo-masculinity" and noted that their approach to sex—and, in a broader context, to human relationships—was "isolated" and "depersonalized." [2]

Not only do domineering men act tough because they're essentially weak, but their strong-man act itself also renders them vulnerable. Jay Haley, research associate with the Mental Research Institute of the Palo Alto Medical Research Foundation, explained this paradox:

> I don't think you can give one person all the power and his mate all the weakness. Because the weaker you make her, the more powerful you make her. Because you become more and more dependent on her doing exactly what you say. She can "hang" you with very little resistance then.

This basic flaw in the concept of male superiority is applicable not only to the pathologically authoritarian male but also generally to the patriarchal type. It's heightened by the rigid division of roles so dear to the patriarchal heart—with the husband relegating to himself most or all of the functions that have to do with the outside world and delegating to his wife most or all of the duties centered on the household and child-care areas. It results in making him far less powerful than he imagines in the very area in which his supremacy is largely taken for granted—the family constellation. By eschewing direct involvement in these vast areas of decision making, he unwittingly cuts himself off from direct influence on them. To put it bluntly, he kids himself (and is kidded) into believing that he runs the show when his wife may easily be—and often is—the family's real powerhouse: Remember the Viennese mother who adroitly manipulated the kids off Father's chair?

Neither one anecdote nor one psychiatrist's experiences are sufficient in and of themselves to explode the myth of the mighty patriarch. But additional ammunition, I discovered as I dug deeper into patriarchal times, is everywhere at hand, both here and elsewhere in the world, both in the present and in the past. The noted anthropologist Ralph Linton wrote:

> It is a common belief that women in "primitive" societies are downtrodden drudges, treated like domestic animals. I have worked in a number of such societies, including some which were supposed to be strongly patriarchal, i.e., man-dominated, and I am convinced that one finds as many dominant women in these societies as in our own.[3]

There is the famous English essayist John Ruskin, product of a typical upper-middle-class Victorian family, who wrote in *Praeterita* that his father became his guide—"happily, though with no definite intention other than of pleasing me, when he found he could do so without infringing any of my mother's rules. . . ." Significantly, it was Ruskin's mother—not his father—who compelled him to read the Bible and instituted a course of Bible study for him, yet Ruskin's background is considered not only Victorian but also highly authoritarian.

And there's the New York psychoanalyst, a man in his late forties, who has done a thorough job of examining his own patriarchal European family background, concluding:

> My grandparents followed the outward forms of the patriarchal society to a T. My grandmother would tell the children, "Hush up, your father's coming." And everybody would hush up. And there was all this outward fear of him. But I assure you, knowing this family extremely well, he was of very little importance to it—of very little importance. Oh, he was the one who growled and so on. But to consider that the family was in any way dominated by him was nonsense. His wife—my grandmother—was the central figure. And as the years went on, this was more and more openly acknowledged. So, finally, in the middle and older years he was a shadowy figure in the background. The fact that the kids ran for cover because he'd scold or he'd spank or he'd whip meant very little to them.

He did the growling; she carried the weight. The culture sanctioned his authority over hers, but indirectly she exhibited more of it. I was to hear this theme repeated time and again upon interviewing both men and women, within and without the behavioral sciences, after they had searched their memories deeply enough to get beyond their first unthinking assertions that Father or Grandfather was the more powerful member of the family.

Puerto Rican families, to give another example, are considered quite patriarchal. The Puerto Rican father, both on his native island and in the United States, generally assumes ultimate authority and responsibility for his family. Particularly among low-income families, he allows himself far more freedom than he does his wife. He comes and goes as he wishes, and he doles out an allowance to her. She has to account for her movements, keep up with all the housework whether she has an outside job or not, and get up before he does to prepare his breakfast.

Despite all this, the mother in her indirect way has a good deal of influence. In her book about Puerto Rican migrants living in New York, *Up From Puerto Rico*, anthropologist Elena Padilla tells a revealing—and typical—incident. A Puerto Rican father caught his two boys, ten and twelve, playing with a knife they had found in an alley. The father gave the two boys a good talking-to, then flatly asserted he was going to throw the knife out the window. At this point the mother spoke up for the first time and said that she'd take the knife to use in the kitchen, whereupon the father told the boys, "If you find another knife, it must be brought immediately to your mother to see if she can use it in the kitchen." To be sure, the arbitrary command was the father's—and no one dared question it—but it was the mother who made him change his mind in midstream. It is a small incident, but it illuminates one of the ways the woman's influence comes into play in a patriarchal family.[4]

At the Community Service Society of New York, which

113

counsels many Puerto Rican families, I was told that the authoritarian fathers among these families often do a lot of blustering but aren't really controlling their families. The following case history is representative. What caused this family to seek help in the first place was the fact that the firstborn son had become a drug addict and was hospitalized. Before his release it was deemed advisable to give his parents some counseling.

The father, a taxi driver, was harsh and aggressive. His job was eminently satisfactory to him, for it provided an outlet for his aggressions: He could curse the traffic all day long. By contrast, the mother was a somewhat depressed, retiring person, mousy-looking and quiet. When the two were together, it was the father who spearheaded everything and, so to speak, made all the noise. He was a real table pounder. In fact, initially he spoke in such a loud voice that caseworkers had to ask him to quiet down; he was disturbing everybody in the office.

After the Community Service Society caseworkers had had some opportunity to study the couple, it became very evident that the wife was the one who really possessed all the power in the family. She made every decision regarding the children, including those affecting the boys. She was the one who decided when they would have their haircuts (the young addict hadn't had his cut until he was three or four because she liked him in curls), what schools they would go to, how much allowance they would get. She was the one who controlled the money for the entire family; in fact, the father brought his paycheck home to her.

In short, the father impressed everybody he met that he was the strong one, the real head of his family. Actually, it was the mother who ran everything. She was unobtrusive about it. She never said, "I'm going to decide this." She always said, "I'm going to talk it over with my husband," but before doing so, she already knew what the decision would be.

There's a tendency among some professionals and many laymen to view money and power in a one-to-one relationship:

Money means power; the individual in the family who controls the money controls the family itself. This is too simple an approach, for influence and the decision-making power within a family are always a subtle interweaving of a variety of factors. It may nevertheless be said that when a wife is habitually handed her husband's paycheck, she inherits a considerable amount of power that she might not otherwise have—though whether this has an emasculating effect on her husband depends on how closely they associate money and masculinity.

When Blood and Wolfe did their comprehensive study of Detroit marriages, they found that "keeping track of the money and bills lacks a generally accepted pattern of allocation" but that "there is a high correlation between money-handling and decision-making." As for the specific place of this administrative function in the making of decisions, they said:

> Apparently keeping track of the money and bills is a crucial administrative function in the home, standing midway between the making of financial decisions and carrying them out through actual purchases. . . . Apparently making decisions about money and keeping track of money are two functions which tend to reinforce each other. They are not easily separable between one partner as boss and the other as bookkeeper.[5]

In this connection it should be noted that among Polish miners in Appalachia, who are considered patriarchal, the wife traditionally doles out the money; German and French workers, both patriarchal in their own countries, give their salary checks to their wives; the patriarchal English working husband, at least in the north of England, does the same. These husbands may very well *delegate* the money-administering function to their wives, but in the process they become far less the patriarchs than they imagine themselves. Ideally, of course, money control is allocated on the basis of which marital partner can do the more competent job, money's symbolic meaning in terms of masculinity or power notwithstanding. Some marriages certainly would be—and are—better served when the wife handles the family funds.

Among low-income families particularly such marriages may be more stable than in families whose husbands control the money but dissipate it in drinking, gambling, and the like. Howard University sociologists Dr. Hylan Lewis and Camille Jeffers explained:

> A comparison of the management of money in the marriages judged stable with those judged relatively unstable, indicates a higher proportion of unstable marriages when husbands control money than when wives control. Among the possible factors operating, is the likelihood that the wife, more oriented to the home, is more committed to see that the basic survival needs are met out of limited income; and that the man, less oriented to the home, is more likely to surrender to other pulls.[6]

Insofar as English working-class husbands are concerned, there's more to be said about them than merely the fact that they turn over their pay to their wives. Two British sociologists scrutinized the English blue-collar family structure during the mid-1950's and came up with the surprising information that the wider family of grandparents, uncles, aunts, and the like is still very much a part of life there. And who's at the center of this anachronistic extended family? Mum—the wife's mother—is the one who provides advice, succor, and an occasional scolding, who looks after the sick, who minds the babies, and who does 101 other things to give the entire family its meaning, its direction, and its vital energy. The British sociologists concluded: "The mother is the head and centre of the extended family, her home its meeting place." [7]

Among Italian-American families adhering to Old World patterns, the strong mother supporting a supposedly stronger father is very common. So is a rigid division of roles that leads the mother to assume an inordinate amount of decision-making power. According to Dr. Salvatore Ambrosino, "The Italian father issues the sharp edicts about how things are going to be done. He'll say when the children have to be in, how much money has to be spent, and so on. But the implementation, the child-rearing practices the mother employs to create harmony in the home—everything is left to her." Dr. Ambrosino added, "It's a false kind of authority he has."

Significantly, when Professor Herbert J. Gans turned his sociological eye on low-income Italian-Americans living in West End, a section of Boston since torn down, he found that wives often referred to the family apartment as *"my* rooms" and that husbands talked to their spouses about *"your* sons." On the other hand, even though child rearing was strictly the mother's job and even though the father often wasn't around much, she respected him and instilled this respect in the children. In one way or another, according to Gans, she continually identified the father as a "model of masculinity" and referred to him as the "male authority." [8]

An Italian friend of mine who has been a member of New York City's middle-class Italian-American community for about four decades takes a much more subjective—and pessimistic— view of the Italian family power structure. "In Italy the father *thinks* he has the power," this man says. "In the United States, few families even bother with the pretense."

But surely if we make an abrupt shift in time and place to prerevolutionary China, the very epitome of a patriarchal land —symbolized by the cruel practice of binding the women's feet —surely there we'll find the male displaying undiluted patriarchal power. Yet a renowned novelist and social observer, as thoroughly steeped in Chinese lore as any Asian scholar, cannot find such power there. Pearl Buck writes:

The women of Asia are strong and independent. . . . Their place in society was, and is, defined but powerful. In the family the woman was the de facto ruler, although she was trained to defer outwardly to her father, her husband or her older brother. Men exercised their authority within the accepted limits and did not interfere with women in the home. . . . True, women's place was in the home, but then the seat of power in Chinese society was the home.[9]

As for those bound little feet, the Chinese woman slyly made use of them as the instruments of her reign over men:

> And when modern times came, it was women who did not want to give up their little feet. They had for a long time wielded their power over men by those little feet. Women had grown very powerful. Within the confines of their lives, narrow in space, they had gone deep and climbed high. They had come to understand completely the nature of men. They knew men's every weakness and used such weakness ruthlessly for their own ends, good or evil. Lacking other education, they had devised cunning and wile and deviousness and charm, and they had men wholly in their power, confounding simple men by their wisdom and learned men by their childishness. Men had to feed, clothe and shelter them. Men had to work for them, fight for them, and protect them. Man's one reward they gave him. It was to allow him a feeling of superiority because he was a male, and as they granted him this in seeming generosity, they hid their smiles behind their pretty embroidered sleeves.[10]

The story is the same wherever a system of male superiority is coupled to a rigid differentiation in sex role functions, with the wife being assigned the roles that have to do with home and children. The husband-and-father is the *de jure* leader; the wife-and-mother is—or is close to being—the *de facto* leader. The Middle European Jew (at least prior to the advent of Communism) provides another proof of this. Successor to the Biblical patriarch, he lived a traditional Jewish village life. The culture was male-oriented. The father stood for the values of the community. He represented tradition, mind, and spirit. He was, as Mark Zborowski and Elizabeth Herzog describe him in a fascinating account of Eastern European Jewish life, "the household spokesman of God's law." His wife, on the other hand, represented flesh and blood. She was "the source of warmth, succor, emotional response." She was subordinate to the mighty male, traditionally his inferior. But this was the societal structure as seen from the outside. Once one peers inside, as Zborowski and Herzog do, the view is somewhat different:

> The woman's informal status is more demanding and more rewarding than that formally assigned to her, for in actual living the complementary character of her role is always to the fore. She is the wife, who orders the functioning of the household and provides the setting in which each member performs his part. She is the mother, key figure in the family constellation. Moreover, the more completely her husband fulfills the ideal picture of the man as scholar, the more essential is the wife as realist and mediator between his ivory tower and the hurly-burly of everyday life.

As realist, she was apt to work at some kind of job, in addition to managing the house, for employment in the Eastern European Jewish community was sexless. She dealt with the merchants. If there were things to be bought or sold, she was apt to do the buying and selling. As for which member of the family ran it, Zborowski and Herzog leave no doubt:

> It is the woman who manages the fiscal affairs of the family. It is proverbial that a true scholar "doesn't know one coin from another," but even in *protesh* families the woman usually stores and dispenses the household cash, and to a large extent decides how it shall be used. She is the chief counselor, likely to have power of suasion and of veto in any matter outside the World of the Torah. "What do you say?" is the husband's familiar query and a common response is, "What can a silly woman say? I have only a womanish brain, but if I were in your place . . ." Often enough, the opinion so modestly prefaced is decisive.[11]

Inferior the woman may have been, say Zborowski and Herzog, but she asserted herself "not merely in spite of her subordinate status, but often through manipulating it."

Transplanted to the United States, this lady with the "womanish brain" becomes a Molly Goldberg, of radio fame. She is the big-bosomed mother on whom everyone leans—all-embracing, all-knowledgable, all-giving—yet is shrewd enough to carve out a seemingly important place for her husband.

Even among the Mormons—in whose church doctrine patriarchal authority is a fundamental tenet, for it is held to be divinely ordained—this authority is far from absolute. A Mormon wife often has a great deal of influence, according to a sociological study of thirty Mormon couples. True, nearly all of the husbands and three-fourths of the wives agreed that the husband is—and should be—the family leader. But once again there was a wide gap between attitude and practice or, as the sociologist aptly put it, "a curious discrepancy between the concept of patriarchal authority and its exercise," which he found to be the case in fully seventeen of the thirty marriages he scrutinized.

In one case a wife had just finished stating that her husband was the final arbiter in all family disputes when she turned right around to correct him "with an air of finality" on a point of church doctrine—even though religion is supposed to be exclusively the Mormon male's area of competence and authority. In another case a wife told her son that he could go to a friend's house even though the boy's father had refused to give him permission. In six of the marriages the wives handled the family finances and doled out money to their husbands—hardly a shining example of male authority. Nor is it the mark of the strong patriarch to use his wife as a sounding board for his opinions; yet this was observed in a number of instances.[12]

Even this admittedly spotty survey of patriarchal family relationships, past and present, makes it abundantly clear that the all-powerful authoritative patriarch is largely a myth when he is looked at closely. He's a myth because his power and authority are based on a false premise, that of arbitrary male superiority. He's a myth because, as has already been noted, to confirm one's strength on another's weakness is to make the weak person strong and the strong one weak. He's a myth because, although he may have his society's sanction to be the undisputed boss in the family, this sanction is worthless unless his wife supports his authority instead of undermining it. Authority based much more heavily on outer structuring than on inner resources, while effective in part, is nevertheless on shaky ground. He's a myth, too, because the head of the house cannot largely remove himself from many family functions and decision-making areas without having his wife acquire a substantial amount of power and influence in the process. In rebuttal it may be stated that the patriarch assigns his wife to certain roles, allows her whatever authority she may have, and has the power to withdraw this authority when and as he pleases. Sociologist William J. Goode, of Columbia University, has noted:

> Readers who have observed first- or second-generation immigrant families from Italian, Greek or Eastern European Jewish backgrounds are likely to have noticed that though the rhetoric of male dominance is common, the middle-aged or older matriarch is to be found in many homes. The woman seems to be the center of initiative and decision. However, the male head of the family seems to be *conceding* this authority, reserving the right to take it back when he wishes. If he wants to oppose her will, he can do so successfully. That is, a distinction should perhaps be made between day-to-day initiative and direction, and negative authority—the right to prevent others from doing what they want.[13]

Yet what must be taken into account is that since cultural norms prohibit the wife from showing too much authority directly, her power and influence become iceberglike—only a fraction of the total is apparent to the naked eye. Authority can be far more potent for being circuitously, manipulatively used. A patriarchal husband may think that he has the power to give power and the power to take it away, but he doesn't realize the extent to which his wife often learns to acquire influence. What is most salient, it would seem, is not who has the final decision-making powers but whose *influence* predominates in making the decision.

Yet a man *is* often vaguely aware of the fact that a woman is much less easily managed than he might like, even if outwardly she appears to be compliant. He's aware of the fact that she can frequently get him to agree to things he was utterly determined not to agree to. He makes jokes about it, half believing them, half not. ("In our family I make all the big decisions —what to do about Vietnam, how to solve the race crisis.") He's somehow uneasy around women, as if they may in some way get the better of him, although he isn't necessarily able to say how or why. All he knows is that he's much more comfortable being with his own sex. It's a common phenomenon at social gatherings within every socioeconomic group for the men to congregate at one side of the room and wives at the other.

Herbert J. Gans noticed quite a bit of this sort of thing going on among the Italian-American West Enders of Boston. The men tended to be "distinctly uncomfortable" around the women. If the women tried to initiate conversations with them at socials, the men hurried to the safety of their own group. According to Gans, the men "explained that they could not keep up with the women, that the women talked faster and more readily . . . and that they tried to dominate the men. The men defended themselves either by being hostile or by retreating. Usually, they retreated." Gans put the blame for this directly on the patriarchal system with its double standard of freedom for the males. Since the women couldn't express their wishes directly, they had to use women's wiles to influence their menfolk. This meant that they had to learn how to talk— and to talk more expressively than the men—for "talk is the woman's weapon for reducing inequities in power between male and female." [14]

As for the wife of the patriarchally oriented husband, unless she's grossly lacking in self-perception, she has a fairly good idea of how much power she really wields and to what extent her husband kids himself about the family power balance. (At times, however, even she may be misled into thinking that her husband has more power and influence than he really does.)[15]

Take the classic study of a typical American town, Middletown—really Muncie, Indiana—made by Robert S. Lynd and Helen Merrell Lynd in the 1920's. According to the Lynds, Middletown husbands were inclined to refer to women as "purer" and "morally better" than men, but this didn't keep them from adding that the females were "impractical, emotional, unstable, given to prejudice, easily hurt, and largely incapable of facing facts or doing hard thinking." Were the women in this historic town fazed by this stereotyped view of them? Not at all. The women smiled knowingly and opined, "Men are nothing but big little boys who have never grown up and must be treated as such." [16]

The American Patriarch

In point of fact, the contemporary American male who looks back to his nation's history for confirmation of what the American male once supposedly was may be in for a shock—and not just because the American woman learned to get her way indirectly through the acquisition of influence. No, the power she accrued in certain vital aspects of life came directly and resulted in part from specific conditions arising out of the development of the nation itself. To be sure, the United States was, from colonial days, a patriarchy. Woman's legal and educational rights and her rights to property and the like were severely restricted until almost the middle of the nineteenth century, when the first solid cracks in the armor of male supremacy appeared. But within the patriarchal framework her scope and influence were not only wider but also more overt than elsewhere in the Western world. Let us see how it happened, keeping in mind that the patterns to be described evolved cumulatively, rather than being defined by clear-cut demarcations of time.

To begin with, consider the colonial women. They had to be a more courageous and aggressive lot than their sisters who remained behind in England. Even if they started out meekly following husbands determined to leave the known rigors of the Old World for the unknown rigors of the New, they had to toughen up if they were to survive (many didn't, of course). Furthermore, under pioneer conditions, there was no room for narrow sex-role differentiation. The Puritans, as is well known, were a business-oriented body of people within the context of their strong religious convictions. "Business," anthropologist-historian Eric Dingwall has pointed out, "was a sacred calling, and if it were carried out in accordance with God's will and direction it would have the divine blessing." Success in business —wealth itself—was merely evidence of God's goodwill. So some of the women pitched in to help their husbands with their businesses. Some others, whose husbands or brothers became sick or died, took over entirely. This didn't seem to make the Puritan men feel emasculated; on the contrary, married couples were far warmer toward and more companionable with each other than they were to be a century later. Insofar as the home was concerned, according to Dingwall, the mother was "the unchallenged head of the home, although her husband was nominally the head of the family." [17]

Three factors served to strengthen the American woman's position in those early days. They were: (1) the deterioration of the basic Puritan ideology, near the end of the eighteenth century; (2) the scarcity of women; and (3) the westward migration.

The decline of Puritanism meant a shift from an emphasis on faith and works to a concentration on works themselves. In other words, in a confrontation between religion and Mammon the latter eventually won out, as so often happens. The men became increasingly occupied with trade and commerce and with the building of the nation, leaving more and more non-business matters to women, a trend that was to grow as the years went by. Under the circumstances there was created an unfortunate overemphasis on materialism. This has to be viewed in conjunction with the scarcity of women, for that which is scarce is prized, and that which is prized usually acquires an exaggerated symbolic value when it is defined in material terms. When the nation had barely been born, then, some of its women were already learning to be vessels of conspicuous consumption, something that was to increase considerably in the nineteenth century. As far back as 1777 an officer with the British Army in the colonies wrote:

> . . . one of the necessary evils of the world, which we men-folk know how to accept admirably . . . is the domination of the women over their husbands. This petticoat rule is spread throughout America, but in quite different type than in Canada, where it aims at the welfare of the man, while here it seeks his ruin. The wives and daughters make a display beyond the income of most of the men. The last penny from his pocket must be yielded for the purpose—there is no help for it.[18]

We may suspect that he was exaggerating, perhaps because he was homesick for a docile lamb of a girl across the ocean. We may also suspect that the pattern was then no more one-sided than it was several decades later, when in upper-middle-class circles it became much more pronounced. When women are gold diggers, men are rarely helpless victims of their trepidations. To shower their womenfolk with luxuries is for many men a mark of status, an affirmation of masculinity.

The expanding American frontiers further expanded women's roles. Frontier conditions required role specialization if the myriad tasks that had to be accomplished were to be done most effectively. Men fought the Indians, gouged communities out of the wilderness, set up their trades, and instituted commerce. Women suckled their young, spun cloth, did the washing, made sure there were chintz curtains over the windows, helped fight off the Indians when necessary, and saw to it that there was some order within the disordered frontier life. Was it only their other tasks that kept the men from participating in this latter endeavor? The answer is negative. As the distinguished psychoanalyst Erik H. Erikson observed in a discussion of the American identity, the men who opened up America's frontiers had for one reason or another felt stifled in their countries of origin. They wanted to be free, and the imposition of order, either external or internal, frightened them. So "these men insisted on keeping their new cultural identity tentative to a point where women had to become autocratic in their demands for some order." [19]

Therefore, it was the frontier woman—not the man—who became "the cultural censor, the religious conscience, the aesthetic arbiter, and the teacher. In that early rough economy hewn out of hard nature it was she who contributed the finer graces of living and that spirituality without which the community falls apart." [20]

The frontier experience was, according to historian Frederick Jackson Turner, the most profound experience in America's history. Indirectly, its impact is still with us. In Europe and in America during colonial days, culture and education were male endeavors; during frontier times they became female, and this is the way it has remained. In 1965 author-poetess Phyllis McGinley could write, with a large measure of truth if with an unfortunate implication of approval of this sexualization of a cultural life that should be shared more or less equally by both sexes:

"It is our [housewives'] influence which will determine the culture of coming generations. We are the people who chiefly listen to the music, buy the books, attend the theatre, prowl the art galleries, collect for the charities, brood over the schools, converse with the children." [21]

The frontier experience was, of course, neither uniform nor isolated. Wave after wave of immigrants from the East struck out over the prairies; wave after wave came to the East from Europe. The American patterns and traditions slowly being shaped in the new land were by no means similar in all parts of the country. It wasn't until 1860, for instance, that Eastern schoolteachers were predominantly women. In the South the wives of plantation owners faced pressures different from those of frontier wives. Life was slower and more languid in the South than in the West. Nevertheless, the Southern women too had to be strong; in many instances their husbands were away on business trips for months at a time, and it was up to them to run the plantations.

In the East unique patterns brought over from England were also to pervade the psyche of the nation. Victorianism was taking hold, even before Victoria was actually established on the British throne. Middle- and upper-middle-class families—those who could afford it—adopted the pretensions of female helplessness and the dogma of female purity. Lower-class women couldn't easily accept all the Victorian conventions—swooning isn't exactly compatible with factory work—but they tried. These conventions made their slow way to the outer limits of the frontier, a most improbable place for them. In *The Natural History of Love,* Morton H. Hunt tells of a young man who arranged to have several dozen eligible young ladies brought to the Puget Sound area. The feat won him a seat in the Oregon state assembly. "I had been taught to believe, and did believe," he is quoted as saying, "that practically all the goodness in the world came from the influence of pure-minded women. At that

127

time there was not a single woman of marriageable age on Puget
Sound . . . [and] the bachelor element was almost wholly beyond the reach of female influence and its wholesome results." [22]

The American wife in Victorian times, therefore, not only
exercised her power circuitously but in large measure did so
directly. This was the case in all areas of family life, including
even those over which the husband and father supposedly held
unilateral decision-making powers. Thus, in the case of many
middle- and upper-middle-class families the husbands involved
themselves so thoroughly in their business affairs that the wives,
although subjugated in many important respects (far more than
pioneer or frontier wives were), nevertheless were forced to
take on many parental tasks that were supposedly the father's.
After examining scores of items on American childrearing practices published between 1820 and 1860, Robert Sunley (now
with the Family Service Association of Nassau County, New
York) came to the following conclusions:

> The role of the father received little attention in contrast to
> the great emphasis placed on the role of the mother. . . . The
> father in such families, whether from prior disposition or as a
> result of his wife's absorption in motherhood, then became
> more occupied with his work. Writers often mention how many
> fathers spent most of their time away from home and had little
> to do with their children. The father gave such reasons as the
> need to frequent bars after working hours in order to make
> business connections. While some writers on the subject still
> tried to give the father the position of the instructor of the
> children, even this function seems to have been declining. The
> mother not only was taking over the teaching of the young
> child, but also was handling the daily disciplinary problems
> rather than waiting for the father's presence in the evening.
> Daily religious observances, previously conducted by the father
> as head of the family, were less and less practiced, and the
> mother tended to take over what was left of this function.[23]

The oppressive nineteenth-century sexual double standard put the Victorian woman in a position of sexual inferiority—but, as we have seen, very much in a position of moral superiority. The deference paid her by the men was enormous. In his analysis of *The American Woman*, Eric Dingwall referred time and again to foreigners who left our shores bewildered by the way the women were catered to. Upper-class women dominated the social scene and, for all their supposed helplessness, ventured into other areas as well. In 1855 a social observer, N. P. Willis, had this to say about life in the United States as he saw it:

> It is the women who regulate the style of living, dispense hospitalities, exclusively manage society, control clergymen and churches, regulate the schemes of benevolence, patronize and influence the Arts, and pronounce upon Operas and foreign novelties; and it is the women . . . who exercise the ultimate control over the Press.[24]

The question is, How much accuracy can we place in observations like Willis's? Maybe this particular nineteenth-century writer was a dispassionate observer; then again, maybe he was a beleaguered male of his time, unable to accept the conventions of the era and seeing feminization wherever he looked. But even if we evaluate his appraisal conservatively and chop off a bit of its credibility to allow for exaggeration, the fact remains that there were many statements like his, emanating from many different sources, all attesting to the power of the upper-middle-class Victorian woman.

Consider the following remark in a mid-nineteenth-century novel set in the United States; A French maid comments to the footman, "Monsieur is man of business, Madame is lady of fashion. Monsieur make the money, Madame spend it. Monsieur is nobody at all—Madame, everybody altogether." [25] Consider the intriguing point, made by Dixon Wecter in his definitive work on the rise of American society, *The Saga of American*

I

Society, that in the Old World aristocracies, when a man married, "he endowed the woman with his social rank. . . . Quite different has been the trend in American society, by which rich Astors, Vanderbilts and Belmonts have risen from social nobodies to nobility by marriage with patrician women from the Livingston, Armstrong, Schermerhorn, Kissam, and Perry families." [26]

Consider, too, the extravagant comments about motherhood in the child-rearing literature—and the popular psyche—of the time. The following appeared in an 1849 issue of the magazine *Mother's Assistant*: "Yes, mothers, in a certain sense, the destiny of a redeemed world is put into your hands; it is for you to say, whether your children shall be respectable and happy here and prepared for a glorious immortality, or whether they shall dishonor you, and perhaps bring your grey hairs in sorrow to the grave, and sink down themselves at last to eternal despair!" And in another issue of the same magazine: "You [mothers] hold the sceptre in your souls in which, more than the laws of a legislature, now repose the futurity of the nation, the world, and the destinies of the human race!" [27]

Such advice presumably was directed at the educated middle-class women who bought such ego-gratifying journals. The newly arrived immigrant wife-mother didn't, but societal factors operated to increase her importance almost at once insofar as her children were concerned, if only because the father's prestige was lowered. For many first-generation immigrant families it has proved difficult to adapt to American ways. The children, however, usually want to adapt immediately, to discard the old ways in favor of the new. Does this cause them to reject both their old-fashioned mothers *and* their old-fashioned fathers? No, just the father is rejected. As sociologist Geoffrey Gorer pointed out, the immigrant mother "might be as old-fashioned and tainted with European ideas as the father; but these drawbacks could not interfere with her provision of care and succor and food and love." [28] Pop was expendable.

But power is relative, and none of the above is to suggest that the Victorian woman ran the show in the broad sense. Her direct influence was great—much greater than that of European women—in a narrow but highly significant band of activities. She was, nevertheless, living in a firm patriarchy that circumscribed her with all kinds of humiliating restrictions—from such major ones as civil rights and education to such petty prohibitions as engaging in mild exercise. The Victorian male's overall supremacy was affirmed by the society and supported by his wife. He was his family's economic leader, an aspect of his functioning that ought not be minimized. Financially, his wife was totally dependent on him. Like his supremacy, her subordinacy was affirmed in many respects. Nor to be minimized is the simple fact that he worked at or near his home; propinquity served to confirm his importance and authority in relation to wife and children.

What can be said with some degree of certainty is that the patriarchy, as it evolved in the United States, is unique in regard to the power and responsibility that it has assigned its women in the areas of child rearing and culture, in the shaping of the personalities of the young. This is of tremendous importance in exploring the condition of the contemporary American father, who so often these days is accused of having abrogated his paternal responsibilities.

V. The Paradox of the Contemporary American Father

Fathers Are Parents, Too, by Dr. O. Spurgeon English

"The Vanishing American Father," *McCalls Magazine*

"What Ever Happened to Daddy?" a chapter in *Suburbia's Coddled Kids,* by Peter Wyden

Has Anybody Seen My Father? by Harrison Kinney

"Putting Down Father," *The New York Times Magazine*
—partial list of critical literature about the contemporary American father.

"It's easier to make money than it is to be a good father. If you're willing to put in the hours, willing to stick your nose to the grindstone, you can really bring in the greenbacks. This applies to every strata of society. I think that for many fathers making money is something tangible, something that can be shown immediately, at the end of the week. 'I made this much money, and it shows what a man I am.' Now, to be a good father, what are the tangible rewards? For many people the rewards come much later, when the kids are grown up and out on their own. Then, too, the family is a risky proposition in terms of rewards and self-enhancement. The kids might not turn out well—while on the job you get paid."—Dr. Paul Vahanian, in a conversation with the author.

Every Day Is Mother's Day

Comparisons between men and women on which sex has it rougher in this world are both onerous and pointless. Yet it is fair to say that in at least one area men face far more difficult problems than women. I refer specifically to the parental role.

It is no easier, of course, to be a mother than a father. The important difference is that while the mothering role has remained essentially the same throughout the ages, the father's role has been changing radically. The mother has always nurtured her children, exercised discipline over them, and involved herself deeply in their socialization, in seeing to it that they grow up more or less adjusted to the requirements of society.

The role of the contemporary American father, however, is inconsistent with the patterns of the past. Since he works outside the home and often has to travel a considerable distance to get to his place of employment and back again, today's father has little opportunity to be with his children or even to make his presence felt by them. The trend to the equality of the sexes is rapidly doing away with the external scaffolding of authority that used to structure him in the past. The shrinking of the wider family unit to its nuclear base focuses the spotlight of paternal responsibility directly on him, and this responsibility has enlarged in inverse ratio to his authority. In other words, his duties have expanded while his rights have diminished. Today's father no longer teaches his children his craft, as he did in rural America. He no longer apprentices them to others. He no longer controls their education, nor does he even have the illusion of doing so. He has little, if anything, to say about their marriages. On the other hand, he's expected to exhibit a wide range of fatherly responses. He's supposed to support his youngsters financially, as always; support them all the way through college and even graduate school, if possible; be firm with them but understanding; involve himself in their problems; help his wife care for them physically; baby-sit with them occasionally; discipline them effectively, but be a pal to them as well; present an authoritative masculine figure that his girls will admire and his boys will emulate; act as friend of and wise counselor to his brood; be warm and affectionate with them; and be their link to the wider community.

Countless books, magazine articles, speeches by child-care specialists, parent-training manuals, and pronouncements by psychologists tell him of these responsibilities and make him feel guilty—or, more likely, spur his wife on to make him feel guilty—about not meeting them adequately. Advice and criticism have been coming in thickly and heavily for the past decade or so. It seems that there's little he does or *can* do right. If he moves his family from city to suburb, he's placing them in a "manless" environment. If he concentrates on being a pal to his son, he's evading his role as authority figure. If he has a nurturing bent, some of the psychiatrists call him a motherly father. If he doesn't do any nurturing to speak of, he's accused of distancing himself from his children. If he's the sole disciplinarian, he takes on, in his youngsters' eyes, the image of an ogre. If he doesn't discipline them sufficiently, he's a weak father. If he's well off and gives his children all the material advantages he didn't have, he's spoiling them, leaving them unprepared for life's hard knocks. If he's well off but doesn't spoil them the way other fathers in the community do their boys and girls, he gains the reputation of a latter-day Scrooge. If his work keeps him away during the week and he tries to compensate by spending extra time with his children on weekends, by doing special things with them, this is also wrong. He's told either that he's making himself into a goody-goody figure with them, while his wife has all the dirty work of really bringing them up, or that he'll eventually come to resent the concentrated time he spends with them because he'd rather be out playing golf. And, repeatedly, the accusing voices tell him that he has given up his rightful place as head of his family, as guide and mentor to his children.

If the advice is contradictory at times, and the criticism more so, it is in part due to the fact that the experts themselves have widely divergent opinions on the proper role of the father. So does the society in general. In fact, American society is somewhat schizoid in its attitude toward fatherhood. This is the result of another one of the innumerable ironies springing out of the patriarchal system. The Victorian mother might have shouldered most of the responsibility for the children's care and upbringing, but she gained in turn a powerful form of compensation: She was glorified. She was idealized. Her virtues were praised to the skies, and of faults she was deemed to have none. To an extent we have inherited this glorification of the mother. True, vituperation is often hurled at the possessive, castrating, domineering Mom that Philip Wylie first thrust into the spotlight some twenty years ago, and currently there are attempts by some neofeminist writers to downgrade the mother's importance. But theirs isn't a winning battle. The "cult of motherhood," as Wylie aptly described it, is still fairly potent. In fact, when sociologist Helena Lopata at Roosevelt University in Chicago asked more than 600 urban and suburban wives what a woman's most important roles are, in order of importance, the great majority of the ladies voted first for "mother." ("Wife" came in second; "homemaker," third.)

As for fatherhood, there is no cult. Nobody votes the father's role as the most important in a man's life (although it's highly questionable whether either sex should consider the parental role the most important in its life). Despite all the demands that contemporary society makes on the father, despite all the expectations it has regarding his performance, fatherhood in America is accorded remarkably little respect.

An anonymous saying goes, "God could not be everywhere, and so he made mothers." In a nation in which Mother's Day not only is a yearly ritual but also generates $1,500,000,000 worth of business, such an aphorism is devoutly believed. From the mother-child mysticism stem such clichés as "Nobody knows a child the way its mother does" and "A boy's best friend is his mother." There's some truth to them, of course. Why shouldn't there be, if Pop hasn't been around much and traits like sympathy and understanding are labeled feminine?

Orthodox psychoanalysis, which has had such a pervasive influence on American culture, tends to elevate the emotional response between mother and child to impossibly lofty heights —heights to which no mere father could aspire. Consider Dr. Marynia Farnham's declaration: "The special genius of women has always been that of nurture, for which man has no talent whatsoever." [1] Consider Dr. Erich Fromm's phenomenally successful analysis of love, *The Art of Loving,* which states, "Mother's love is bliss, is peace, it need not be acquired, it need not be deserved. . . . It is for this altruistic, unselfish character that motherly love has been considered the highest kind of love, and the most sacred of all emotional bonds." [2] Consider Dr. Ashley Montagu's pronouncement in another work that has garnered a huge readership over the years, *The Natural Superiority of Women:* "The sensitive relationships which exist between mother and child belong to a unique order of humanity, an order in which the male may participate as a child, but from which he increasingly departs as he leaves childhood behind." [3]

Even the nation's child custody laws prove how potent the cult of motherhood still is. In almost every state both the law and court practice give the mother a clear and almost insurmountable advantage in divorce cases in which there's a battle between mother and father over custody of the children. Unless it can be shown that she's a distinct hazard to the health or welfare of her offspring—something very difficult to do—most courts in most states award full custody rights to the mother under the blanket assumption that a child needs to be with its mother. It is the case even when the father is just as willing and just as competent to raise the children as she is. In some courts it is the case even when the mother is obviously the less desirable parent from the standpoint of both morals and competence. It could be argued that men want it this way, that it precludes saddling them with the physical responsibility for the offspring. This may have been true at one time, but the frequency of child-custody battles shows that at least for some fathers times have changed. (Both lay people and legal authorities in some states are trying to correct the situation. Attempting to effect legal reforms in his state, for instance, an Ohio jurist, Judge Roy C. Scott, has observed that "a man's status in divorce cases and domestic problems is not an enviable one" and that "the father in many cases is just as well equipped to have custody since he, too, can hire a baby sitter.")[4]

It should be possible to acknowledge the vital role of love and nurture that a mother plays without giving it the inflated stress that borders on caricature, without making the father's role seem peripheral and inconsequential by comparison. But this has not been happening. Not surprisingly, the *Thesaurus of Quotations* lists thirty-one "apt thoughts" and "felicitous expressions" for motherhood and a scant ten for fatherhood, the most felicitous of the sparse lot being the proverb "It's a wise child that knows its own father." Not surprisingly, either, psychiatrists and sociologists complain about the dearth of solid data on fatherhood, pointing out that the behavioral sciences have concentrated primarily on motherhood. Even the mass media, grown so critical of the American father, make their own intriguing commentary on the condition of fatherhood today merely by the way they present this criticism. The majority of articles pointing out what's wrong with the contemporary father appear in the women's magazines, which most men don't read. Speeches on the subject are frequently given by women—and to an audience of women. In 1965 a series of television programs on the problems facing the American male, including those concerning his role as parent, took place on a midmorning show whose viewing audience is composed primarily of housewives. The ludicrous conclusion one could come to is that fatherhood is somehow feminine!

A goodly portion of the professional literature that exists on fatherhood suggests that the best father is the one who has relatively tenuous emotional ties with his young ones. When the child is in infancy, according to this viewpoint, the father's primary role is to protect and support (both psychologically and financially) the new mother. As the child grows older, it's permissible for him to show love, provided that this love is exclusively conditional—that is, strictly earned, given as a reward for good behavior or accomplishment. Woe to the father's image if he diapers the baby, feeds the child, or displays in any way the kind of warmth we have come to associate with motherliness. His image, many psychiatrists still insist, will turn motherly. It goes without saying that in such patriarchal eyes the father who has a nurturing bent, who enjoys helping take care of the little ones, who doesn't withdraw love from his children even when he exercises discipline, and who gets considerable emotional gratification out of their love for him is somewhat lacking in masculinity—and will create unmasculine sons.

As psychoanalyst Irene M. Josselyn is frank to admit, a great deal of psychological literature "tends to minimize the significance of any possible psychological response specifically called fatherliness." Pointing to a definite psychological existence of fatherliness, she includes among its elements the child as a narcissistic extension of the father, as proof of the father's manliness, as rival, and as an object of "tender love." Dr. Josselyn adds, "Unfortunately, when this emotion acts as a cohesive force in men, it is too often considered evidence of the repressed femininity of the man." [5]

The very term "tender love" within the context of fatherhood still sounds somewhat strange, so seldom is it used. It is not that the contemporary father fails to display warmth and affection to his children. By and large he does, at least when they are young. We have come a long way from the nineteenth-century aloofness, when a studied coolness was the mode between father and child. Today there are warmth, laughter, and spontaneous affection. Today some fathers delight in sharing with mothers in the care of even very young infants.

Still lacking is a really basic awareness that a father can enjoy, wholly as a man, the give-and-take of psychic nurturing that we tend to associate primarily with mothers. Actually, the father who permits this give-and-take to occur finds his own scope widening as a result. As Dr. Milton R. Sapirstein has pointed out, this kind of participation allows the father to resolve his own "residual dependencies," affords him an opportunity for "fulfilling his creative drives," and helps him to open up emotionally, for "many a father has learned to be a healthy emotional human being only through contact with his children." [6] Despite scattered insights such as these, there is still little real intellectual crystallization of father love.

Furthermore, the most recent sociological studies on the subject show that the boys who see their fathers giving warm positive affection, as well as providing discipline, are more likely to identify with them than the boys who don't. Hence, these are the boys least likely to have problems with their masculine identity.[7] Important as these findings are (and they're beginning to be publicized), it certainly seems as important to stress the joys of fatherhood—the emotional rewards it provides for the father—as to stress the duties and obligations the paternal role imposes on him. Too often the emphasis is on what the father must do, with little or nothing said about what he can receive. Then, too, unless he's profoundly involved with his children on an emotional level, today's father is apt to have ambivalent feelings about them, for unlike youngsters in a rural setting, they constitute economic liabilities, and he must work all the harder to provide for them than he would otherwise. If the involvement isn't there, he's likely to feel, if a bit guiltily, "Is it all really worth it?" Here, then, is another reason for stressing the fact that fatherhood is potentially a two-way street, that it provides rewards, as well as imposes obligations.

The Dagwood Bumstead Syndrome

"What about the father? As far as his biological role is concerned, he might as well be treated as a drone. His task is to impregnate the female and then to disappear," wrote the great anthropologist Bronislaw Malinowski. The contemporary American father isn't being looked on as a drone, of course, but the atmosphere surrounding him is oddly jeering or contemptuous. So lacking in essential dignity has Dad become (except on Father's Day, when his presence makes a healthy impact on the gross national product) that he's tailor-made for the sneer approach. Whatever his shortcomings and however much he may have fooled himself about his power, the patriarchal father of 50 or 100 years ago at least didn't have to sit by and watch the mass media amuse themselves at his expense. Nor, one suspects, would he have permitted such a thing to happen.

For one thing, he wasn't exposed to the denigrating magazine cartoons prevalent during the past several decades. *Playboy's* "Love, Death and the Hubby Image" surveyed the cartoon scene as it reflects the contemporary father image and found the American male lampooned in dozens of cartoons in magazines like *The New Yorker, Look,* and *Good Housekeeping.* Author William Iversen concluded that "examples of such down-with-Daddy husband razzing are so numerous that it would take no more than a few minutes to fully document a charge of pictorial sadism, verbal castration or symbolic patricide." [8]

141

One of the favorite techniques, both in cartoons and in articles, seems to be the portrayal of Dad as something other than human, the anthropomorphic insult. Needless to say, the image is never flattering. The June, 1965, issue of *Family Circle* is a case in point. It carries an article entitled "How to Get More Mileage out of Daddy," which compares the family man to the family jalopy. The blurb entices the housewife reader as follows: "Like a station wagon that isn't paid for, a daddy needs constant loving maintenance to keep him in good working order. Remember—appreciation helps cut down depreciation." [9] The advice in the body of the text is just as patronizing, just as condescending. Yet, on reflection, the piece leaves one with the impression that likening father to a car may not be such a bad idea after all, at least not if the intent is to convey subliminally the idea that mother is fairly well ensconced in the driver's seat.

Comic strips do their considerable share to make Pop the butt of the joke. Whereas most of the unmarried comic-strip heroes are adventurers, swashbucklers, and romantics, with virility oozing out of every pore, the married ones with few exceptions are good-natured buffoons. A Temple University professor has described the typical male comic-strip character as "a Dagwood Bumstead, a well-meaning idiot who is constantly outwitted by his children, his wife, and even his dog." [10]

Television provides another practically endless stream of verbal and visual insults that yesteryear's father was lucky enough to do without. Some of the commercials take such deadly aim that it's difficult to believe the sponsors aren't deliberately trying to offend at least the male segment of the viewing audience. A detergent commercial, for instance, shows two married men doing their families' wash in the basement laundry. There is nothing wrong with men throwing the wash into the machine but there's everything wrong with deliberately caricaturing them as gushing-housewife types, men who clearly ape their mates. A commercial sponsored by a salt company shows two men discussing the relative merits of various brands of salt. Again, there is nothing wrong with this—except for the fact that the two men are portrayed as simpering mother-attached caricatures of the American male. Columnist William S. White commented, in discussing the male who's so consistently denigrated by television commercials:

> For him, the apogee of enchantment, the very mountaintop of bliss, is attained when, happy, happy moment, he is able to show that his wife approves his choice of deodorant, and even uses the same one herself. This for him is the highest measure of their togetherness; he is, after all, something of a fellow, is he not? [11]

Nor is the viewing time *between* commercials often more uplifting to the male. This is clearly apparent in television's tiresome parade of situation comedy shows, another insult that yesteryear's father was lucky enough to do without. In most of these shows, Father can be classified as the village imbecile. When he tries to fix a faucet, he winds up with a flooded basement (either his bride or a husky repairman comes to the rescue). When he attempts to fend for himself, he nearly sets the whole house afire, trying to cook a meal. Bring a beautiful sexpot into his orbit—usually a teacher he is all set to give hell to because she has been picking on Junior—and he degenerates into a drooling adolescent.

The sad-sack state of the contemporary television father is summed up in the ending of one of the *Danny Thomas* shows. Pointing to a plate of hors d'oeuvres, a housewife asks, "What's that ridiculous-looking thing?"

Without thinking, the other woman points to her own husband. "That's Charlie," she answers.

Maybe in time the men of the nation will tire of such emasculation and will let the offending parties know their feelings in no uncertain terms. Until it happens, though, the mass media's mass castration will proceed apace, and the contemporary American father will be ever more emphatically confirmed as a vestigial figure.

The Biological Myth

The father's status as a vestigial figure and the mother's much greater prestige derive from some popular and, in part, debatable interpretations of biology. These interpretations are based on one unquestionable fact: The father impregnates, but the mother conceives. She's the one who has the fundamental biological connection with the child. Fatherhood, it has been emphasized by Margaret Mead and others, is a "social invention" learned "somewhere at the dawn of history"—society's way of providing protection for mother and child. Some behavioral scientists—Dr. Josselyn for one—challenge the view that, as she put it, "the role of fatherhood is a psychologically foreign one, artificially imposed by the culture for the survival of the race." [12] Nevertheless, the fact remains that in any popular comparison between the roles of mothering and fathering, the latter —being far less based on biological ties—seems relatively unimportant.

One may ask whether the mothering role does indeed find its wellspring entirely in conception and parturition or whether learning plays a more significant part than is popularly granted. Is woman born with a full array of maternal feelings which grow and mature in conjunction with her physical maturation? Or do these feelings take on shape and form during the process of enculturation? As with all other aspects of the biology versus culture dilemma, there's no simple answer. "It simply is not possible to dissociate the two aspects of mothering—biological and social," Dr. Nathan W. Ackerman has observed. Referring to studies which have attempted to measure the existence of a maternal instinct in women, Dr. Ackerman has noted that the results do not lend themselves to definite conclusions:

> The constitutional factors influencing mothering are difficult to estimate in and of themselves, insofar as their manifestations can never be observed in pure form; their influence can only be inferred because their effects are always clothed in socially structured patterns.[13]

The fact that she *can* become a mother may give a woman *some* inborn psychological tendency toward motherhood and maternal response. It's this tendency—if it exists at all, and many authorities are inclined to doubt it—that's so often exaggerated and idealized, so often paralleled with the much more clearly delineated mothering instincts found in the animal world. A woman is not a salmon, struggling bravely upstream finally to deposit her eggs and then, spent, to die. A woman is not a rhesus macaque that gives birth approximately 50 percent of her life. A woman is, as Morton M. Hunt has pointed out in his balanced exploration of the subject, a human being and is therefore "born almost completely unequipped with rigidly patterned instincts." Although she has "powerful amorphous drives toward food, comfort, sex, and so on," she nevertheless has no "inborn, predetermined mechanisms which automatically come into play to satisfy those drives." [14]

She isn't *automatically* a mother, with all the subtleties and complexities of attitude and action the word implies. All these she learns from her culture, absorbing its particular ways of motherliness. The learning process doesn't begin the moment that the rabbit test shows positive; it doesn't begin when the pubertal breasts first ripen and the menstrual flow initially starts. It begins, as the result of countless cultural clues, much farther back, from infancy on. As Hunt observed, a human mother, unlike an animal mother, must "*learn* how to be kind and loving, and how to want and to care for a child."

Here, then, is a crucial point to consider in this exploration of fatherhood: When we view the maternal role in the context of a learning process, the dichotomy between it and the paternal role becomes far less striking. *Both* mothers and fathers are— and must be—culturally prepared for their child-rearing functions. The differences between motherhood and fatherhood become even less striking when we consider the relative ease with which women can suppress their mothering tendencies—can, in effect, learn *not* to want children or at least not a sizable number of them. The alacrity with which women latch on to each new advance in contraceptives specifically designed for them—like the famous pill—shows that the maternal drive (if there is any such thing) isn't so powerful that nonmaternal wishes can't supersede it.

Missing: The Concept of Fatherhood

Seen in the light of learned maternal behavior, American males are on the whole woefully shortchanged when it comes to learning and being encouraged to learn their paternal roles. Preparation for motherhood is, as we have seen, a cumulative experience. It starts in very early childhood and is progressively reinforced until the girl actually becomes a mother. By comparison, men are clearly disadvantaged in their preparation for fatherhood. Since their potential for the paternal role isn't structured by a biological framework, boys ought to be made especially cognizant of the multifarious parental responses they'll be called on to exhibit one day. Instead, they see—in their own homes—that fatherhood either assumes narrow dimensions or is more or less irrelevant. They don't get the feel of fatherhood the way a girl gets it for motherhood. The result is that, as psychoanalyst Bruno Bettelheim has said, "Only very occasionally, for boys, is fatherhood added like an afterthought as part of their self-image as mature men." [15]

No wonder fatherhood so often and so quickly bores a man. No wonder a research study into what preadolescent (eight-to-eleven-year-old) boys consider the appropriate images for themselves and for girls shows enormous differences in orientation. These boys think girls must stay close to home; keep clean; play more quietly and gently than boys; are prone to cry when scared or hurt; and are afraid to venture to hazardous places like rooftops and empty lots. Girls play with dolls; fuss over babies; talk about clothes; need to learn cooking, sewing and child-care—but it's much less important for them than for boys to learn such things as spelling and arithmetic.[16]

The fact that the girls would become mothers someday was implicit throughout. Contrast this with the way that the same boys viewed their own roles. Only in the most indirect fashion did they acknowledge their own potentialities for fatherhood—and then only in terms of the breadwinning (protective) role. Boys "have to be able to fight in case a bully comes along; they have to be athletic; they have to be able to run fast; they must be able to play rough games; they need to know how to play many games—curb-ball, baseball, basketball, football; they need to be smart; they need to be able to take care of themselves." They should also know all of the things girls don't know—how to climb, make a fire, carry things. Furthermore, "they should have more ability than girls; they need to know how to stay out of trouble; they need to know arithmetic and spelling more than girls do." [17]

One wonders how a boy building up a mosaic of stereotypes like these (suitably laced with male chauvinism) will grow into a man able to handle the various paternal challenges, big and little, that come along to test his mettle as a father and a male. How, for instance, will the father handle the first major crisis—the birth of his first child? Unprepared for the new demands that will be made on them, lacking readiness for the new roles they'll be called on to play, many fathers face the prospect of parenthood with real foreboding and genuine feelings of inadequacy.

The insecurity such a man feels is heightened by the fact that he's suddenly shoved out of the favored position in the family as his wife necessarily identifies much more closely with the needs of the new baby than with his. He may then withdraw psychically or become a submissive, loving, but easily manipulated third party to the symbiotic mother-child dyad.

How, being relatively unprepared for the fathering role, will he handle the close attachment that his young sons are likely to develop for their mothers? Freud postulated the existence of an Oedipus complex, stating that each boy, from the ages of (roughly) three to seven, passes through a difficult phase in which he views his father as a rival for his mother's affections. In Freud's terms, it's the crucial phase in the formulation of the boy's masculine identity. There's considerable skepticism among a portion of the psychological community about the reality of the Oedipus complex as an innate phenomenon. Anthropological data denies its existence in many other cultures. But there can be no doubt that in our society a triangle situation often does develop between the boy, the mother who gives him so much attention and provides for so many of his needs, and the father. Frequently the father considers himself—or is made to consider himself—extraneous to this close relationship between the two others and withdraws even further from the fathering role. Alternatively, he meets the boy's hostility and moodiness toward him with his own hostility and moodiness. Either way, a lack of balance is created in the family. The boy misses a male figure whom he can respect and identify with and who will help him grow out of this phase. If the situation persists—if the father remains passive, weaker than the mother, or rejecting as the boy grows up and if the mother remains or becomes dominating and overprotective—the boy either develops into a weak, passive man basically fearful of women or actually becomes a practicing homosexual.

To an extent, of course, a mother sensitive to the situation can compensate for a father who absents himself physically or psychically. She can maintain his identity in the home, his presence and importance, as it were, by the way she refers to him in front of the children when he isn't there. But if she herself feels cheated by his absence—as is sooner or later likely to happen—the tensions that build up aren't going to predispose her to refer to him affirmatively. On the contrary, consciously or unconsciously, she's apt in time to denigrate him and tear down his image.

How will the unprepared father handle the feelings of rivalry likely to come when his son is a teen-ager anxious to display his own burgeoning masculinity? The boy may be a source of pride —but also a threat. By his very presence he tells the father, "Your strength can't go on forever. I'm here challenging you." Some competition may be inevitable, and on the boy's part it may be a healthy aspect of growing up. If the father feels inadequate as a parent or as a male, he's likely to show ambivalence: urging the youngster to do well, but trying to crush his ego at the same time. Many fathers are "thrown" by a son's first request for the use of the family car or for a bigger allowance for dating purposes or by other manifestations of approaching manhood. The Crestwood Heights study of suburbia showed fathers becoming pals with their sons as a "cultural ideal" because the community's "concept of time makes ageing and the looming prospect of the termination of the career a very real threat to the man; the prospect can be softened by playing down the actual gap in years between father and son." [18]

How will the man who has little concept of the fathering role handle his relationship to his daughter—a relationship presenting its own delicate problems? To his daughter, the father represents, so to speak, the first man in her life. He's largely responsible for the way she forms her general attitude toward men. If he is fearful of women and shows it either by retreating into passivity, by using brutal authoritarianism, or by insisting that the females in his family adhere to rigidly patriarchal patterns, she soon senses it. It doesn't take her long to discover that—directly or via the manipulative approach—her mother is the real, the only, strength in the family. Her images of masculinity and femininity, of the male-female relationship, develop accordingly. In an intriguing study of maternal overprotection made by psychiatrist David M. Levy, twenty classic Philip Wylie-type Moms—all of them highly dominating women who had badly overprotected their sons—were put under the psychiatric microscope. In almost every case, Mom had a history of father deprivation in her childhood. In several of the cases, Mom's father had either died or deserted the family when she was a very young child. Most of the other Moms had "passive," "cold," "stern," or "tyrannical" fathers, with whom no meaningful relationship was possible, and they grew up in households in which their mothers were the dominant figures.[19] Thus, the combination of dominating mother and ineffectual father creates not only weak sons but also dominating girls, who turn out just like the girl that married dear old Dad.

How is the father going to handle the most difficult and crucial job—that of giving his children the materials they need to fashion a coherent, mature, meaningful set of personal values for themselves? How is he going to provide them with the guidelines that will help them recognize the differences between freedom and license, assertiveness and anarchy, self-worth and self-seeking? This is the crux of the matter, the area of his paternal functioning in which his failure to exercise sufficient authority and initiative shows the most blatantly deleterious results. That he *is* failing is hardly surprising. History has given him a powerful nudge in that direction, but there's more to it than this. When the pace was slower, life's changes less kaleidoscopic, and the pressures for success and for security less intense than they are now, a man had the *mental* leisure to acquire, assimilate, and pass on—or have his wife pass on—meaningful values. He was also supported by the fact that his range of choices was fewer and his life—both on inner and outer levels—more clearly delineated. He knew much better who he was and what he was, so it became much easier for him to offer his identity to his family. Caught in compulsive, contradictory patterns, the contemporary father is hard put to define himself and his own values, much less convey them without confusion to his offspring.

A goodly number of American fathers follow one or the other of two courses of action: (1) They leave the guidance and decision-making aspects of fathering pretty much to their wives, or (2) they involve themselves, but narrowly—concentrating on instilling the achievement motive in their youngsters. Let us consider the probable results of the two courses.

The Children Take Over

Without the old supports she used to have, eager in many instances to assume *less,* rather than *more,* responsibility in the home, the wife is ill equipped to be the sole family authority. She nags her husband, understandably enough, to do more in this area. Reluctantly, he leaves the home workshop—which he set up in part to isolate himself from too much family involvement—and mouths the standard verities to his children. But unless he practices what he preaches, reciting a kind of Boy Scout Promise has little effect, and what the children swiftly grasp is not the verities but his own bewilderment. Increasingly, the wife goes elsewhere for help. She devours reams of material on child rearing. She becomes unspontaneous, afraid to act on her own initiative with her children. She relies more and more on outside sources—such as teachers, counselors, and even babysitters—to assist her in playing the mother-father role. The obvious result is that the children tend to look less and less inside the family for the structuring they used to get there. Dr. Otto O. von Mering put it this way at a meeting of the Family Service Association of America:

> The maze of youth clubs and councils, recreation centers, and agencies, presided over by child specialists, and the widespread collective membership in streetcorner and schoolyard societies have encouraged children to adhere prematurely to extra-familial values and norms of behavior. Together with and reinforced by the welter of merchandise and pulp literature, movies, and television presentations with the youth brand stamped on them, they have all too often provided the only form of "supervision" and the only standards by which today's children are asked to live.[20]

In effect, the sequence of events goes like this: the parents feel inadequate to assume authority in the home and evade that responsibility; this creates a kind of power vacuum; as in any vacuum, somebody steps in, and in this case it's the children themselves; since the young people have taken over the stronger role, the parents now count on them for a sense of direction; the mass media, the advertisers, and the manufacturers feed the situation and capitalize on it by aiming their sales guns with ever-increasing fervor at the burgeoning youth market; the youngsters themselves gain an ever-increasing sense of power; and, presto, you have a child-centered culture.

All this makes it apparent that the marketplace is an integral part of the phenomenon. While some of the experts still debate whether husbands or wives have the greater consumer-purchasing influence, the youngsters themselves are stepping in to take command. B. S. Durant, president of the giant RCA Sales Corporation, stated publicly that although American youth was doing "a $24 billion business above the surface, we estimate that their total buying influence extends to four times this amount." Referring to a handsome increase in the sale of portable phonographs, Durant added that teen-agers are no longer content with $20 models; instead, "they seem to be persuading their parents to buy them our $150 models." [21]

The spectacle of father depending on mother depending on the children themselves to say how they'll be brought up and how much to spend on consumer items is dismaying to behold. The youngsters are pushed to make decisions they simply aren't equipped to make; the accent is on instant gratification; the emphasis in the parent-child relationship comes to be rather more on materialism than on essential communication. Frequently, teen-agers seem to know more about their fathers' money than they do about its source. Dr. William A. Schonfeld, past president of the American Society of Adolescent Psychiatry says, "Many modern youngsters can't even describe accurately what Father does between 8:10 when his train leaves and 6:20 when it brings him back." [22]

It may be said that in America the young have always led the way, their elders (particularly among immigrant groups) looking to them for help in assimilating to the American way of life. It may also be said that in the face of industrialization and urbanization some loss of parental authority is unavoidable. This is true, but the point is that the pendulum has swung too far. In recent years the reliance and concentration on—and the exploitation of—the young have become intense enough to create a peer-group culture so potent that now even many parents who *want* to assume authority have a hard time bucking it. Some of the more thoughtful parents among my interviewees were sincerely troubled by the situation. Many of the experts I talked with were also troubled. Typical of them was Dr. Gertrude Hengerer. Acknowledging that in some students today there is a growing social awareness, she nevertheless stated:

> I'm worried that we're not geared at this time in our nation to teach responsibility as early as people ought to have it. Children are being pushed out much earlier without the protections they used to have. I'm very much concerned about our creating

an irresponsible, immature, undisciplined people. Here we see many, many more impulsive young persons. This is the trend.

When inexperienced youngsters look for guidance to other inexperienced youngsters, when children don't even know what their fathers do for a living, this trend is hardly astonishing. The peer-group culture is admittedly difficult for parents to compete against at this late stage, but the less communication there is between them and their offspring, the more difficult it becomes. A father cannot control his children's education these days, but he can discuss with them some of his business problems; can possibly bring them to his place of employment from time to time; can take them to political meetings, government offices, and the like; and can give them closer contact with what Dr. Paul Popenoe calls "the serious side of the family's undertakings" by providing them with an understanding of leases, installment contracts, insurance policies, and the family's budget. Few fathers take the trouble to engender this kind of communication. It is, of course, easier to be a pal.

A number of psychiatrists contacted while this book was being researched saw in the current lack of paternal authority the root not only of immaturity but also of male passivity and of a disinclination in the contemporary American male to take risks. The indulgent father who exhibits no meaningful authority, they said, thereby engenders more terror in his sons than even a really harsh father could. Dr. Ralph Greenson explained this seeming paradox:

> A strict father is a very tough father to deal with. But no father is far worse, because then the child's fantasies have free play and it creates another father who is so frightening that he's much more terrifying than the really harsh father could be. A child's instincts are far more primitive and destructive than an adult's behavior. If you don't have a father who corrects your notions about your fantasies, you will create a much worse father by yourself.

For some time, probably as a reaction to the authoritarian Victorian concepts of fatherhood, the experts have thought that children who were given a great deal of freedom and permissiveness would grow up to be psychologically healthier. But the opposite is occurring. When no limits are set, no rules established and no punishment meted out, a child becomes frightened of all authority because he has no experience within the family to cope with it and grow with it. Such a child projects his own fearful instincts onto this blank surface, as it were—or becomes so instinct-ridden and impulse-ridden that he cannot set up any controls for himself. According to Dr. Greenson, males who have had very good-natured and easygoing fathers— fathers who never contended with them, never fought with them—often become quite terrified of violence. The terror originates in "projections of their own violence which were never corrected by the realities of father."

The Success Motive

Many American fathers today—particularly in the middle and upper-middle classes—pride themselves on the fact that they're not being too good-natured, too easygoing. They're sure that they display authority. So they do, but it's on narrow and erratic terms, for the men involved are the ones for whom masculinity is very strongly tied up with the success motive and for whom status becomes the validation of success. They know that you can no longer get anywhere in life without a college degree (although they may not realize that such men as they have created this closed-shop intellectual system), so they push their sons to get good grades in school. They push very hard, as though grades were all that mattered, and the compulsiveness with which they insist on the high marks, the good schools, the right classes, and the proper fraternities (if possible) bespeaks more than an interest in readying their offspring for the rigors of the world. Some of these fathers have "made it" themselves and want their sons to do as well or better; many others haven't been notably successful but at least want to take credit for producing offspring that are.

Mothers, too, abide by the success motive. At the Family Service Association of Palo Alto and Los Altos, California, I was told that frequently this pushing "is the parents' only common area of agreement. To get Johnny up, up the ladder," At the Family Service Agency of Marin County, California, a caseworker said, "I've never seen anything like it as a syndrome in the San Francisco peninsula and in Marin County. You push them in school, haul them to horseback-riding lessons, to music lessons, to tennis lessons. . . . The kids have got to accomplish."

On the East Coast, but surveying the national scene, Dr. Dan W. Dodson, director of the Center for Human Relations and Community Studies at New York University, put the pushing syndrome into perspective: "The thing which is bringing status today is whether the children are leading their classes in making grades in school. Whether they are academically curious or not is of small consequence; the grades represent goals of status rather than goals of growth or achievement." Dr. Dodson told me of suburban parents who give their children trips to Florida and winter vacations if they attain high grades—a form of academic payola.

The competitive pressure to get the boys into college is, according to many observers, fantastic; the pressure to get them into graduate school is becoming increasingly so. Whether a young man is college or graduate-school material is irrelevant; the important thing is to be admitted, to obtain the degree. Once again the competition is of a distorted kind; the goal is not individual excellence but making the top grades in class or, at the very least, manipulating things to get by.[23] One perceptive lad, victim of the status-competition game remarked:

I've always had the feeling that I was an employee of my parents. I was supposed to be something—like their car or their house—that they could point to with pride.[24]

From any standpoint and for both sons and fathers this exaggerated emphasis on competition and status, on the externals, is a loser's game. If the lad is docile and good and true, if he makes the top grades, if he gets into the finest schools, if he always does better in comparison with others in his peer group, and if this represents his meaning as a person, his success pleases himself and his parents and his community. It gives him a sense of accomplishment. But it also engenders grave problems in identity, and the sense of accomplishment remains curiously ephemeral. He can never really be himself, a person with a core, someone who believes in something. The problem is that he has been highly conditioned to associate success with approval (love). To succeed—first at school, later at work—means to be loved. Success being transitory and love being necessary, he becomes the proverbial man on a treadmill, the compulsive one who can never relax and stop running.

Referring to "yardstick rearing"—the continuous comparison of one's child to others—the Episcopal minister Gibson Winters notes that such a child "comes to see himself only as a doer—a performer" as he becomes an adult.

He is a bundle of performances which can be called forth by the right signals. . . . A person's insides shrivel in this atmosphere. . . . He becomes increasingly worried about failure. Every failure is a tragedy, because one belongs only if one succeeds. One must not fail. One has to succeed, because this is who we are—those who succeed. Successful jobs have always depended on effective work. This is nothing new. What is new to our way of life is the feeling that we can only belong as long as we succeed.[25]

So the lad who tries like hell but just can't measure up to his parents' expectations faces a real inner struggle when, say, he winds up at Podunk U. instead of at Princeton. He'll find it tough to get rid of the guilty feeling that gnaws at his psyche—that he has let Dad down. He'll find it even tougher still to rid himself of the gnawing suspicion about himself—that he really doesn't measure up as a man.

It's less than a surprise that the compulsive approach to competition—this radical shift of emphasis from the joy of learning to the quest for a high mark on the report card, which is being pushed by the school, as well as by parents and peer groups—is occurring at a time when the rate of cheating, nervous breakdowns, random violence, normless Beat rebelliousness, and even suicide soars among middle-class youths.

The father in such a case is, of course, painfully aware that he has somehow failed in the father-son relationship—failed, that is, as a man. It may be the first time he really, consciously, associates fatherhood with masculinity.

VI. Potency and the Sexual Revolution

"Today, millions of women, freed by technology from many household tasks, given by technology many 'aids to romance,' have become pioneers, with men, on the frontier of sex. As they become knowing consumers, the anxiety of men lest they fail to satisfy the women also grows—but at the same time this is another test that attracts men who, in their character, want to be judged by others."—David Riesman, *The Lonely Crowd*.[1]

"The basic fact is that they're all babies. . . . They just don't seem to have true masculine qualities. They're always and forever deferring to you. They never make up their own blinking minds about where to eat, where to go, what to do. It drives one dotty. . . . They even ask you, under the most propitious circumstances, if they may kiss you. Fancy a European or an Englishman ever doing that. . . . From all my observations, and those of all the girls I know here, it's the fault of the American woman. She babies him and wears the pants. It's as absurdly simple as that."—An English secretary working in New York City.[2]

New Light on an Old Standard

The contemporary American male as lover is caught up in a welter of contradictions. The masculine stereotype demands that he be sexually virile and attentive, but he devotes most of his psychic and physical energies to making a success of himself in the breadwinning role. To make love freely and spontaneously, he must acknowledge his sexual partner erotically; yet too often his stereotyped view of her gets in the way of real eroticism. He lives in a society that exposes him to an unceasing array of sexual stimuli, yet severely limits his response to them. He expects to be the dominant figure in the sexual relationship, but the social and sexual patterns he follows tend to make his woman the controlling figure. He enjoys bragging a bit about how much he likes the girls, but many of his attitudes reflect rather more hostility—or at least suspicion—than they do liking. He considers himself a pretty sexy fellow, but in some of his actions he betrays a fear of, and antagonism toward, sex.

The contradictions are either engendered or exacerbated by a phenomenon of the profoundest importance in the sexual relationship between the sexes: the American male is witness to, and sometimes unwilling participant in, the breakdown of the sexual double standard. As a result, many of his comfortable notions about female sexuality are turning out to be will-o'-the-wisps, and insofar as women are concerned, he faces even greater challenges in the bedroom than in the world outside. Indeed, this is the crux of the sexual revolution so often and so indiscriminately discussed these days—the slow, erratic, anguish-filled, but implacable march of women toward sexual equality and the changes this is bringing about.

The woman's sexual revolution demands adjustments and adaptations on the part of both sexes. However, since the male has always insisted on his freedom and since—in terms of visible trends, at least—the American woman is now insisting on hers, the burden of adjustment and adaptation falls on him. In some ways he likes this new state of affairs. He has more sexual partners available; they participate actively, instead of conforming to a sexual ideal of passivity; in marriage, he and his wife achieve a sexual adjustment much sooner than in the past; the sexual climate is much freer and much more healthy than it was during the Victorian gloom. But in other significant ways the woman's sexual revolution is proving highly disconcerting to him—and to her as well. Equality implies choice of action; choice implies responsibility; responsibility demands perspective. The old ways of the sexual double standard were easier; they were less demanding.

On an intellectual level a majority of better-educated American men may say that sexual equality is fair and just and may nod approvingly over the continuing erosion of the double standard. But when they are faced with this equality on a more starkly personal basis, their reaction often is emphatically un-equalitarian. This is to be expected. The American male does not, after all, live isolated from any of the traditional patterns in the relationship between the sexes, and the sexual double standard has been in existence for thousands of years. It has had currency in primitive societies and in highly developed civilizations, in sophisticated centers and in remote parts of the world. It is by far the predominant sexual pattern in the relationship between men and women. In effect, the history of the interaction between men and women almost everywhere in the world and far back into the reaches of time includes overwhelming and sometimes really extraordinary measures on the part of men to dominate or to control the female's sexual behavior or to allow uncontrolled behavior only under conditions socially degrading to her.

It would be a surprise if the contemporary male, having the weight of this pattern on his psychic shoulders and being, moreover, the product of an antisexual Victorian culture, were to feel at ease about the sexual equality of a woman who meant something to him. By and large he's not at ease. Any random conversation on the subject at a cocktail party bears this out, and so do a variety of professional observations.

Scrutinizing adolescent dating patterns in ten Northern high schools, sociologist James S. Coleman found that the double standard still is very much institutionalized there. Another

161

L

social scientist, Ira L. Reiss, surveyed premarital sexual standards on the college campus and found that most college men still adhere closely to at least some facets of the double standard.[3] Perry J. Gangloff, executive director of the Family Service Bureau of Broome County, New York, made an illuminating comment on the subject of infidelity and the double standard: Wives are apt to accept unfaithfulness in their husbands if they otherwise carry on within their families as usual. Husbands, on the other hand, are much less tolerant; they "tend to bring their unfaithful wives to the agency for counseling, expecting that the agency will persuade the wife to stop her unfaithful behavior."

Curiously, a host of psychiatrists and family service counselors presented me with virtually the same casework material regarding married couples whose wives, as well as husbands, had had premarital sexual experience. During the counseling session it's usually the husband who comments on his wife's premarital affairs, not the other way around. Despite the fact that he brought up the subject in the first place, he's likely to hide his real feelings by assuring the caseworker that he's not at all bothered by his wife's lack of chastity at marriage. He'll also say that it plays no part in their present marital difficulties, although this is clearly not the case. Often he's markedly suspicious of his wife's fidelity to him, even when suspicion isn't in the least warranted.

Such men are in the clinical population, but the apprehensions they unconsciously feel about their wives' premarital and extramarital sexual experience are no different from those overtly voiced by men everywhere for many centuries. Why has the female rarely been entrusted with her own sexuality? A number of plausible answers have been forthcoming. It takes little imagination to realize that the male, being bigger and more muscular than she is and not being encumbered by pregnancy and childbearing, would among preliterate peoples and in the beginnings of civilization establish himself as the dominant—therefore controlling—figure in all aspects of life between the sexes. Having established his superiority over the female, he viewed her as more or less a servant, much as he did his cattle and other effects. He required her to be intact upon acquisition. Afterward, she was to be available for his use only —unless, of course, he wanted to use his prerogative of sharing her with others, as is the case in some cultures.

As for the woman, she really had little choice, not only because she was weaker and needed his superior strength to protect her, but also because she needed protection for her children. In effect, she was trading her freedom for male protection.

As for the offspring themselves, they're another factor often mentioned in any discussion of the double standard, for closely allied to the notion of property is the notion of inheritance. After all, paternity is inferential. Males in patriarchal societies —where inheritance always passes from father to son—had to establish some degree of certainty that the chosen sons were actually their own. This reinforced the proscription against extramarital sexual activity for wives. Still another reason advanced for the establishment of the sexual double standard is that unbridled sex for everyone in the community would lead to so much rivalry and jealousy as to threaten the community's very existence, and it has always proved easier to control the sexual desire of women than that of men.

These are reasonable explanations for the formation of the sexual double standard, and all may have played a part in it. Yet it's difficult to believe that repressive measures of the kind directed against women, so sharply focused on her sexual behavior and so consistently applied for so many centuries, do not, in addition, have a more fundamental reason behind them—a reason perhaps buried in the unconscious mind of the male. Analyzing primitive man's virginity taboos, Freud wrote: "Where primitive man instituted a taboo, there he fears a danger; and it cannot be disputed that the general principle underlying all these regulations and avoidances is a dread of women." [4] Analyzing the meaning of feminine purity, a favorite double-standard concept often used over the past 125 years both as a sop to woman and as a lever to make her conform, psychiatrist Abram Kardiner wrote:

> It connotes either, "You, the woman, shall have no pleasure at all," or "I alone shall give you pleasure," or "I don't care whether you have pleasure or not; you shall give me pleasure and me alone." [5]

Why the dread of woman? Why this obsessive concern about her sexual pleasure? Maybe the puzzle of the sexual double standard and its longevity over these thousands of years take on more clarity if one narrows on one of the elemental and irrevocable biological differences between the sexes—the penis compared with the cunnus. During coitus, his penis puts the male to the test in a unique way—a way the female isn't tested. She can pretend arousal; he must obtain an erection. She can think of totally nonsexual matters and still carry on with the sexual act; he has to be in a specifically erotic frame of mind to sustain his erection. She can pretend pleasure; for him, little pretense is possible. If she's so inclined, she can mask failure to reach an orgasm with make-believe; he can't: his sexual success is highly visible, and so—humiliatingly—is his failure. Furthermore, sexual functioning can occur without her active participation; it cannot without his. Upon reaching an orgasm, she doesn't ejaculate; that he loses semen (unconsciously equated with strength) is a very obvious matter. In his case a multiple orgasm is a relatively rare phenomenon; in hers, not at all. He's subject to detumescence, the loss of sexual capacity, very soon after reaching an orgasm; she can, if she wishes, simply keep on going. This leads to an age-old fear in man that she can't be satisfied and either drains him dry or turns to other men, once thoroughly awakened. The sum of these differences in male and female sexuality has, it would seem, given men a tendency to anxiety in relation to the female.

This anxiety comes sharply into focus when we take into account the two diametrically opposed—yet strikingly similar—viewpoints that men have always held regarding the female sex drive. Most of the time they've taken her to be an insatiable creature, whose power it is to make putty of otherwise grown males—the conclusion being that she had best be kept in check. This held true for the Hebrews, Romans, early Christians, and Arabs. For instance, a study of historical changes in sexual attitudes, *Sex in History,* quotes a little-known passage from Ecclesiastes: "Women are overcome by the spirit of fornication more than men and in their heart they plot against men." [6] The Victorians, however, disregarded the hitherto consistent view of supercharged female sexuality. In that time of great social and economic change, attitudes toward sex underwent a profound alteration: Sex went underground. Convention had it that woman's sex drive was far weaker than man's, if it existed at all, and that decent women neither enjoyed sexual intercourse nor were aroused by it. Actually, when one follows the two historical trains of thought about female sexuality to their logical conclusions, they wind up at the same safe spot. If woman is insatiable, she can't be satisfied; if woman is unmoved by sex—well, then, she can't be satisfied. Either way the male is, sexually speaking, off the hook.

That the sexual double standard is—at least in part—based on the male's anxiety about the unique sexual testing process to which he's subject doesn't mean the female isn't also put to a sexual test. At the very minimum she has to draw the male's interest, if not actually make a bold attempt to excite him sexually. She must, as one psychoanalyst picturesquely explained, "find ways of making this place of hers attractive for the man." The testing she's subjected to clearly engenders its own anxieties. But men have generally recognized the fact that the greater responsibility for, and greater proof of, sexual readiness is theirs. And they have interpreted this biological fact as a challenge, a trial of manliness.

It's precisely at this point, the point at which the male's copu-
latory ability becomes tied up with his notions about himself
as a man, that concern about his potency begins. A vigorously
competitive society in which particular emphasis is placed not
on how well a person does, but on how well he or she does in
relation to others, intensifies these associations between sex and
male pride and increases the resultant anxiety. The male is
forced to keep comparing his performance with that of other
men. The American boy of seventeen who still hasn't toted up
his first sexual experience feels much less self-assured than his
more experienced classmates, feels that there must be something
wrong with him. So does the married man twice his age who is
perfectly content with the quantity and quality of sex he and his
wife have had until he learns of another man's having twice
that amount of sex. Prompted by his newly crystallized anxieties,
he may go to his doctor and seek drugs to increase his potency.
This kind of request is hardly uncommon in physicians' offices
these days. When the first two Kinsey volumes on sexual behavior were published, some social scientists kept exclaiming in
surprise over the fact that the books were so popular with the
general public despite their profusion of dry statistical data and
tables. It was precisely this data that was so fascinating—and
potentially anxiety-provoking—for one could compare one's
own scores against the tables and come away with a sexual
rating of sorts.[7]

In the sexual revolution of the twentieth century, women are
beginning to emerge victoriously from the sad, twisted anti-
sexualism of the Victorian era to affirm the force and equality
of their sex drives. For many a beleaguered American male the
growing emergence of the sexually emancipated woman is more
than a profound threat; it's a definite distortion of the natural
order of things. Yet nature doesn't bear him out as he would
like it to. Although the female sex drive isn't as constant as the
man's and although it's more easily inhibited, once it has the
freedom to express itself and is awakened, it proves fully as

strong as the man's—if not stronger than his. The female animal in heat expresses her sexuality with unmistakable vigor, and in the few cultures where women are allowed full sexual freedom, they are as sexually inclined and as initiating as the men.

Yet, in a curious way, the beleaguered male is perfectly correct. A distortion does exist—because sexual equality, as it's shaping up in America, is no equality at all. Not when the pendulum has swung all the way 'round, and as with the ancient Hebrews, Romans, early Christians, and Arabs, the contemporary male's plaint, increasingly heard these days, is that his female counterpart is sexually far too grasping, greedy, and aggressive.

The Modern Woman's Demand for Sexual Pleasure

What is working the most fundamental change in the sexual relationship between the sexes—what is making the greatest impact on the male and giving vent to accusations of sexual aggressiveness—is the fact that the vast majority of American women now want the sex act to be pleasurable for themselves, as well as for the men.

This expectation holds true for virgins and nonvirgins alike, for women in every age group and all social classes. It is the inevitable result of the wedding between the feminist movement and the libido and sexual repression theories of Freud, and it is given further impetus by the commercialization of sex. The image of the plodding, unimaginative, selfish husband who rolls on a wife more dutiful than responsive for a quick act of sex—and who then rolls over and falls asleep, sexually sated, while she tosses and turns for a long time—is an enduring one in American sexual folklore. But it's obsolete in spirit—although not, of course, in fact. Women know that there's sexual pleasure

to be had for the female of the species, and they hope to get—
or, increasingly, insist on getting—it for themselves. It's to be
expected that the middle- and upper-middle-class women, the
ones most exposed to—and the most sophisticated about—the
sexual revolution, would emphasize their own sexuality. But so
pervasive has the woman's-right-to-sexual-pleasure movement become that it's being emphasized in blue-collar reading material
as well. More and more sin-suffer-and-repent stories in the con-
fession magazines, mostly read by women from a low-income
group, accent what one confession-magazine editor described to
me as "the thrills sex gives women" and sex scenes emphasizing
women's "rapturous response." Articles in these magazines also
reflect concern for women's sexual pleasure; they deal with
frigidity, impotence, wedding-night problems, and the like. In
her *Blue-Collar Marriage,* Dr. Mirra Komarovsky notes that
most wives "think that men are more highly sexed than
women," but even though it's sometimes communicated indirectly "there is no mistaking their feeling that ideally wives
should also experience sexual enjoyment." [8]

The recognition that the woman, too, has the right to pleasurable sex is a rewarding one for men. It means that their
partners are more responsive than they were before. It means
the freedom to experiment in the conjugal bedroom with the
less conventional forms of sex, rather than to look to the bordello
(as the Victorian men did) for sexual spice and variety. But the
positive side of the picture is marred by the new responsibilities
the male faces and the new image of womanhood he must get
used to. For many men it's a difficult adjustment. They discover
that women's sexual freedom means not only the right to respond but also the right to initiate. And more girls are becoming less shy about initiating, less veiled about their desires, than
they were before.

To a man whose yardstick is the traditional, somewhat inhibited girl who, even if she is experienced, always waits for the
male to be the clear-cut, direct initiator and aggressor—that is

to say, if he's like most males—the girl who is candid about her own sex desires appears sexually menacing, rather than sexually exciting. Drs. Phyllis and Eberhard Kronhausen, conducting a sex study of American college men, noticed that a number of them gained their initial experience with older women but that some were so taken aback by the spectacle of a female frankly wanting sex that they rejected the invitation. The same thing occurred on the campuses themselves, when a girl made her sexual interest in a boy too plain for (his) comfort.[9]

The Kronhausen assessment was made in 1960. Four years later, author Gael Greene, doing a study of sex and the college girl, found the situation unchanged. Conceding that "a girl's perception will, of course, be distorted by her own fears and prejudices," Miss Greene had to admit, upon taking stock of the current campus scene:

> One of the most striking characteristics of sex on the campus in the sixties is the widening gap between the conservatism of the college boy and the increasing sophistication of the coed. It plagues the girls. It threatens and paralyzes the boys.[10]

At least some of the boys evade the issue in much the same way that their adult counterparts do—by concentrating on outside achievement for confirmation of masculine identity. In 1963, at a time when there was a great deal of furor about campus sex, a large northeastern all-male university considered liberalizing its rules regarding visiting rights. The powers-that-be consulted one of the professors, asking him whether, in his opinion, such liberalization would result in orgies. He told me that he had replied, "Orgies? A lot of these students don't even know how to hold hands, they're so focused on intellectual activities!"

But the campus is only a segment of America, after all, and the American woman's growing reputation as a sexual aggressor springs only partly from what goes on behind the walls of ivy.

It's a reputation confined—so far—mostly to the middle class, and it bids fair to supplant the American woman's earlier reputation for Momism—that is, in the late 1940's she was reputed to devour her sons emotionally; in the mid-1960's, to devour her menfolk sexually.

There *is* a parallel. Most of the more virulent critics of the domineering Mom barely mentioned the man she was married to; he wasn't even important enough to criticize, although his passivity was partly responsible for her ravaging her sons emotionally. Similarly, the critics of the sexually emancipated woman of the 1960's find plenty to say about her supposed rapacity, but for the most part they refrain from placing the problem in a wider framework that encompasses both sexes. When psychoanalyst Theodor Reik tells a *Playboy* panel that he's astonished by the way "women, more and more, are taking over the active roles in sex, which was not so before," he prophesies that the men are finally going to resent it, but it behooves us to at least wonder whether *any* activity on the part of the sex with the supposedly lesser sex drive would unnerve some men and whether the women are becoming increasingly active because the men are becoming increasingly inactive. When author-raconteur Alexander King tells the same panel that sexual equality has gone too far, "so that women are sitting like district attorneys to see what the man can or cannot perform," and adds that this has put men tremendously on the defensive, we're entitled to question this assumption that the sexually emancipated woman has run wild with her newfound power and to ask whether the entire patterning of male-female relationships today actually forces women into a dominant position sexually.[11]

We can certainly infer that a sexual vacuum of sorts is being created and that the patterning isn't at all conducive to sexual equality by considering the change in the nature of sexual complaints over a period of several decades. This qualitative change has been tremendous, and a number of the authorities with whom I discussed the American male had something to say about it. A quarter of a century ago the typical female patient complained that she didn't like sex and couldn't achieve sexual satisfaction. The typical male patient complained of premature ejaculation or outright impotence. Both sexes were somewhat in the same plight: they wanted sex but couldn't have it. Today, increasingly, the women are saying, "My husband doesn't try hard enough. He doesn't want it often enough." And the men are saying, "What can I do with this woman? She's so demanding. Why doesn't she let me alone?" Dr. Ralph Greenson's conclusion is that men "seem to have become more security-minded, rather than pleasure-minded."

One of the recurrent themes the experts I interviewed voiced time and again was the reluctance (or inability) of many American husbands to accept any sexual condition other than male control and male supremacy. They function perfectly well within the limits defined by the sexual stereotypes of masculinity and femininity. But if their wives, perhaps carried away during a moment of passion, take some of the sexual initiative, they become offended. For such men, too, any coital position that places the woman symbolically or actually in the dominant position is anathema. Voicing her dilemma in the face of such male sensitivity, one middle-class wife among my interviewees said, "I want to please my husband. I want to make him feel comfortable. But sometimes I feel like I'm having to walk on eggshells."

In point of fact, clinicians are finding that in a number of their cases involving frigid women the problem is by no means all it seems to be on the surface. It's not a simple matter of a sexually inhibited woman frustrating her sexually eager husband, although both partners may see it that way. The clinicians are discovering that in these particular cases the woman certainly has her own problems, but so does the man. Without realizing it, he gives her to understand—either consciously or unconsciously—that he would be terribly threatened were she to respond freely to his ardor. A psychiatrist in New York City told me of one frigid female patient who articulated this feeling beautifully after she had been in therapy for a number of months. She said, "You know, I don't trust my husband. I'm afraid to let myself go. If I did, I really don't think he could take it." [12] To judge from my interviews, many American wives are secretly afraid—justifiably or not—that their husbands can't take it.

A Quest for the Sexual Ideal

Does the foregoing mean that a man can't function adequately and give his sexual partner pleasure under a system of sexual equalitarianism? This is the opinion of a number of observers, who view with dismay the unfortunate consequences of equalitarianism to date. The authors of a study of esoteric Eastern and African sexual practices summed up this pessimistic viewpoint that either men or women must dominate—that equality is impossible:

> Feminine equality may only be achieved by masculine abdication and at the price of masculine subjugation. The sexual consequences of the subjugation by the "equal" female are well defined and have often been described: the male, in varying ways and degrees, is "unmanned." It would seem that a great many men, and quite likely the majority of men, are able to function at peak level sexually only with women who are submissive and who willingly accept, or skillfully pretend to accept, the domination of the male.[13]

The trends developing in the United States and beginning to develop in Europe would seem to bear this out. Yet it is a degrading portrait that is painted—that of a male so weak that he can only function adequately at the price of female inferiority—and it overlooks one very important factor. *There*

*must be congruity between role expectation and the prepara-
tion for the role.* It's perfectly reasonable to expect a man and
woman to engage in vigorous, mutually satisfying sex and to do
so under conditions of equality—provided that circumstances
are congenial to this expectation. Some couples do enjoy precisely this kind of sex life within an equalitarian setting. Many
do not, however, because the conditions are not at all conducive
to it.

There are a number of reasons to explain this. Although
they certainly don't apply equally to every man, in the aggregate
they account for the difficulties the male has in coping with the
sexual revolution.

The Old Stereotypes—The American male has to keep adjust-
ing his stereotyped images of what a woman is and isn't with
the realities he comes face to face with in everyday life. In
effect, the more beleaguered he feels himself in the nonsexual
aspects of his relationships with women, the less chance he has
of being the relaxed self-assured lover he's expected to be. He
has to adjust, for instance, to the fact that in early childhood
he's taught girls need to be protected—and that later he finds
them competing scholastically with him for grades, achievements, and the like. He's taught that women are the more
virtuous sex, and he can't help feeling a bit shocked whenever
they turn out otherwise. He's taught that certain tasks are
masculine and women show no talent for them, then feels
threatened when he meets women who do. He's taught that
women are "naturally" homemakers and mothers, and he finds
it incomprehensible that there's a growing problem centering
on women who find little fulfillment in being exclusively housewives and mothers. He's taught that his primary function—
earning a living—is what makes the world go round, then finds
out the "little woman" thinks her problems are equal in importance to his.

In short, he has to grapple with the fact that women are refusing to conform to the stereotypes. Since his masculine identity is at least partly based on the validity of these stereotypes—since he confirms his maleness at least as much by what women *aren't* as by what men *are*—the whole thing is apt to have a fairly unsettling effect on him.

Antagonism Toward Women—Nor does it help in his role as lover if, when he was a youngster, his parents poured on the pressure to make sure he was acting in a properly masculine fashion. The greater the emphasis on masculinity, the greater the likelihood that the child will develop an unconscious antagonism toward anything resembling femininity—including women themselves. A man who has learned to be defensive about things female is hardly apt to be relaxed and confident about females in a sexual situation.

Early dating, one of the ways boys are supposed to show their budding masculinity these days, is a case in point. The boy whose mother and whose peer group pushes him into a parody of adolescent dating when he's only nine, ten, or eleven, before he really has an inclination to date, is put into a precarious position. According to Oscar Rabinowitz, the practice sets up a distorted basis for future heterosexual relationships. The preadolescent who dates because he's supposed to, because this is the way a man should behave, will still be dating for this reason when he's twenty-five. Frequently, when he takes out girls, such a man's attitude is: "What can I get out of her?"

Defensiveness about and antagonism toward women are developed in boys who grow up in households in which the mother is clearly the dominant figure and the father is passive in the areas of influence having to do with home and family. According to Dr. Josselyn:

> However he may conceive of the important role of the father figure out of the home, that is of minor significance to him dur-

ing childhood as long as the father is so relatively unimportant in the home. As a boy, he cannot feel adequate if he accepts an anemic image of himself as an imitation of the powerful mother figure. Rather he prefers to make a noise as if it were the man that is powerful in spite of the fact that to him, in childhood, reality would imply that the woman is the real power.[14]

So he repeats the pattern he was exposed to as a child, seeking to become active and important outside the family unit and remaining relatively passive in it. It shouldn't be assumed, however, that a passive man is simply and uncomplicatedly a meek, unaggressive individual. He may be timid, yes, but Caspar Milquetoast often has some unexpected dimensions. Underneath the surface meekness lives an angry man, a man resentful of what women (in effect, his mother) have done to him. His hostile aggression is negative, circuitous: He provokes his wife into dominating him; he uses adroit ways of stalling her when she wants him to do something around the house; he becomes very efficient in the use of "Yes, dear," without really listening to her at all; he makes fun of her in public, slyly hitting her in the weak spots. Nor should it be assumed that the passive man is necessarily sexually inactive. His wife or girl friend is likely to take the initiative most of the time—in effect, to lead him to bed. When he has a mistress, he's apt to be even more dependent on her than on his wife. But as long as he doesn't feel threatened, he can maintain an erection, functioning fairly adequately in sex. Of course, he feels threatened more readily than more assertive men do. And if his dependency on his wife becomes too great, he's apt to see her more as mother than as wife and, consequently, fail to be aroused by her. Impotence is one means a passive man has of showing indirect aggression. "Every time you see one of these impotence cases clinically," says research associate Jay Haley, "you find that although the man expresses great distress about his misfortune, he also finds a little pleasure in it. He has a way of really hooking his wife; she can't get a response from him, can't get an erection from him."

The Idealized Mother—The mother who's both powerful in the home and greatly idealized—the female head of a patriarchal household—presents even greater danger to her son from the standpoint of his potency than his wife does. It might actually be said that the more a man has been taught to idealize his mother, to invest her extravagantly with concepts of purity and goodness, to focus on her very narrowly as a maternal-housewife figure in the typical double-standard way, the less likelihood there is that he'll be an adequate lover with his wife, especially when she herself becomes a mother. In his mind there occurs a confusion that has its roots in the incest taboo; mother and wife become in a sense merged in his mind. For him, more than for most men, the world is divided into good women and bad, virgins and nonvirgins, women who engage in sexual inter-course primarily for procreation and women who engage in it for pleasure. The good woman for such a man resembles his mother (and possibly his sister); he marries her, but since he concentrates so much on her housewife and mother roles, it's extremely difficult for him to view her in a sexual way as well. For sex (which he considers dirty) he's drawn to the "bad" woman—the one so unlike his mother that there's no chance his incest fears will be activated.

Double-Standard Dating—The fact that all statistics show the sexual double standard to be breaking down steadily shouldn't obscure two important facts: (1) The bulk of the population still adheres to double-standard attitudes, particu-larly when it comes to premarital and extramarital sex, and (2) no matter how many girls engage in sex before marriage or even do so at increasingly younger ages, most start out dating on a double-standard basis. The issue to be taken up here is not the familiar one of chastity versus sexual liberalism, but the relationship hazards that present themselves when the two sexes have such divergent aims and attitudes as the double standard imposes on them.

For one thing, girls still, much more than boys, are imbued with guilt feelings about sex. If these guilt feelings prompt a girl to repress her sexual urges, it may take her many years of living with her husband and growing secure enough as a person before she can shed her inhibitions, before she can feel herself free enough really to enjoy sex relations. By then her husband may very well be preoccupied with his work, devoting the major portion of his energy and attention to it, and far less interested in sex than his newly awakened wife is. Here, then, is another factor to account for the contemporary American woman's growing reputation as a sexual aggressor. Unlike her counterpart in Victorian times, not only does she shed her inhibitions and learn to enjoy sex, but she also learns that it's her right to expect and demand it.

Strong guilt feelings don't necessarily keep a girl from engaging in coitus before marriage, of course. Even so, these guilt feelings can work their destructive magic after the wedding day. Clinicians often see women who insist that they enjoyed sex before marriage but find it dull and themselves unresponsive once they marry. One frequent reason is that what such a woman really enjoyed during her single status wasn't sex itself but its forbidden-fruits aspect.

Again, it's still girls, much more than boys, who are saturated with notions of illusory romance, who are encouraged to make marriage their primary goal in life and to seek in family life the justification for their being, who are taught that sex is an expression of love. A number of studies of adolescents show that until they go steady or become engaged, most girls don't enjoy necking or petting as much as they pretend to their boyfriends. Their overriding concern is: "How far shall I let him go?" The result is that responsibility for the extent of a couple's sexual

177

M

intimacies rests primarily or exclusively with the girl, while the boy's responsibilities are largely confined to his own needs and desires. It also means that this dichotomy creates a tendency in many girls—consciously or unconsciously, maybe with a little subtle assist from mother—to use sex as a manipulative device to get the boy to the altar. As for the boys, it creates a tendency to pretend love and a desire for marriage in order to get the girl to have sex. And, once marriage has taken place, sex is apt to mean something quite different for the husband and the wife; for instance, he may see it more in physical terms while she views it more as a demonstration of love.

It has often been said that the American dating pattern is a kind of sexual ritual: the boy tries to get all he can; the girl puts her budding femininity to work, keeping his sexual interest high and his sexual accomplishments low. It isn't as grim as it seems in cold print, of course. More often than not, the ritual is carried out with the softening effects of humor. Moreover, the girl would be slightly insulted if he didn't try, while the boy might just possibly be a bit relieved if she stopped him—depending on how far along they were in their relationship—at the point of kissing, necking, or petting. Sociologist James S. Coleman has pointed out that the girl uses the hint of sex to gain dates and to "keep the boy partly at her bidding." Sex is a currency, which she uses to exercise some kind of control over him; thus, when she's too free with her favors, she debases the currency. As for the boy, it's just the opposite: the more currency he accumulates, or the more sexual conquests he makes, the more status he gains as a manly figure.[15] Although the girl has the primary responsibility for deciding how far they will go sexually, the boy is apt to use her need for dates as a lever. According to a study on teen-agers made by Grace and Fred Hechinger, dating has become a "social 'must,' the expected way of teenage life," and popularity is "the big prize and an obsession." [16] So the boys are in an excellent position to dictate some of the terms; girls say it's not uncommon for them to be warned that if they don't pet on the second or third date, they will be dropped.

Boys and girls need to test themselves against each other in their growing-up years, but the very divergent attitudes created or reinforced by the double standard make sex far too much a manipulative, exploitative, competitive tool. It's not surprising, then, that often, later on, sex is used as a controlling or competitive device by marital partners who have not matured and in whom these patterns remain ingrained. There is, for instance, the common example of the wife who wheedles a favor or a present out of her husband, by the artful use of sexual denial or sexual promise. There is the example of the wife who uses sex systematically as a way of doling out rewards and punishments: if "Hubby" has been a good boy in her eyes, he can have it; if not, he'll just have to do without until he behaves himself. There is the example of the husband who remains faithful to his wife just so long as he doesn't feel threatened, but when he faces trouble, maybe on the job, he finds another woman to sleep with because a sexual conquest boosts his sagging ego. And there is the example of the husband who absolutely insists on having sex with his wife when he feels that she has paid too much attention to another man at a party or has otherwise made him feel insecure, and he must prove his dominance over her.

These examples could go on indefinitely; the irony is that whenever sex is consistently used in an exploitative or competitive manner—as a weapon—it's less sexy. The erotic element is diluted, and eventually there's likely to occur some impairment of sexual functioning. This may mean impotence, curtailment of sexual interest, compulsive sexuality, or simply a mechanized, joyless coupling that leaves one somehow unfulfilled.

The Sex Bombardment—The ceaseless emphasis on and the commercialization of sex—via the mass media, songs, dances, advertising, and even the social sciences—are a powerful force in intensifying the competitive aspects of sex and are destructive in other ways as well. This sex-obsession feature of contemporary American culture is frequently attacked on humanistic and moralistic grounds—*i.e.,* it leads to sexual depersonalization and has unpleasantly voyeuristic connotations. Actually, the obsession with matters sexual is a perfectly understandable phenomenon. Since one extreme reaction usually invites another, the Victorian denial of sex and the current compulsive affirmation of it are simply two sides of the same well-worn coin. If any proof is needed that the American psyche is still imbued with a heavy dose of fear and guilt about sex, this compulsive need to affirm it—to show ourselves "liberated"—is sufficient evidence. Contemporary America is no more sexually liberated than the Don Juan who has to sleep with every woman crossing his path or the self-styled pornography policeman who sees hardcore smut wherever he turns. Parenthetically but not insignificantly, despite all the so-called sexual freedom, there's still no realistic, comprehensive sex-education program for young people in the nation's schools.

The constant preoccupation with sex does more than demonstrate how much fear and guilt still surround it. In another ironic turn, the very preoccupation has a decidedly negative effect on having a good time in bed, quite apart from the possibly castrating effects of the fear-guilt syndrome itself. I use the phrase "having a good time in bed" advisedly. The remarkable increase in leisure time has given rise to the fun approach to life and to a number of studies and surveys which show that Puritanical impulses still cause Americans to transform fun into work. Nowhere is this more evident than in sex. We're told, over and over again, in a truly remarkable multiplicity of approaches by the mass media, professional sexologists, and even some members of the clergy, that sex should be fun. Indeed, sex *should* be fun, among other things. More to the point, it should be a joyful, lusty act performed in fun—that is, performed at least somewhat spontaneously. Spontaneity, one might say, is the life-blood of the libido. The less spontaneous a male is allowed to be, the less potent he *can* be. If his sexual expression is severely overregularized, his ability to function sexually may easily disappear altogether. In somewhat different form this is also true of a woman; she *can* have sex all the time, of course, since she need not produce an erection, but the more inhibitory rules and regulations are woven around her sexuality, the less able she is to reach orgasm or, for that matter, to enjoy the sex act in any sense.

But the incessant barrage of sexual symbolism that emanates from books, magazines, television, motion pictures, radio, and newspapers destroys real spontaneity. All of it is a cornucopia of sexual stimuli, a never-ending reminder that sex is fun, fun is sex, sex is for people, people ought to be sexy, sex will make you free. Yet the very constancy and the never-endingness of it rob sexuality of freedom. In effect, both sexes are brainwashed. The female is obliged to walk around in a perpetual state of half expectancy (only "half" because the double standard still exerts its inhibitory influence); the male is obliged to walk around with a perpetual psychic erection. And he does this under the most erotically depressing conditions. He's continually reminded that he has to measure up to a certain norm of attractiveness if he's to wind up with the prettiest girl, for not winding up with her constitutes a failure of masculinity on his part. One might say, on reflection, that he's not so much kept in a state of psychic erection as in a state of fear that he doesn't have what it takes sexually, that the girl isn't pretty enough, that the erection won't be adequate, that other men are more virile than he is, or that, way down somewhere in the nether regions of his self, may lurk a homosexual.

Exploiting Male Anxieties—David Riesman has pointed out that college men these days are much more fearful of possibly being homosexual than they were in earlier generations; actually, this fear is pervasive in the middle class generally. The many homosexual jokes that keep making the rounds, each one accompanied by peals of laughter at once uneasy and relieved, are one indication. The continual speculations that are made about classmates or coworkers who don't exude 100 percent Grade A virility—*Is he or isn't he?*—are another. Some men find themselves subtly motivated to marry in order to prove their heterosexuality or are pressured to do so by their employers. While researching a study on the erosion of privacy in the United States, I came across numerous instances in which corporate pressure was quietly put on bright—but single— young men to marry. The reason the employers usually gave was that married men are "more stable." Stability, in this sense, means there's less likelihood of married employees being homosexuals.

The advertisers have not overlooked the sales possibilities in male anxiety, thereby expanding both sales and anxiety. As Philip Wylie noted a considerable time ago, all the fashion and cosmetic advertisements directed at the yearning female seduce her with the simple, unmistakable message "Madam, are you a good lay?" [17] It was only a matter of time, obviously, until the manufacturers and advertisers woke up to the fact that feelings of sexual inadequacy know no sex. Thus, the message from Madison Avenue is now: "Mister, can you lay 'em good?" And, increasingly, the advertisers play on that other deep-seated fear of the American male: "Mister, sure you're not a homosexual?" In a stroke of genius, this anxiety is being manipulated to excellent effect in an area where it might be least expected to—the male cosmetics industry. The secret of this particular success seems to lie in a reverse twist: any connotation of effeminacy on the part of the consumer is ingeniously avoided by presenting the product as so "gutsy" that only a real man would dare use it. For example, an ad for Fabergé's Brut, a new shaving lotion, ran: "Now comes bold new Brut for men. By Fabergé." And underneath, in the same heavy type, the ad read: "If you have any doubts about yourself, try something else."

Competitive Sex—The competitiveness with which sex is imbued today presents the worst possible condition for real sexual enjoyment, whether in marriage or out of it, whether in a love relationship or not. There's great concern among some social scientists over the increase in the practice commonly referred to as sex-for-sex's-sake—that is, sex had solely within the framework of desire, not of love or affection. But much of what passes for sex (even in so-called love relationships) is really a way of proving something, a way of being competitive, a way of rationalizing fears, a means of controlling, a device used for exploitation, and a technique for not being left out of things, so that it's essentially removed from love, affection, *or* desire. This is really the most extreme dehumanization of sex.

It's by no means uncommon these days, for instance, for people to go to bed with each other not because they really *want* to, not because they really desire each other, but because if they didn't perform sexually, they would somehow be left feeling too vulnerable—too much at the mercy of the internalized voice of anxiety, asking, "Just what is the matter with you? Aren't you like other people? Aren't you normal?" The outer-directed man who wants to be judged by others and is therefore attracted by the test of satisfying a modern sexually knowledgeable woman provides another example. What he's doing is more akin to entering a competitive meet than to engaging in an act meant to be enjoyable, meant to be a physical release and a form of communication. If he loses, defeat is ego-shattering. If he wins —well, under the rules of the game, he's only as good as his last sexual performance.

Even with sexual preoccupation rampant then, there seems to be lacking a real appreciation for sexual intercourse, a genuine savoring of it. What is tragically absent, despite all the concern about sex-for-sex's-sake, is a true gusto for sex.

The Fifty-Fifty Orgasm—Surely gusto for sex cannot be shown as long as every act of sexual intercourse is expected to send both partners into transports of maddening delight, marriage-manual fashion, with the bells ringing and the flags flying. When the rigidities of the past were shattered and it was recognized that both men and women had the right to sexual pleasure, the feminists and the sexologists did exactly what they might have been expected to. They rushed from one black and white situation to another. They equated the male and female orgasms as though they were exactly alike, demanding that sex become a fifty-fifty proposition—one for you, one for me. In doing so, however, they failed to take into account the facts that there's a tremendous variation in orgasmic response during coitus in women; that the female orgasm—unlike the male one—is a learned, rather than a reflexive, response; that it's subject to hormonal fluctuations; that it's more diffuse and more easily inhibited than the male orgasm; and that women who don't feel under competitive pressure to attain a coital orgasm on every single occasion are apt to feel satisfied (by the closeness with the man that the sexual act engenders) even when they don't make it all the time.

This physiologically unrealistic demand men and women were led to make on themselves and on each other came to be further codified. Thus, it wasn't sufficient to recognize the right of the American female to sexual pleasure—a realistic and admirable ideal flexible enough to allow for a wide range of possibilities, making both the type of pleasure and the means of reaching it an individual matter. Instead, there has come into being a sort of sexual standard which defines female sexual satisfaction solely in terms of the orgasm—not only the orgasm, but the orgasm every time; not only the orgasm every time, but the orgasm attained solely via coitus; not only the orgasm reached every time strictly during coitus itself, but an explosive kind of orgasm closely approximating the male's; and not only an explosive orgasm achieved directly as a result of intercourse on every occasion that intercourse takes place, but this selfsame orgasm achieved simultaneously with the man's climax.

Let it be acknowledged at once that the average couple doesn't engage in the sex act fully determined, do or die fashion, to achieve every last item on this strict sexual agenda. Let it be acknowledged, too, that some of the social scientists—seeing too many men intimidated and too many women left frustrated by the frenetic or futile quest for the female orgasm, seeing too many couples less concerned with sex than with technique—now advise a more relaxed and individualistic approach.

"We've looked on sex as a panacea—'get them adjusted sexually'—because we're an inhibited society," one psychotherapist told me. "We've emphasized sex too much in our initial concern for marital adjustment. Hopefully the woman will reach orgasm, but there's no guarantee she will every time she engages in the sex act, and there's no biological urgency for her to." Nevertheless, sexual equalitarianism—with its narrow concentration on the fifty-fifty orgasm—is working a profound and dismaying change in what might be called the sexual self-image of the American male.

The Tyranny of the Female Orgasm—In point of fact, the male's sexual self-image is no longer based on the self. It is based on the response evoked from the sexual partner. Now, there's nothing unusual in the fact that a man takes pride in and joy from having brought his partner to the heights of erotic ecstasy. It has always been thus. Her excitement both feeds his ego and is itself erotically stimulating to him. Therefore, the purveyors of advice on sexual matters from Roman times to ours have told wives to simulate rapture even if they didn't really feel it. The experienced prostitute, wise to the ways that she can enhance her professional reputation, has at hand a whole repertoire of sighs, moans, and little screams, which are, to her thrilled clients, the mirror of their virility. But there's a subtle—if highly significant—difference between gaining ego gratification from the response one is able to evoke in one's sexual partner and basing one's entire sexual self-image on this response. Yet this, in terms of noticeable trends, is what is happening to the American male. More and more, not only does he feel that he must prove himself sexually, but he also bases the sexual test primarily or exclusively on his partner's pleasure and satisfaction. In other words, his sexual success or failure is *dependent* on her. If she figuratively gives him an *A,* he's a real man. Any lesser grade, as measured by her response, leaves him somewhat doubtful of his sexual capabilities.

"Some men begin to wonder if they're sexually potent enough when they don't get the same kind of performance out of their wives that the gamekeeper got out of Constance Chatterley," Dr. Dan W. Dodson commented when we discussed the suburban sexual scene. He added that there's tremendous pressure to make sex the mark of masculinity—and to make it, under the most difficult conditions, what it's idealized as being in the media.

In many cases, of course, the male isn't alone in expecting to elicit such a performance. The woman too measures both her femininity and his masculinity by the degree to which she responds. But even if she has a more relaxed, less mechanistic view of sex and doesn't insist on the orgasm for herself, the male still is apt to be unhappy unless her orgasm occurs to confirm his sexual capabilities. In the Komarovsky study of the blue-collar marriage this came through clearly in the replies of many of the respondents, male and female. For instance, a taxi driver's wife said, "It's no fun for him unless I come across, so I try." And a plumber's wife commented, "You can't enjoy it all the time. . . . He gets all let down when it's blaa." [18]

To be sure, such replies don't indicate pure self-concern on the male's part. Another element is involved, particularly when there's affection or love between the sexual partners. This element is sexual sharing. The man wants his partner to share his enjoyment, wants her to have pleasure for her own sake. But as a result of the tremendous emphasis placed on the female orgasm, it's the lesser motivation. One might say he really isn't being given psychic room to want to share spontaneously. As clinical psychologist Joseph Stein expressed it, "Her orgasm is important to his own feelings of adequacy. He is never quite sure that he is a thrilling lover until her arousal culminates in this climax." [19] As a result, in many cases sexual technique preempts sexual spontaneity and feeling.

It was inevitable, too, for the pendulum to swing from one extreme to the other in this respect: for the American male to make the incredible shift from a Victorian preoccupation exclusively with his own pleasure to a present-day preoccupation with his partner's orgasm. However, this is a self-conscious approach, and if there's anything that reduces sexual adequacy for either sex, it's self-consciousness about it.

A case in point, a common one, concerns the man who concentrates on a variety of techniques to delay orgasm and who does so, not to prolong pleasure, but exclusively on behalf of a very inhibited partner who requires an extremely lengthy buildup before she's able to achieve a coital orgasm. When these delaying tactics develop into a regular and unvarying routine (especially with the same woman) and when, as Dr. Stein put it, "both cater to her inhibited state," then the whole thing eventually becomes a chore and the man impairs "his spontaneous ability to arouse the female and become aroused himself." [20]

Another pattern increasingly seen by clinicians is the reverse of the traditional one in which the husband insists on his sexual rights regardless of his wife's inclinations. Among some middle-class couples it's now the wife who insists on *her* sexual rights irrespective of her husband's mood or feelings. She wrongly takes it for granted that men are always and instantly in the mood to have sex anytime the female is. She makes little or no effort to stimulate him, or she becomes insulted and incensed if her efforts to arouse him don't always succeed. In short, her definition of sexual equality is naïvely literal, and she confuses sexual imperiousness with sexual initiative. She forgets that there can be delicacy in the sexual relationship even between equals. The result, more often than not, is the direct opposite of what she intended: by commanding an erection, she psychologically emasculates the male. Not that the man in question is necessarily blameless. He intensifies the situation by his reluctance to be candid about what is wrong. It's difficult for him to admit that he isn't in a perpetual state of sexual readiness, for to admit this would be to go against the stereotype, to seem less the man.

The male for whom the pressures of the sexual revolution have become too great may be driven into actual impotence. More likely, he severely curtails his sexual activity, explaining he has simply lost interest in sex, a curtailment which may not, however, prevent him from resuming masturbatory practices. Then again, he may turn to brief homosexual encounters, affairs with other women, or visits to call girls.

The Whore in Every Woman—That sex with their wives has become a duty, rather than a pleasure, is seen by the marked change in the reasons that men give for going to prostitutes and call girls. Men once blamed unresponsive wives or wives unwilling to participate in a specific sexual technique. But these are the days of the sexual revolution, and increasingly, the men who require the services of prostitutes say that they have wives who are *too* responsive and demanding. In effect, the pressure of having to please has become too great; the men "cop out." They prefer a one-sided arrangement with themselves on the receiving end. " 'It burns them up not to be lords and masters in their own beds, and so they try to make believe they are in ours,' " a perceptive call girl is quoted as saying in a recent study on prostitution in New York. She observed that her sole task is to make her clients feel good, and that unlike their wives she's not concerned about getting anything but money in return. " 'Take this two-hundred-and-fifty dollar baby comes to see me one or two times a week. Always says he enjoys being with me instead of his wife, because when he's with her he's so busy trying to please her he hardly has time to think about himself.' " 21

Is the prostitute significant solely in terms of the haven she provides for men who feel cornered by their wives? Or does her attraction for such men—for all men who seek her out—have something more fundamental and general to say about the sexual relationship between men and women? I noticed a curious reaction during my off-the-cuff interviews with men. When the conversation turned to sex and we ruminated on female response during intercourse, many of my interviewees came up with the same insight, which they expressed in almost identical words: "Way down deep, there's a bit of the whore in every woman." Nor is the concept unfamiliar in psychoanalysis. Helene Deutsch, Karl Abrams, Harold Greenwald, and others in the field have indicated the existence of prostitution fantasies in ordinary women. Many psychoanalysts relate these fantasies to the masochistic tendencies supposedly found in all females. However, the men I spoke with—both blue-collar and middle-class—didn't seem to have masochism in mind. The way they spoke made it evident that they were less concerned with female psychology than in projecting their own wishes: They *wanted* women to want to be treated like whores.

Why should they want this? The answer lies in what it is that the whore represents. She represents sex in its primitive sense, untrammeled and undiluted by feelings of guilt, fear, sentimental love, respect, and competition. In short, she represents pure eroticism: men sleep with her solely for her sexual self. Never mind that in reality most prostitutes are actually frigid with their clients. Never mind that many of the men who patronize call girls and prostitutes suffer from sexual disturbances of one kind or another. It's the prostitute's *image* that counts, and the image the prostitute holds in the public eye is that of a person focused on the erotic in herself and in her clients.

This focus on sheer sexuality—this relinquishing of the self to sex—is surely at the bottom of the woman's wish to be a whore and the man's wish to have her be one. What it shows is this: Even if she's unable to acknowledge it consciously, she wants to feel that her man is aroused by, consumed by, possessed by, and compelled into the sexual act by her sexual desirability and her desire. She wants to feel that it's his sexual love of *her* —uncomplicated by the fact that she's his wife and the mother of his children—that triggers off his dramatic primitive urges. I'm not suggesting that she doesn't also want the man to care for her on an affectional level; of course, she does. At its best, in a mature relationship, sex involves a healthy interchange of feeling, as well as physical passion. But what stimulates her desire is to be desired sexually, as well as soulfully. And she wants to return this earthy sexual love in kind.

As for the man who expresses his belief in the whore in every woman, a parallel situation applies. He's confirming his own deep-down wish to be simply and directly and primitively sexual when he's in the sexual situation. He wants her to be the whore so that he can act with her as unself-consciously as he imagines he acts (or would act) with the genuine prostitute. It's not at all uncommon, when one refers to the sexual revolution, to point out that these days a man can have *with his wife* the varieties of sex he used to have only in a brothel. This is an interesting rephrasing of the old statement about the whore in every woman. But he cannot have these kinds and varieties of sexual experience—at least not with any real sense of fulfillment—unless he and his partner respond primitively to each other.

Furthermore, the emphasis our culture places on explicit sex obscures the fact that an erotic interchange isn't circumscribed by the dimensions of the bedroom. A look, a touch, walking along the street together, or enjoying a meal together—all such acts can evoke a sensuousness, quite satisfying in itself, in two persons free enough within themselves and aware enough of each other to allow such a basic response. The emphasis on sexual intercourse—the close association between sex and masculinity—often causes the American male to forget that sexuality isn't limited to coitus. When I asked the clinicians to tell me what is the chief complaint of wives about their husbands, the most common reply was: "'He doesn't look at me as a woman. He doesn't make me feel like a woman.'" Needless to say, many such wives complain bitterly about their lack of a sex life. But much more than sex is involved when they are sexually ignored. Their main feeling is one of being rejected as women. When the husbands begin to pay them more attention and overtly acknowledge their wives as desirable females, the women themselves often become much less concerned about actually engaging in sexual intercourse. They no longer cast doubts on their husbands' potency or keep badgering them to exhibit it.

Yet a free, spontaneous, primitive sexual response between men and women who look on each other as individuals, rather than as walking stereotypes, is enormously difficult to evoke. We have seen the many factors responsible. Actually, these factors cannot be isolated from one another. So interrelated and interconnected are they that only in their complex, conjoined state do they really make sense. The problems of potency facing the American male in the midst of the sexual revolution aren't sexual problems pure and simple; they involve all aspects of his relationship to himself and to the opposite sex at a time when the patriarchal sources of his masculine identity are seriously weakened or disappearing altogether.

VII. New Ways to Manliness

"I don't think it's an accident that throughout history women have been subjugated. It almost seems as though man had a fair chance if women had their feet bound and no legal rights and were practically tied up. Now that they've been freed—have the same rights as men, the same opportunities—the question of the balance seems to be thrown off. And I begin to wonder if a woman doesn't perhaps have a wider range of tactics than a man has. Women have more flexibility, and in a fair encounter a man can't handle them. Men aren't able to handle weakness as women are, for example."—Jay Haley, of the Mental Research Institute, in a conversation with the author.

"To me freedom involves the ability to participate in change, in having the flexibility to change, in the ability to perceive in new forms and manner, in being as self-critical as we are critical of others, of joining others to solve problems, being able to deal with crises, either individually or by social means, of creating institutions capable of meeting both the needs of nurturance of our fellow men and the adaptive problems of man in his relationship to man and his environment."—Dr. Leonard J. Duhl.[1]

The Breadwinner

When sociologist Helena Lopata of Roosevelt University queried more than 600 women in the Chicago area to find out how they viewed their roles in life, in order of importance, she discovered that they considered themselves mothers first of all. When she asked them to do the same for their husbands, their replies were an even greater revelation. Did these women— suburban wives in their thirties, with a family income between $6,000 and $10,000; urban wives with a median age of forty-nine and a family income from $5,000 to more than $16,000— see their mates primarily as husbands? As fathers? Or as bread-winners? The answer, startling though it is, isn't difficult to guess. Nearly 65 percent of the wives in both groups stated unequivocally that the most important role of the man of the family is, in their eyes, his breadwinning one. Father came in second; husband, a poor third.[2]

These statistics lend themselves to a very plausible explanation. Since the American male bases his masculine identity so narrowly on the breadwinning role, since it occupies—both psychically and physically—the central position in his life, his wife naturally is inclined to see him in the same utilitarian way. If one leaves aside the implications this has for the emotional relationship between husband and wife, the fact is that by depending so heavily on his breadwinning role to validate his sense of himself as a man, instead of also letting his roles as husband, father, and citizen of the community count as validating sources, the American male treads on psychically dangerous ground. It's always dangerous to put all of one's psychic eggs into one basket.

This is not to deny the meaning and importance of work in a person's life. Ideally, work is an outlet for creative energy, a way of channeling aggression, a tie with reality, and what Erik H. Erikson has called the backbone of identity formation. What is suggested here is this: (1) The other roles a man plays in life may also be very valuable in these respects; (2) present-day working conditions do not permit fulfillment of the traditional psychological aims of work to any significant degree; and (3) a narrow concentration of work in terms of his identity does not allow the male enough scope and flexibility to deal with the complexities of the times.

In a bureaucratic, technological society with its insistence on rote and specialization the psychological meaning of work undergoes considerable reduction. With roughly 80 percent of the working population of the United States employed by someone else, most breadwinners are to some extent alienated from their work. Sociologist Robert Blauner defines alienation along four principal lines:

1. The breadwinner feels a sense of *powerlessness* because he has no say over the end result of his efforts, no control over his actions, is at the mercy of the machine or the front-office brass.

2. The breadwinner feels a sense of *meaninglessness* because all he knows are his specialized little tasks, which he can't relate to the various other departments, to the organization as a whole.

3. The breadwinner feels a sense of *isolation* because he can't really identify with the firm or its goals.

4. The breadwinner feels a sense of *self-estrangement* because there's little or no integration between his work and other aspects of his life.[3]

Although Blauner was referring principally to industrial workers, it's clear that his definitions are—to a greater or lesser degree—applicable at all levels of the working world. There aren't too many men who have the autonomy or the freedom to make decisions that is the hallmark of individual initiative. Nor are there many people—whether in business, industry, or even the professions—who can fully escape the feeling that they are cogs in some impersonal machine. Furthermore, the more work is fragmented, the less able a man is to relate to people not in his immediate specialty. To be sure, many breadwinners are interested in their work, but on a comparatively narrow level. For the most part, what challenges there are lack real dimension. Truly creative jobs—those in which the individual feels a sense of autonomy, a call for his best efforts, a solid sense of accomplishment, a real recognition of his particular services, *and* a knowledge that what he's doing is truly a worthwhile contribution to the world—are relatively few in number. On the whole, men are more acceptant of their jobs than actually caught up in them. Thus, for the tremendous ego investment a man makes in his job, the great emphasis he places on it in terms of his masculinity, the work he does will not, generally speaking, reward him commensurately. And he shows it. The growing problems of pilferage, restriction of output, malingering, "putting something over" on the company, expense-account cheating, and heavy drinking at lunch or after work—all are, in part at least, manifestations of job alienation. It may well be that in some instances strikes are also a manifestation of the psychic distancing between a man and his job.[4]

Actually, these days it is not the task itself that the majority of American males are primarily involved with when it comes to their breadwinning role. The *fruits* of work are what the male considers more meaningful to him in terms of his manliness: the pay he gets, the prestige the job has, the status it gives him in the community, the possessions it allows him to buy, and the better life it enables him to give his family. His wife views his breadwinning role the same way; many wives have little comprehension of what their mates actually do for a living.

As Vance Packard put it, "Ever more people . . . find their main life satisfactions in their consumptive role rather than their productive role."[5] In such circumstances the work itself becomes "instrumental," to use sociologist Harold L. Sheppard's description of the phenomenon. It "becomes the means by which a man is able to achieve valued goals unrelated to the job. A 'good job' thus is one that allows the maximization of these goals with a minimum of effort and with as good physical conditions as possible."[6]

Here may be one very good reason that so often and so justifi-

196

ably is heard the complaint "Men don't take pride in their workmanship any more." Whatever rewards a highly affluent consumer society has to offer, pride of workmanship isn't one of them. There are other things that make the man.

Here, too, is one reason that so often these days one hears the comment "People are afraid to stick their necks out on the job, to make decisions, to rock the boat." With the intrinsic rewards of the tasks one performs much less important than the extrinsic rewards they provide, it behooves one not to rock the boat. This doesn't mean less competition; it means, for many men, intense competition of a different sort: they play it safe; they "play it cool"; they become more adept at manipulating the environment than in pursuing excellence or even, on an overt level, the other man's job. They develop the skill of fending off the competition—the younger men under them on the way up, the eager beavers on their own level. They learn the art of being present without being seen, of doing nothing that would make their superiors really take notice of them. Such men are trying to create an anxiety-free environment for themselves, but they wind up with the worst possible case of anxiety. A therapist in Connecticut told me about one such patient, a man working for I.B.M.:

> He's under constant fear and tension. He's constantly worried about whether he's going to get ahead or isn't he? He's not worried about being dropped, but he's very worried about what people are thinking about him. He's been with I.B.M. for something like eight years, and he hasn't moved ahead. He's putting the pressure on himself. It's him in relation to the society of I.B.M. He's afraid of taking the risk of getting a promotion, afraid he might not be able to handle the new responsibilities. He's also afraid of the competition. His idea is that if he fails, he'll look worse than if he didn't try at all. So he doesn't try. The failure becomes much more difficult for him to handle.

One of the most important things a democracy has to offer is the freedom for a man to choose his own line of work. Economics, lack of training, or other factors of this kind limit his choice, of course; often he has to take the first thing that comes along. But at least there's no government agency to tell him what he must do or where—no one shipping him off to pick crops in California, say, or putting him to work on space projects in Houston when the need arises. Yet the masculine stereotypes themselves serve to delimit job choice. This is especially the case with occupations having a feminine or an artistic connotation. When masculinity is closely bound up with job status, as is so very much the case today, there's even more constriction of job choice. A study of middle-class fathers and sons shows that such fathers usually say that their sons are free to take any jobs they want, although further probing elicits the fact that what they really mean is that their boys are free to take any jobs that are safely middle-class. So many a middle-class boy who loves to get his hands dirty working on cars and who would make a skilled mechanic winds up in the pristine surroundings of an office, working at a job really not much to his liking. This also works in reverse: Some blue-collar workers who would otherwise enjoy their jobs can't allow themselves to do so because these jobs don't have middle-class status.

The rating of jobs in terms of prestige is probably inevitable; it occurs in all industrial nations. But its built-in hazards are intensified when the society is very competitive. It isn't the job that really goes on the rating scale; it's the man who holds it. This automatically creates a lot of losers. By definition, any rating scale can only accommodate X number of prestige positions; this means that about 80 percent of the working population is more or less disqualified. Dr. Marvin Bressler, professor of sociology at Princeton University, pointed out that when there's a hierarchical system in which the bulk of the population holds positions which aren't highly esteemed "the occupational structure itself systematically generates a sense of failure in many men. A janitor who does his work with skill and fidelity nevertheless remains a janitor and he may convert the low prestige attached to his job into a generalized estimate of his own self-worth. Men are peculiarly vulnerable to this process. Women may escape harsh self-judgment by invoking the durable symbols of feminine virtue—wife and mother—that by public and private consent still redeem their lives. The alternative of shrinking the universe to family size is not now a viable male option."

Even if the job carries a goodly measure of prestige—or, at any rate, enough to satisfy the man who has it—he isn't off the hook. The trouble is that prestige isn't a stable element. Once achieved, it has to be maintained, leaving the man who banks on it at the mercy of all kinds of competitive pressure and changing circumstances. For instance, Walter Buckingham, a specialist in automation, makes the point that in the past workers were dirty while managers were clean. This gave managers a prestige that automation has done away with, and they don't like it. He tells of a U.S. Bureau of Labor Statistics survey of an insurance company that was in the process of installing computers—machines that would displace many of the white-collar workers. The survey showed that it wasn't the workers who objected. Dissent came from the vice-presidents, who felt their own status would be diminished.[7] On every level of the executive pyramid in the larger corporations there has evolved what Vance Packard calls the "intense preoccupation" with "symbols of status." He quotes the comment of a Cleveland corporation president that "often the little privileges that go with an office are more important to an executive than a raise. You'd expect executives to be more mature, but they frequently aren't." [8] In effect, competition these days doesn't necessarily mean climbing up the ladder of success. It can also mean making one's particular rung as safe and plush and comfortable as possible.

The American male looks to his breadwinning role to confirm his manliness, but work itself is fraught with dehumanizing

—*i.e.,* unmanning—influences. With the growing impact of automation, they're bound to increase. The very fact that leisure time is already becoming a social problem in America, a problem getting a great deal of expert scrutiny (several major universities have centers for the study of leisure, and the American Psychiatric Association has a standing committee on leisure), is a manifestation of how an overemphasis on work in terms of identity has a boomeranging effect. Most factory workers don't want more free time; this is reflected in the fact that the majority of unions have stopped bargaining for a shorter workweek. It's the threat of being displaced, however, that makes automation a major threat for most people. That threat is felt not only by low-level workers but also by white-collar workers and junior executives. A contributor to *Mass Society in Crisis* observes in discussing the new computers:

> [They] combine high technical competence with just enough of an I.Q. to keep them tractable. They do precisely the kind of work to which junior executives and semi-skilled workers are usually assigned. . . . Many middle management people in automated companies now report that they are awaiting the ax, or if more fortunate, retirement.[9]

Scientists themselves are becoming obsolete in terms of their present skills. Many scientists—especially those in government defense work—are overtrained in one specialty. As their jobs are being eliminated, these Ph.D.'s and technicians face serious adjustment problems, for circumstances require them to retrain so as to put their expertise to work in a new field.

Eventually, automation is expected to make some profound changes in the work role. Depending on which expert you talk to and which crystal ball he uses, everybody will work, but only a few hours a day or week; or most people will only be occupied in research and services; or every person will acquire several different skills and jobs in his lifetime; or one-third of the population will always be in school; or the definition of work itself will undergo radical changes, encompassing some of the activities we now call leisure-time activities. Such changes, however, won't come about in the very near future. As for now, the man who invests his entire identity in the work role is rendered extremely vulnerable. Dr. Bressler summed it up this way:

> Many people invest too much of their psyches in work. A wide variety of circumstances—limited native capacity, skills that become obsolescent, impersonal socio-economic forces, capricious judgments by superiors—make the prediction and control of occupational success very hazardous. Accordingly, a prudent man would do well to develop other sources of ego-gratification.

Dealing With Adversity

The more flexible a person is in terms of his life roles—that is, the greater his ability to commit himself to a wide repertoire of roles—the less vulnerable he is to temporary setbacks in the playing of any one of them. The more flexible a person is in his relationships with other people—that is, the fewer preconceived notions about appropriate male and female behavior he has— the greater his ability is to deal with adversity.

A personal crisis—sudden unemployment, for example—demonstrates clearly and dramatically the stunting effects of inflexibility, of a rigidly patriarchal outlook. If further evidence is needed that for the majority of American males, work is at the center of their conception of themselves as men, their reaction to the abrupt loss of their jobs proves it amply. Often their immediate reactions are remarkably like those of war casualties or victims of sudden accidents. Almost everything on which they have based their inner security is shattered. They're bereft.

When the Packard automobile plant shut down in 1956, for instance, many of the workers showed "stupefaction, bewilderment, a feeling of being 'lost.' " One employee said, "I felt like a bomb hit me . . . no place to go." Another commented, "I felt like someone had hit me with a sledge hammer." And a third told an interviewer, "I felt like jumping off the Belle Island Bridge in the river—put that down, you put that down." [10] When news broke in the closing months of 1964 that the New York Naval Shipyard, in Brooklyn, would be shut down, one worker told a *Herald Tribune* marine reporter, expressing what many of the workers felt, "We've been bombed out." When sociologists looked at the dislocations caused by the Studebaker automobile plant shutdown a year earlier, they found a high number of suicides taking place among the former workers—a rate far higher than would be the case in the total population with people having the same characteristics.

According to Dr. Harold L. Sheppard, of the W. E. Upjohn Institute for Employment Research, many former workers shut themselves inside their houses after the Studebaker plant had closed down. They never went out. "It was," Dr. Sheppard told me, "like a sudden, unexpected death in the family." He pointed out that not only had these men banked so heavily on the breadwinning role in terms of their image of themselves, but they also had a unidimensional view of that role:

> When a man has been an auto worker or a miner for twenty or thirty years, he can't picture himself as being anything else. We need some new counseling techniques to shake these men up, get them out of the rut, get them started thinking of new possibilities.

This pattern of a man who has lost his job shutting himself up in his house for days or weeks at a time, shutting out the world, is by no means an unusual one. It occurred in California when a Lockheed Aircraft Corporation plant laid off 500 engineers. Many of the men—who had worked at Lockheed for eight years or more, who had nice houses, expensive furniture, and several cars, but who hadn't yet consolidated their gains—could not handle the stress situation. One man left his house and came back home at the normal times each day, just as though he were still working, but he spent those eight or nine hours sitting in the park. This went on for two weeks. As luck would have it, a friend of his learned of a fine job opportunity, something the man was ideally suited for, but didn't tell him because he assumed from this going-to-work-as-usual pattern that he was in fact still working.

Dr. Gertrude Hengerer told me that financial counselors in her area, Palo Alto and Los Altos, California, become swamped with work when there are mass layoffs. One reason is that many of the people who lose their jobs are bogged down with debts, frequently in order to keep up, to buy the essentially unneeded homes, cars, expensive vacations, and the like that become very much needed as a result of an overemphasis on the fruits of work. Wives may have to go to work precipitously to bring in some money. The whole family, including the children, become anxiety-ridden. The man who was laid off watches others still on the job, and the overriding question in his mind becomes, "Why me?" The men still on the job become terribly anxious, too. Their fear is, "Will I be next?" Dr. Hengerer said, "You can't get away from that question, 'Why me?' It really hits at your sense of self-worth, of masculinity."

Dr. Sheppard pointed out that the loss of job or even a sharp cut in pay is apt to be far more traumatic today than it was in Depression times. Then, nobody was asking, "Why me?" It was happening to everyone, and this took some of the psychological sting out of the stress situation.

The loss of job is obviously never a cause for rejoicing. In a youth-oriented culture it's especially agonizing for a man over the age of forty, who not infrequently is made to feel as though he has reached the extremes of decrepitude as he goes job hunting. But men vary widely in their ability to deal with adversity, and it has been demonstrated time and again that men who see their identity in the narrowest of terms, see it based principally in their breadwinning role, are in the greatest psychological trouble when they are suddenly deprived of this role.

The Depression is a relevant phenomenon to explore in this connection, for a number of depth studies—both psychological and sociological—were made in those bleak times. In study after study what keeps showing up is that the experience of a sudden job loss was far more of a shock to the men than to the women, although the loss of income would affect both equally. It was the men who had been primarily making money. It was the men, now out of work, whose main role had disappeared, who lacked anything to involve themselves in, both physically and psychically. Revisiting Middletown during the Depression, about a decade after their initial trip there, sociologists Robert and Helen Lynd noticed that for women the reverse often held true. The women's roles didn't contract; they expanded. Not only did the wife have to go on with the household routine—cooking, cleaning, taking care of the children—but frequently the wife was also the one who held the family together when her husband was prone to go to pieces.[11]

Paul Lazarsfeld, another noted sociologist, found somewhat the same situation when, in 1931, he scrutinized a small Austrian village that two years earlier had lost its one and only industry, a textile plant. Of a population of 1,486, 80 percent were out of work. Again, it was the men who were hardest hit psychologically, the ones who now had nothing to do and nothing to invest themselves in. They drifted helplessly and apathetically in the streets, looking dully for some means of rescue. On the other hand, the woman's world—the world of cooking, cleaning, mending, and childrearing—remained intact.[12]

Since the women weren't deprived of their principal roles in life, it stands to reason that they would be less shattered than the men. Possibly if they were suddenly unable to fulfill their housewife-mother roles, they would also tend to fall apart, although I suspect that the very roles women concentrate on—the expressive, emotional ones, in terms of temperament—render them more adaptable. But there remains the point that a narrow concentration on role poses considerable psychological danger.

The subjects of the Lynds' study, and Lazarsfeld's, had strong patriarchal orientations. They conceived themselves as men principally in terms of being their families' breadwinners. When no bread was there to be won, they lacked the ability to make a shift, to obtain greater psychic rewards from their roles as husbands and fathers. On the contrary, since his supremacy was structured by externals, often an unemployed man's prestige as husband and father, as head of the household, deteriorated badly. "I still love him, but he doesn't seem as big a man," says a Depression wife about her husband in Dr. Komarovsky's classic study of *The Unemployed Man and His Family.* Dr. Komarovsky gives a poignant description of such a man's loss of power and prestige at home:

> The general impression that the interviews make is that in addition to sheer economic anxiety the man suffers from deep humiliation. He experiences a sense of deep frustration because in his own estimation he fails to fulfill what is the central duty of his life, the very touchstone of his manhood— the role of family provider. The man appears bewildered and humiliated. It is as if the ground had gone out from under his feet. He must have derived a profound sense of stability from having the family dependent on him. Whether he had considerable authority within the family and was recognized as its head, or whether the wife's stronger personality had dominated the family, he nevertheless derived strength from his role as provider. Every purchase of the family—the radio, his wife's new hat, the children's skates, the meals set before him—all were symbols of their dependence on him. Unemployment changed it all. It is to the relief office, or to a relative, that the family now turns. It is to an uncle or a neighbor that the chil-

dren now turn in expectation of a dime or a nickel for ice cream, or the larger beneficences such as a bicycle or an excursion to the amusement park.[13]

When there is prolonged unemployment, as in depressed areas, the erstwhile breadwinner's reaction can take a different turn. Witness what the unavailability of jobs over a protracted period has brought about in Appalachia. With unemployed miners unable to get other work——and unwilling to work in nearby textile mills because they considered what they would have to do woman's work—their wives have become the chief breadwinners in the family. But according to Dorothy Cohen, executive director of the Family Service Association of Wyoming Valley, Pennsylvania, there's no real role reversal:

> In many instances, the women are faced with carrying the responsibility for home and children in addition to their jobs. Often, the care of the children is haphazard. Sometimes, relatives help. Day-care facilities are almost completely lacking in Wyoming Valley.

Some of the unemployed miners have fallen victim to what observers in the area call the depressed-area syndrome. They no longer feel degraded by their lack of employment. They don't involve themselves in home responsibilities. They congregate and drink together, while their wives work.

But it doesn't take as traumatic and explosive an experience as sudden unemployment to demonstrate the hazards of a firm belief in rigid patriarchal standards. Retirement also proves the point. There are, in fact, some strong similarities between retirement and unemployment. Retirement too brings out different reactions in men and women. The woman has already had her functions reduced when the children left home, but she never really completely retires; she must still cook the meals, clean the house, and take care of her husband. It may have been a very difficult moment for her when the last child departed for a life of his own, but she still has a somewhat familiar routine to pursue.

> As she goes about her daily routines [observes Donald E. Super, an expert on the psychology of careers], the husband is occasionally in her way, and both of them become uncomfortably conscious of the fact that she belongs there, that—whereas she has a role to play and ideas as to how she should play it— he does not belong there, he has no role to play. His role has changed from that of breadwinner to that of do-nothing, while his wife is still a homemaker. The self-concept which goes with the role of do-nothing is not a comfortable one to try to adopt after thirty-five years of working and of being a good provider.[14]

Thus, the man who adjusts least well to retirement is the one who identifies himself—as a man—most closely with the breadwinning role. Conversely, the man who adjusts best is the one whose psychic investments have throughout the years been multidimensional:

> The physician-artist finds it easy to keep on painting, for he took up painting in the first place because of his interests; medical and artistic interests have been shown to tend to go together. Indulging these interests is purely avocational; it contributes nothing to his status as a physician; it brings him no fame or fees, merely satisfaction and friends. On the other hand, the executive does not find it easy to keep up his golf, his yachting or his cards, for he took these up originally not so much out of interest in the activities themselves as for the associations they would bring him. Mixing with the right people at the club brings clients, customers, contracts, and the right people are glad to mix with him for the same reasons. Once the business motivation is removed the association no longer has the same mutual appeal, and the activity itself loses point. There are exceptions, of course; businessmen have real friendships, as

well as friendships of convenience, and some businessmen like golf, yachting or cards for their own sakes. But these are probably the exceptions.[15]

If avocations help the male adjust to retirement, it stands to reason that a flexible view of what it is that constitutes masculinity, a fundamentally equalitarian approach to the marital interaction, will also help enormously. The husband who doesn't look at himself or his wife in terms of roles, who's neither demasculinized by doing the dishes or by having a working wife or by showing tenderness and love—the man who in his conception of himself finds genuine rewards in being a successful husband and father, as well as breadwinner—is hardly going to feel, after he retires, that he doesn't belong at home.

Equality, Flexibility, and Marital Happiness

The functional psychiatrists and sociologists don't quite see it like this. They don't approve of the loose-knit equalitarian marriage. Their way is to pigeonhole men and women into neat categories. They envision the ideal family, from the mental-health viewpoint, operating on the basis of clear-cut role differentiation. The man is the instrumental or task leader, the breadwinner, the authority figure, the one who gets things done, the parent who offers conditional love. The woman is the emotional or expressive-integrative leader, the one who keeps house and raises the children, the one solely responsible for binding the family's psychic wounds, the parent who offers unconditional love.

Such an inflexible division of roles rides roughshod over any individual characteristics. Task division is sharp—people know exactly what their roles are and no mistake about it—but focus on the uniqueness of individual personality is very blurred.

Moreover, in today's world, it isn't even really functional.

It isn't functional because the way the American pattern is going—especially in terms of ecological shifts—the American family absolutely needs strong, flexible men *and* strong, flexible women to get things done. Most middle-class people and a growing number of working-class families are fleeing the cities, establishing themselves in the suburban way of life. In the suburbs a great deal of reliance must be placed on the wife. If something goes wrong, who's to see that it's taken care of? The husband is fifteen or twenty miles away at his job and is possibly working late. As Dr. James A. Peterson points out, if the wife is weak, if she can't get things done, if she can't handle situations, the family is in real trouble. Of course, a city wife has to be strong, too: few husbands can take off from work to handle every domestic crisis that comes along.

Studies at the University of Southern California, Dr. Peterson's bailiwick, show that when marriages have a strict division of roles in the traditionally functional pattern—that is, when the husband is solely the task leader; the wife, solely the expressive leader—the family as a functioning unit ceases to function. He explains:

> Unless there's an interpenetration of roles, the whole thing doesn't work—that is, if the wife cannot play the instrumental role, can't do the tasks that previously the man would insist on doing, the family breaks down. But likewise, if the husband is not an expressive leader, emotional leader, and gives his wife these things, the family breaks down, so that the roles not only become confused in our day, compared to earlier days, they've also shifted somewhat.

To be sure, society may insist that a man who responds emotionally enough to give this kind of leadership has a considerable feminine component in his personality. It may insist on a whole sequence of elaborate rules and standards for what constitutes appropriate masculine and feminine response, for the most part erroneously and arbitrarily connecting them to innate

209

o

sex-linked traits. But to the extent to which such elaborations require demonstration as proof of sexual identity, to this extent many individuals will suppress portions of their personalities, or they will try to conform to the rules and standards but feel insecure because not all aspects of themselves really fit in with what is expected.

However, gaining a feeling of security about one's sexual identity doesn't really require such heavy reliance on any superficial or narrow set of standards or such great emphasis on the tasks one performs. Secure sexual identity depends far more on how fully one incorporates the notion that one is a male (or female)—how comfortable one feels in one's sex, how acceptant one is of it. This incorporation and this acceptance in turn depend very much on how fully the individual's family of origin accepted him, accepted his sex, and allowed him to develop at his own rate of speed.

Discussing this vital point at a symposium conducted by the Child Study Association of America, Dr. M. Robert Gomberg noted:

> We are moving towards an era when it will be progressively less important to distinguish between male and female on the basis of social activity and responsibility. When the emphasis is put on inner personal fulfillment, it will be less important whether the social roles are diametrically opposed or overlap than that the inner image of oneself be that of a person who is respected, loved, wanted. If a small child in his littleness feels wanted and respected, it is natural for him as he grows to know himself as a loved male child, protected by a family that supports his values, even if society is in transition and is confused in some of its dictates. He will find the strength from within, buttressed by the family, to find his own way and to play out his own role. Conversely, an individual may learn the stereotypes of masculinity. But if he has acquired them in a family that is angry, frightened, and competitive, though he sounds assertive and male, he may be inwardly frightened and need

the loud sound of yesterday's maleness to disguise an inner hollowness.[16]

The person who has grown up learning to accept himself and his sex—who learned this acceptance without pressure or compulsion—is the one best able to deal with the demands of a society that has worked out a whole sequence of sex-role elaborations. He's the one best able to take it and leave it, to conform to sex-role demands when conformity is in accord with his personality or does no violence to it and to reject the rest without feeling threatened.

If a man is real—if he is fundamentally secure in his manhood—women do not threaten him; nor does he need to confirm his masculinity at their expense. If his manhood is secure, then, as one young woman writes, "there is nothing the destructive part of me can destroy or hurt, so I can relax and enjoy being a complete woman, revel in my femaleness and enjoy his complete maleness." [17] If he's secure, he can live his equalitarian life in an equalitarian marriage without fear of having his sexual identity shattered because roles merge or overlap. The secure man is warm, expressive, tender, and creative, yet quite capable of showing a sufficient amount of assertiveness when assertiveness is called for. The secure man can wash a dish, diaper a baby, and throw the dirty clothes into the washing machine—or do anything else women used to do exclusively—without thinking twice about it.

It's only when a man depends on arbitrary mechanisms outside himself to determine whether he's appropriately masculine, when he uses the stereotypes as strict guidelines to his identity, that he comes to feel somewhat beleaguered by the changes taking place in the roles of men and women. He reacts by belittling the female or by surrendering his autonomy to her. It's true that the blurring of the roles creates a great deal of identity confusion in both men and women at present, but it's a confusion brought on by the fact that neither sex has actually been as-

211

similating the continuing changes in the condition of—and relationship between—the sexes. Nor may this assimilation be expected to come easily. For centuries woman's place was in the home, whereas her relative emancipation has existed for a comparatively small fraction of time.

Many people fear the phenomenon of role blurring because they earnestly believe that it will eventually spell the complete eradication of sex differentiation in role and in personality. This seems a needless fear. The biological differences between the sexes will, after all, remain. So will the psychological drives rooted in biological structure. In fact, sex differentiation may in one sense be more acute when it's not camouflaged by the stereotypes. Robert Sunley, assistant director of the Family Service Association of Nassau County, New York, noted:

> My impression is that the more the roles are blurred, the more the superficial functional differences are eliminated, actually the more essential sexual differentiation occurs. In other words, your more truly masculine and feminine attributes emerge. I think the artificial distinctions don't really fit the people's personalities, and they also don't fit the essential sexuality involved. It confuses it, if anything. I think if you eliminate the arbitrary kinds of role distinctions, then the real sexual attraction—if there is any—emerges.

We may also surmise that the wonderful human diversity in temperament and in total personality structure will itself ensure the maintenance of many traditional psychosocial patterns of masculinity and femininity, as well as the patterns truly grounded in biology. The breakdown of the stereotypes therefore doesn't necessarily mean that the patterns behind them will eventually disappear. What it means is that they will not pose a threat. They will exist for people, rather than have people existing for them. This would put sex differentiation on the basis of the individual, not an indiscriminate mass.

To be sure, sex differences are much narrower in the United

States at present than they are—or have been—in patriarchal cultures. Although this may be seen as a loss by some people, it should be recognized that this narrowing enables the sexes to be more friendly and companionable with each other than in the past. Only when each sex accepts the fact that it has components of the other in its personality, only when each individual of either sex learns, in a sense, to act out the other's roles, can the two sexes really and essentially communicate with each other. In fact, identity is built up in part by one's ability to master not only one's own roles, whatever they may be, but the roles of others as well. Furthermore, the very process of learning the roles of the opposite sex enables a person, if he is not threatened by it, to be more comfortable with his own sex— hence, with himself. Dr. Reuben Hill, the prominent University of Minnesota sociologist, explained:

> I happen to think that a family functions best that is able to communicate rather fully. That does not deny the opportunity to communicate at all levels. This permits a much wider repertoire of roles because you can discover what it's like to be a woman from a communicating mother, sister, and, later, girl friend. If you're a young man growing up, it's not as much of a mystery. You make fewer *faux pas* in anticipating their responses and are known as a man who is at ease with women. And similarly, with respect to men, you feel more at home with men because the communication bars that would separate you from womankind are not up but down. Because you can understand what the other's roles are, you can better understand what your own may be.

So far this discussion has centered on the equalitarian relationship between male and female, husband and wife, in terms of its functional and psychological validity. What about it in terms of marital harmony? How harmonious can two people be in their marital union when both are strong and both are flexible and both adhere to equalitarian principles?

213

Dr. Elizabeth Bott, a social anthropologist working in Great Britain, examined a number of families in which there was a great deal of role sharing. They were for the most part in the professional and clerical categories insofar as the husbands' employment status was concerned. These role-sharing families derived a substantial amount of emotional satisfaction within the marital union, much more so than other families in which rigid role segregation predominated. Although they had to make some allowance for the fact that the husbands were primarily breadwinners and the wives were primarily mothers of young children (some also worked), in other respects they didn't view their activities within the context of appropriate roles for men and women. Division of labor was very flexible. Fathers participated quite actively in child care, and family finances were handled jointly. Most significant were Dr. Bott's observations of the way these successful couples—successful in terms of marital happiness—handled the instrumental and expressive tasks. Dr. Bott stated:

> As far as I could tell, these couples did not feel that fathers should be the final authorities and disciplinarians and that mothers should be more warmhearted. They thought husbands and wives should be more or less equal both in authority and warm-heartedness.[18]

However, Dr. Bott was forced to conclude:

> In some cases, so much stress was placed on shared interests and sexual equality (which was sometimes confused with identity, the notion of equality of complementary opposites being apparently a difficult idea to maintain consistently) that one sometimes felt the possibility of the existence of social and temperamental differences between the sexes was being denied.[19]

It's a big job that the equalitarian marriage is being asked to do: to be hospitable to the individual both as individual and as marriage partner; to encompass "complementary opposites," as well as to allow traits shared with members of the opposite sex to emerge; and to allow the expression of dependency needs, as well as to encourage independence. Yet it can be done; it is being done. What true equality means is the equal right to expression and growth, to be a person. It does not mean strict equality of leadership every time leadership is called for. It does not mean a rigid fifty-fifty kind of relationship between the marital partners, who place their lives, so to speak, on a scale to ensure undeviating equality. It does not mean a constant and dangerous tussle for authority, in which each member of the marital pair jealously guards his territorial rights and watches anxiously for any undermining of this authority. *True equality entails a shifting, fluid, dynamic kind of interaction, in which leadership changes from one partner to the other depending on their specific interests and areas of competence and on the specific contributions they're able to make in any given situation.* Leadership, dominance, and dependency—all shift with the particular needs and abilities of the marital partners and with the requirements of the situation.

This doesn't preclude a division of labor and of decision making, of course. Whenever any two persons of the same or opposite sex live together, such a division, based on interest and competence, comes into being. Without it, getting anything done may lead to chaos. But in the equalitarian marriage the divisions aren't frozen: Although it may be more logical, more practical, for one partner to take the responsibility in a given area most of the time, the other partner isn't inhibited from assuming or sharing in it on occasion.

A revealing picture of the shifting, dynamic kind of marital interaction is offered by Ernest W. Burgess and Leonard S. Cottrell, Jr., in their monumental study of marriage adjustment, *Predicting Success or Failure in Marriage.* Among the people the two behavioral scientists interviewed was one couple that rated extremely high in marital adjustment; in addition, a number of knowledgeable outsiders gave this husband and wife high marks for marital harmony. The marriage was equalitarian. Decision making was shared. Yet this was no fifty-fifty proposition. Dominance shifted spontaneously as "husband and wife were able to play superior, equalitarian and inferior parts, parental and dependent child roles, and a number of other roles in their marriage drama, with considerable facility." Significantly, the husband was much more rigid in the early stages of their marriage than he was at the time of the study. That was when he resisted his wife's suggestions and advice, even when he knew she was right ("I couldn't stand having her tell me what to do"), but he showed much more personality flexibility as the relationship progressed.[20]

The heart of the equalitarian marriage *is* personality flexibility. For this reason it provides the kind of marital structure best suited to individual growth: it allows each of the partners the freedom and the scope to expand, to unfold their personalities, to realize their particular potentials. In a world that in many ways is becoming increasingly specialized, bureaucratized, and conformist, it affords the one really fertile soil for the nurturing of the individual. Furthermore, it affords each partner recognition and acceptance of his or her particular strengths, weaknesses, and needs. This means that husband and wife can have from the marriage a much greater degree of mutual emotional support than is possible in other marital patterns. A highly patriarchal male may enjoy—or think he enjoys—a superior amount of power in the family. But it's the equalitarian male, not shackled by a convention that demands him to be *always* strong, who can turn to his wife for comfort at times. It's he who has a great deal of social interaction and the deepest companionship with her. The equalitarian marriage, then, is both expedient and pragmatic.

But more than expediency and pragmatism are involved. The most important thing to keep in mind is that people are first of all human beings—not members of a particular sex—and the initial concern of a highly complex, advanced society ought to be the stimulation of the human diversity that makes for a richness of culture. This means stimulating each individual to develop *all* aspects of his personality *and* affording him the opportunity of pursuing the tastes, attitudes, and occupational preferences most congenial to his particular person. In such a society the artistically gifted man and the man who is a gifted sportsman would be equally valued in terms of their maleness; the more nurturing type of male would not suffer by comparison with the more competitive one; each man and each woman would be given full opportunity to tread, without stigma, the paths temperamentally most suitable to them.

This is not what is generally being advocated now. The functionalists, concerned about role confusion, would have us go back to traditional patriarchal patterns in which roles and personalities are rigidly differentiated. The angry neofeminists of the 1960's discount the possibility of any woman's finding fulfillment in the homemaking-mothering role and demand a single societal pattern that would have all women, as well as all men, out pursuing meaningful careers. But why make one's life roles in American society an either-or proposition? Why not tap all our societal and temperamental resources to create an atmosphere in which all kinds of ways are possible and in which self-fulfillment becomes more than a pretty word? For most people this may well mean the more traditional pattern of the husband as breadwinner and the wife as homemaker. For others it would mean, as it already increasingly does, both partners engaging in outside work, whether for financial reasons or to meet creative challenges or both.[21] And if at some state in their unique family life cycle, the temperaments and circumstances of a particular couple dictate a complete reversal of roles—the husband taking care of the children, the wife earning the living —let them do so without hindrance or onus. All kinds of patterns are to be had. By all means, let us break down the stereotypes and have them.[22]

How to Be Male, Though Equal

In the opening chapter I posed the question of how the male can reconcile the overrefined, sedentary present with the images of the male as he was in the past. There are two answers to this question. The first is that he can't do it. The second is that he doesn't really want to, not at the price he would have to pay. To return to a kind of romantic physical primitivism would mean laying to waste the gains of civilization and starting fresh. This is impossible. That man isn't static is his beauty and genius and uniqueness. He grows, and he builds. He develops, and he evolves. The process is as ceaseless as the rhythms of nature. It's often remarked how far mankind is moving away from the earth, the soil, the elemental facets of life. This is true, and it's an inevitable process. Therein lies one of the dilemmas of modern man. He has a need to build and a longing for what is basic: the green of trees; the brown of earth; the blue of open skies. Yet the more he builds, the more difficult it becomes to realize the other longing. It's the reason that throughways out of cities like New York are thronged on warm-weather weekends, the reason that the national parks are packed in summertime, the reason that a freshly caught bass broiled on the bank of a river tastes incomparably better than in any restaurant.

Many of the men I talked to, business and professional men, as well as men who worked in factories, conveyed the idea that they felt something was missing, something that—although they didn't define it quite so precisely—could be summed up as a lack of primitive contact with life, with themselves. These modern American men, leading their soft and affluent American lives, felt out of touch with their bodies, felt a physical distancing between their bodies and their minds.

Some men try to overcome this feeling by keeping up their muscle tone; they go in for exercise. For others, it's weekend sports or summertime treks in wilderness spots. Nothing seems more anomalous than the well-dressed, carefully groomed businessman who, for eleven months of the year, rides to work in his power-steering, power-brake, automatic-drive car; has the elevator whisk him up to his air-conditioned office; pushes buttons to summon secretaries; barks instructions into the phone beside him; dictates letters into a transcriber; and lunches in plush restaurants—and who, on weekends, tosses a handball around, wearing a dirty sweatshirt, or carries his lunch in a simple paper bag when he goes fishing. Yet nothing could be more understandable. It's a way of replenishing himself, of reestablishing that primitive contact.

While it helps, it's only a partial solution. It doesn't go far enough, deep enough. Such activities aren't really integrated into the modern man's life. They're a thing apart. This is one reason that most men take the less demanding path of spectator sports and that physical fitness becomes a national problem. Many American males, even some who actively disliked the experience, look back on their military service as the one time in their adult lives when they felt in peak shape physically. There's good reason for this, and it goes beyond the fact that the military places much emphasis on physical activity. More important, this activity is integrated into the totality of military life. This was also the case in civilian life—generations ago. When man was hunter, fisherman, hewer of wood—when he had to use his wits *and* his body to meet the challenges of survival—there was an integration of the physical and mental. As Margaret Mead observed when we discussed the subject, males have to learn again to trust their own bodies. She suggested that there should be ways for young boys in our culture to test their bodies as youngsters once did with bows and arrows in hunting.

Psychic Primitiveness—It's a paradox that the more civilized we become, the more creature comforts are available, the more need there is for a primitive contact in physical terms. It's another paradox that the more complex and polished human relationships have become, the more need there is for a psychic kind of primitiveness. This, too, puts a man in fundamental contact with himself and with the world in which he lives. Such primitiveness is somewhat difficult to describe *in toto;* character traits that appear forceful when projected by a living individual tend to reduce themselves to little better than a list of adjectives when set down on paper. *The primitive man, in the sense referred to here, cuts away civilization's irrelevancies and gets to the core of things.* He's able to go beyond the stereotypes and to distinguish people—whether in terms of sex, race, age, occupation, or whatever—as individuals. He has an easy acceptance of himself, whether of his toilet functions or of his noblest aspirations. He's unafraid to exhibit emotion—to exhibit passion, as well as intelligence. He's a paradox: *the complicated man able to respond simply, rather than the simple man who complicates his responses.*[23]

Needless to say, the environmental forces that shape the individual in contemporary society make it exceedingly difficult for such traits as these to be developed to any significant degree. Yet these are precisely the ones that will be required of individuals—if they're to remain individuals—in the world toward which we're heading. By this I mean not only the ever-increasing trend to mass man but also the sheer complexity of life as it's developing.

The future that looms—its beginnings already upon us—is truly fantastic. To refer to the population explosion, culture explosion, knowledge explosion—as is done daily—is to convey a pallid view of what lies ahead. Electronic publishing, the routine use of machine components to replace human organs, and the electronic transference of knowledge from computer to brain—these alone will transform society, and it is already starting to be transformed. We are, in Dr. Leonard Duhl's words, "increasingly going to have to learn to deal with complexity and change, with new arrangements in new combinations of people, with interdependence." We are, he added, going to require a new type of education geared to this kind of learning. All this makes imperative the flexible male, the complicated male able to respond simply.

Reflecting on the complexities facing the individual today, Dr. Reuben Hill remarked, "You have to be a reasonably good generalist in the area of the social-emotional, as well as a specialist in some of the instrumental realms." In other words, in addition to the basic skills of living, a human being these days has to be able to call on a wide range of human responses, to call forth a variety of mechanisms, for dealing with himself and with the world. Pragmatically, he cannot be stuck with a single technique for coping with life, cannot be compulsive in any realm, if he's to function fully and effectively. Here, I believe, is one instance in which the equalitarian marriage is especially valuable; its climate is the healthiest for the development of a large repertoire of responses on the part of its members. And here—because of the very demands it makes—is also the reason that being a husband and father and citizen in today's world is a particularly exciting and challenging experience for those men who allow it to be.

Generally speaking, the American male doesn't think of challenges in these terms. He tends to think of them only in the old, stereotyped way: physical challenges, those involving his job, and those that have to do with meeting his family's obligations. Changes in work methodology, technological advances, and social legislation have done a great deal to eliminate these hitherto masculine challenges. So the male tends to see his roles reduced, his meaning lessened, the world much duller and more monotonous than in the romantic past. But the traditional masculine challenges aren't innate. They aren't inborn. They're historically valid, yes; but history takes shifts and turns. If the American male's orientation to masculinity must change to meet the changing circumstances, it follows that his orientation to challenges, too, must undergo reorientation.

The American male in contemporary times, as part of the larger society, faces problems of enormous magnitude. The wonderful technology that he, along with other peoples in the world, is creating threatens to engulf him. The incredible machines he has developed are, in conjunction with the ever-increasing bureaucratization of his consumer society, threatening to turn him into a cipher. The conflict between the white and Negro races is anguished, and the wounds will need to be healed. There is the fouling of the air he breathes; there is the soiling of the water he needs for drink and sport. The daily headlines show no dearth of matters that demand—nay, that cry out—for solution. These are some of his new challenges.

The most important one of all concerns war and peace. Some fifty years ago, philosopher William James, reflecting on the "Moral Equivalent of War," saw in the fight against poverty and suffering one way of displaying masculinity, saw in this a constructive equivalent to militarism—man in combat against a different species of enemy.[24] His vision has even greater applicability today than it did then—as, on the one hand, more and more nations arm themselves with the weapons of total annihilation and as, on the other, the United States begins, if slowly, its offensive on this nation's rugged pockets of poverty. The fact that modern weaponry can destroy civilization—the very shock of it—acts as a deterrent to all-out war. Could it act as a catalyst to change the concept and direction of masculine aggression? Margaret Mead, taking stock of the contemporary human situation, sees ground for optimism, sees it especially in regard to the children of the times:

> Children today, growing up in a world able to destroy itself, do not have to pretend that they are not afraid of modern warfare. Nor do they have to feel that it is unmanly to work for peace. Their heroes need not be daredevils, but men who can soberly assess just how dangerous the new projects are that mankind must undertake—projects that admittedly may not

work out, that are subject to disastrous accidents. The children whose birthright is this new age will be saved from psychological disaster if they see around them men and women who estimate danger carefully and accurately, who work soberly to prevent war and who invent safer ways of keeping the peace.[25]

The Myth of Innate Feminine Goodness—The feeling that it's unmanly to work for peace is part of the idealization of women. From it stems the myth that women are inherently good and men inherently destructive. It's a mischievous notion, which has served highly destructive ends, for not only does it freeze the male in the essentially negative role in human relationships, but it also tends to minimize his personal responsibility for his actions. When it becomes exclusively woman's function to socialize him—to make him fit to live in human society—doing so robs him somewhat of his own initiative. When the mother is the sole or even the principal agent in the task of civilizing the little boy, the adult male he finally turns into is not all that at ease with his civilized self. He in turn leaves civilizing to the mother of his children, and the cycle continues. Maybe that's one reason that the myth of innate feminine goodness has persisted throughout the centuries. It certainly is still very much alive today, kept steaming hot and ready to serve by such ardent partisans of womanhood as Ashley Montagu ("Woman is the creator and fosterer of life; man has been the mechanizer and destroyer of life. . . . Women love the human race; men are on the whole hostile to it") and novelist J. B. Priestley ("In a true matriarchy, love, personal relationships, homemaking, family-creating and taking root in a settled society are at the top of all lists of priorities . . . and all the things that men are always arguing about come a very bad second").[26]

It cannot be denied that a woman's upbringing and her deep involvement in child care activities lead her to develop to a greater degree humanistic traits like sympathy, understanding, and patience and that the male's struggle in the competitive arena leads him to develop to a greater degree other traits, which give him the strongest supports in meeting the demands of his particular challenges. But that's not at all the same thing as saying that woman's genius lies on the side of the angels and man's on the side of death and destruction. The unintended—but unavoidable—result of such polarization is to keep men displaying their masculinity in negative ways and to place unfair requirements on the conduct of women simply because they *are* women.

The myth of feminine goodness has given rise to the saying that this is a man's world and that if women had a free hand, things would be a lot different—needless to say, a lot better. In this context, Mr. Priestley comes right out and unashamedly plumps for an honest-to-goodness matriarchy to replace the present pattern. Although no one can deny that men have steadfastly held the balance of power between the sexes and that women have been cast into the inferior role, it's by no means a clear-cut case of men and women having vastly different psyches. Women have been the socializers of men; but they have also wielded their own power, behind the scenes, covertly, and their power has in the main not been pitted against the men's supposed demonic drives. In point of fact, if the psyches of the two sexes were actually as starkly differentiated, as totally unalike, as the idealizers of womanhood make them out to be, then there couldn't possibly be a meeting of minds between men and women.

It's true that men have generally done the killing, at least on the basis of a mass war. That men are biologically much better equipped to fight than women is obvious; it may also be the case that men are on the whole more aggressive than women. But not to be dismissed is the fact that the restrictions placed on women have inhibited them from any direct outward displays of mass violence in the manner of men. Random examples of women warriors do exist, of course: there were female battalions in the Soviet Union during World War II, for instance, and in Cuba during the revolution, and there are reports of women fighting on the North Vietnamese side at present.

Biology might have combined with cultural restraints to prevent the vast majority of females from waging active war. As a group, females may be less prone to violence than males, but this doesn't mean they aren't potentially violent. It doesn't mean they're morally superior. It doesn't mean nature has exclusively endowed them with humanitarian impulses.

Evidence that women aren't innately morally superior to men isn't so very difficult to find, after all, now that women as a group have so much more freedom to express the various aspects of their personalities than they did before and now that they are doing so in a time of social upheaval. Each year, at least in the United States, the alcoholism rate for women climbs. So does the rate of narcotics addiction. So does the suicide rate. So does the crime rate. In fact, F.B.I. *Crime Report* figures show that robberies executed by women have increased a whopping 60.3 percent in recent years. Aggravated assault with women as the aggressors has increased 10.1 percent. Thirty years ago only 9 percent of all the people arrested for murder were women. Today, according to a study recently completed by New Jersey's Fairleigh Dickinson University, 17 percent of all such arrests involve women. Here, for example, is the not so pretty picture of family murder in New York City in 1964:

Sixteen husbands were killed by their wives; twenty-seven wives were killed by their husbands.

Nine sons were killed by their mothers; five sons, by their fathers.

Twelve daughters were killed by their mothers; four, by their fathers.

Eighteen common-law husbands were killed by their common-law wives; twenty-nine common-law wives were killed by their common-law husbands.[27]

Certainly anyone who has seen the twisted faces of some of the women who attend prizefights and wrestling matches, faces

225

contorted with the lust for blood; anyone who has witnessed the hate-filled glitter in the eyes of women on both sides of the fence at a racial clash; anyone who has borne the brunt of corrupting bitterness that flows from some of the female activists in the camps of political extremism; and anyone who has observed the frenzy of women at a rummage sale—anyone who, for that matter, has read a history of the feminist movement— might have understandable doubts about the gentler sex necessarily being so gentle, the loving sex necessarily being so loving.

I am not suggesting that women are morally inferior to men, but that neither sex is inferior or superior to the other. It's only to be expected that the more women emerge from the cloistered walls of home to participate in the activities of the outside world, a highly competitive, contradictory world that both sexes have created, the more women will exhibit the traits now so commonly and exclusively attributed to women.

For that matter, even a surface display of idealism and humanitarianism is—at times—used to cover up less noble inclinations. Counselors in social agencies see many upper-middle-class women who appear to be concerned with humanity, with relationships, with cultural values. Money doesn't seem to be at all important to them. In many instances, however, a closer look shows something quite different. According to psychiatric social worker Ruth Fizdale:

> She's gotten hold of a man who'll drive himself like mad to get money, and denigrates him for being too interested in money, and not interested in music, or the arts, or in spending time with the children. But at the same time she's subtly driving him—and doesn't know it.

Miss Fizdale explained that in many cases of this kind both the husband and the wife hold identical values. The difference is that the woman really doesn't like these materialistic values in herself and so gets someone else—her husband—to act them out for her. By disliking him, she can feel better about herself.

Myths die hard, and the ones that spring from the idealization of women still have plenty of bounce to them. That women would save the world if they would only go into the scientific arena or would grasp the reins of government is a well-meaning but unworkable idea. Men will always resist values labeled feminine, and so long as men resist, women will continue to be swept along by the societal values that prevail.

Both men and women have an enormous range of possibilities within themselves for good and ill. If the aim is to eliminate war, abate crime, and foster a more humanitarian and cooperative society, it cannot be accomplished on the basis of sex-differentiated roles or attitudes. Responsibility for such a choice is individual, not sexual. Humanistic values have no sex. The idealization of women notwithstanding; they're simply human.

Masculinity and Choice—If the American male is not to become a neurotic weakling, as anthropologist H. R. Hays already accuses him of being, he has no recourse but to exercise his responsibility for choice on every level. The old roads are swiftly being closed to him, one by one. He can no longer surely and definitively confirm his masculinity in terms of unidimensional and sexually differentiated roles. He can no longer do so on the basis of female inferiority in the practical affairs of the world. Whether or not he knows how to fix the faucet, whether or not he takes to mowing the lawn, such matters are quite beside the point. So is physical configuration. It's remarkable how two men with the same physical conformation, even when they conform precisely to the stereotypes—tall, handsome, broad-shouldered—can project such a different air. One conveys a feeling of confidence and ease, of a person who knows who he is; the other seems weak and easily led. It's largely in the way he handles his choices—indeed, whether he has the autonomy to make them at all—that is at the crux of his manly stance. In this sense there's a merging of masculinity and individuality; in fact, they must be considered together. This also holds true, of course, for femininity. The person of either sex who has a sense of his own worth as an individual and who does not long to assume the mantle of the opposite sex doesn't worry about his sexual identity. It's there automatically, with or without reference to elaborate stereotypes.

Admittedly, the times are not conducive to this sense of self-worth. They're not conducive to the easy acceptance of one's sex, to individualism (except in a narrow, insular sense). As long as men feel that the equality of women will emasculate them, it is exactly what will happen. As long as men identify themselves so narrowly with the breadwinning role, with the competitive demands of their consumer society, with narrow and noncreative work, their psychic equilibrium will be shaky.

The question of identity in the larger sense, of individuality, has been viewed in many contexts and written about from many different points of view. David Riesman's *The Lonely Crowd* saw the American character changing from an inner-directed one to one in which Everyman *is* Everyman, whose outer-directed character is formed chiefly by the example of peers and contemporaries. William H. Whyte's *The Organization Man* saw the individual submerging himself wholly in the needs of the organization—be it corporate, governmental, or whatever —and leading the bureaucratized life in which adjustment becomes the greater good. Erich Fromm, in *The Sane Society,* wrote about the variety of conformist pressures on the individual who, in a democracy, supposedly has convictions and a will:

> The facts, however, are that the modern, alienated individual has opinions and prejudices but no convictions, has likes and dislikes, but no will. His opinions and prejudices, likes and dislikes, are manipulated in the same way as his taste is, by power-

228

ful propaganda machines—which might not be effective were he not already conditioned to such influences by advertising and by his whole alienated way of life.[28]

Implicit in each statement is the view that the technological society which man has created is taking over, is crushing man's ability to make his choices with any degree of autonomy. That is, he cannot stand back. He cannot weigh. He cannot pick and choose, cannot see the whole because of the economic and other pressures which manipulate him to see only the parts. Such books and the studies they reflect are immensely valuable in the perspective they give of the changing American society —a society whose greatness lies in the emphasis it has historically placed on the worth of the individual. But without in the least meaning to, they carry a built-in danger, as this book may well do, too. They seem to make the forces at work on the individual appear so powerful that an air of inevitability is somehow conveyed, that short of superhuman effort, short of really drastic economic or political change, the future will be like the present, only more so.

But is the individual really doomed to be a cipher—well fed, with creature comforts readily at hand—but a cipher all the same? The advertisers advertise, the manipulators manipulate, sex is single-mindedly extolled, a high degree of competitiveness fuels the individual and collective life of the nation, and man comes to see himself primarily as economic man; *yet although the scope and potential for autonomous choice have been drastically reduced, they have not disappeared.* Some people *are* making their choices in life on an individual, not mass, basis. Societal pressures can't be minimized and should be spotlighted, but at the same time individual responsibility must not be totally ignored. This may seem a naïve view. Let me be naïve. Ever since the popularization of psychiatry began, it has been fashionable—and easy—to blame one's own neurotic behavior on an unhappy childhood. As the popularization of sociology proceeds apace, it's becoming fashionable to blame all manner of social and personal aberration on society. Too often forgotten is the fact that each individual, whether by direct action or by default, also bears responsibility for the patterns of his society.

Parents who themselves are disturbed personalities make it extremely difficult for their offspring not to turn into neurotics, and society does bear heavy responsibility for the mental health —or lack of it—of its members. The Calvinistic notion—or, if you will, that of Joseph P. Kennedy—is that the individual can, all by himself, cope with almost anything in life. If that were ever possible, it would be ridiculous to insist that it is possible today. Today it's impossible for the individual to cope with the world all by himself. Today he cannot be totally independent. He need not be totally dependent, but he must be interdependent. Robert L. Heilbroner has pointed out:

> Whereas man made his peace with nature very largely as an individual—as a farmer, a hunter, a fisherman, a sailor—he makes his peace with technology through social organization. The technology itself demands organization in order to function, and the environment it creates in turn calls forth organization in order for men to function within it.[29]

It's not in the cards for individualism in the mid-1960's to be what it was in the nineteenth or eighteenth century, nor is it irretrievably lost. Man has to pay a price for his wonderful medicines that prolong life, his extraordinary gadgets of comfort, but need he turn over *all* his money? Must we say that the individual—as individual—is totally helpless? That he has no alternative but to submit passively to the forces that shape him and that he in turn has helped shape? That there's no point at which he can be expected to take some initiative because the societal pressures are simply too great?

It is a depressing notion to accept, and reality demonstrates against it. However distant the sources of power may be, however confused the day, however loud the din of the television commercials, and however strong the pull to compete and to conform blindly, individual choice is by no means gone. Witness the Peace Corps volunteers. Witness the young men and women who donate their skills in the underprivileged sections of the United States. Witness the many people who work directly and specifically on behalf of civil rights. Witness the enlightened and courageous businessmen, like the Xerox Corporation's president, Joseph C. Wilson, who involve themselves deeply in social problems on a national or international level. Witness the Americans, young and old, who are beginning to shake the apathy of the 1950's, to question, to protest, to become active on whatever side of the fence their political beliefs are grounded. With the nation's population in excess of 190,000,000, they are a very definite minority—if one that is vocal and well publicized. But the people who make choices are there; their numbers are growing; their very existence proves the point that some choice is indeed possible.

Nor does choice necessarily involve intensely pragmatic social commitment, although it's repeatedly borne out that the individuals most healthy mentally are those who have moved away from absorption with self. The American male has some personal choice in the matter of his society's competitiveness. He can let it manipulate him, or he can do some of the manipulating himself. He can place the greater emphasis on "I can better that guy; I can push him right off his place on the ladder"; or, "I'll keep quiet and out of sight; I'll do the best I can to keep him from pushing *me* off my place on the ladder"; or, "I'll try to better myself, to do the best I can and keep on improving all the time." He has the choice of conforming even when it involves a direct violation of personal dignity or of conforming to a meaningful set of values. He has the choice of rebelling meaninglessly, merely for the sake of showing off an immature brand of individuality, or of rebelling at the point where not to do so would demand too high a price in terms of his self-esteem.

231

He has the choice of accepting each marvelous new device uncritically, as it plops off the assembly line, or of assessing its value on a personal basis, determining the extent of its usefulness in his life, and remaining its master. The American male has the choice of viewing his worth to his family and to himself mechanistically—by how much money he makes and how much status he garners or by how meaningful and broad-based is the relationship he establishes with them. He has the choice of making his marriage an either-or proposition—either he bosses his wife, or she bosses him—or of looking at himself and his spouse as persons with individual needs and temperaments. He has the choice of conveying his authority as father by the mere fact that he *is* a father or by not cheating on his income tax after talking to his kids about honesty, by not giving them a swat after conveying the importance of reasoning, and by following through on a promise after lecturing them on the value of a man's word. He has the choice of accepting the fact that he is becoming less hard and rough and that the female is becoming more competent and adventuresome as signs that the sexes are reversing roles or that both of them are becoming more civilized.

There is a new way to masculinity, a new concept of what it means to be a man. It has little to do with how strong the male is physically, how adept he is at ordering people around, how expensive his cars are, how versatile he is with a set of tools, or how closely he identifies with all the other stereotyped attitudes and acts. It has everything to do with the way he manages his life—the way he conducts himself as a human being in terms of his wife, his children, his business associates, his friends, his neighbors, and his compatriots in the community—and with his ability to make decisions, with his courage to say no, as well as yes, with his perception into the consequences of his actions and decisions. This isn't the easy way. It could hardly be called the path of least resistance. But there's no turning back the clock. With the equality of women an inexorable trend, with the traditional male patterns increasingly losing their significance for a variety of reasons, it is—at bottom—the only alternative to what may well become psychic castration.

What I am saying is that no matter how much American males may yearn for the simpler, more clearly defined times gone by, their yearnings are futile. They have the choice of remaining what collectively they are—a sex at bay—or of redefining themselves in the light of the changing culture. Historically, in the relationship between men and women and between men and men, this is a new approach. And it is the ultimate masculine challenge. It's the ultimate challenge because it does away with stereotypes, guidelines, and life plans. It simply requires a man to be more fully human, more fully responsive, and more fully functioning than he has ever before allowed himself to be. This is the freedom that equality of the sexes offers him.

If he's afraid to take this freedom, the American male will wind up enslaving himself all the more. If he grasps it, he may at last come to see that he's not really as fragile as his patriarchal concepts have made him out to be.

Notes

Chapter I. The Male in Crisis

1. Sebastian de Grazia, *Of Time, Work, and Leisure* (New York: The Twentieth Century Fund, 1962), Anchor Books edition, p. 167.

2. Reported by *The New York Times* (September 4, 1963).

3. Packard's picture of the executive type is of a man who wants his home run as precisely as his corporation is, who flies off the handle when encountering the "normal chaos of everyday living," and who has a tendency to deal with his wife and children the way he deals with subordinates. Vance Packard, *The Pyramid Climbers* (New York: McGraw-Hill Book Co., 1962), Ch. 20 (also London: Longmans).

4. Russell Lynes, *A Surfeit of Honey* (New York: Harper & Bros., 1953), p. 49 ff.

5. Mirra Komarovsky, *Blue-Collar Marriage* (New York: Random House, 1964), p. 50 f.

6. Robert O. Blood, Jr. and Donald M. Wolfe, *Husbands & Wives: The Dynamics of Married Living* (London: Collier-Macmillan, 1964), p. 50 f.

7. Milton R. Sapirstein, *Emotional Security* (New York: Crown Publishers, 1948), p. 188.

8. Quoted by Vance Packard, *The Hidden Persuaders* (New York: David McKay Co., Inc., 1957), p. 76 (also London: Longmans).

9. Judd Marmor, editor, *Sexual Inversion* (New York: Basic Books, Inc., 1965), p. 22 n.

10. Charles Frankel, "The Third Great Revolution of Mankind," *The New York Times Magazine* (February 9, 1958).

11. Leonard J. Duhl, "Urbanization and Human Needs," *American Journal of Public Health* (May 1964).

12. Howard Halpern, "Work Inhibition in Children," *The Psychoanalytic Review* (Summer, 1964).

13. *Fortune* (August, 1946). Also, George Gallup, *Gallup Poll* (Princeton: Audience Research, Inc., 1955).

Chapter II. The Masculinity Trap

1. Quoted by Samuel Grafton, "The Twisted Age," *Look* (December 15, 1964).

2. David M. Levy, *Maternal Overprotection* (New York: Columbia University Press, 1943).

3. Both studies reported by Eleanor E. Macoby, "Woman's Intellect," *The Potential of Woman*, Farber and Wilson, editors (New York: McGraw-Hill Book Co., 1963), p. 24 ff.

4. Edward T. Hall, *The Silent Language* (New York: Doubleday & Co., 1959), Premier Books edition, p. 50.

5. Edgar Z. Friedenberg, *The Vanishing Adolescent* (Boston: Beacon Press, 1959), p. 26 f. (Also London: Mayflower).

6. J. R. Seeley, R. A. Sim, and E. W. Loosley, *Crestwood Heights* (London: Constable, 1956), Ch. 12.

7. Clellan S. Ford and Frank A. Beach, *Patterns of Sexual Behavior* (New York: Harper & Bros. and Paul B. Hoeber, 1951).

8. Margaret Mead, *Sex and Temperament in Three Primitive Societies* (New York: William Morrow & Co., 1935), Part One.

9. Morton M. Hunt, *Her Infinite Variety* (New York: Harper & Row, 1962), p. 40.

10. Marmor, *op. cit.*, p. 10.

11. John Paul Scott, *Aggression* (Chicago: University of Chicago Press, 1958), p. 88 f.

12. Roger Brown, *Social Psychology* (New York: The Free Press, 1965), p. 171.

13. Helene Deutsch, *The Psychology of Women* (New York: Grune & Stratton, 1944), p. 222.

14. Quoted by Sapirstein, *op. cit.*, p. 192.

15. Deutsch, *op. cit.*, p. 138.

16. David Riesman, "Permissiveness and Sex Roles," *Marriage and Family Living* (August, 1959).

17. *Ibid.*

18. Komarovsky, *op. cit.*, p. 140 f. Wives also had areas which they were reluctant to discuss with their husbands, some overlapping areas the husbands had listed. But wives were much more prone to self-disclosure than husbands.

19. Seeley, Sim, and Loosley, *op. cit.*, p. 184.

20. Ernest Dichter, *Handbook of Consumer Motivations* (New York: Mc-Graw-Hill Book Co., 1964), p. 146.

21. *Playboy,* "Playboy Panel: The Womanization of America" (June 1962).

22. David F. Aberle and Kaspar D. Naegele, "Middle-Class Fathers' Occupational Role and Attitudes Toward Children," *The American Journal of Orthopsychiatry* (April, 1952).

23. Quoted by columnist Phyllis Battelle, "Assignment: America," New York *Journal-American* (February 27, 1964).

24. Roger Kahn, "Money, Muscles—and Myths," *Mass Leisure,* Larrabee and Meyersohn, editors (Illinois: The Free Press of Glencoe, 1958), p. 267.

25. Max Gunther, "The Female Fears That Bind a Man," *True* (February, 1965).

26. *Ibid.*

27. *Ibid.*

28. Daniel G. Brown, "Sex Role Development in a Changing Culture," *Psychological Bulletin,* Vol. 55, No. 4 (1958).

29. Ruth E. Hartley, "Sex-Role Pressures and the Socialization of the Male Child," *Psychological Reports,* Vol. 5 (1959).

30. Susan W. Gray, "Masculinity-Femininity in Relation to Anxiety and Social Acceptance," *Child Development* (June, 1957).

31. See, for instance, Walter B. Miller, "Lower-Class Culture as a Generating Milieu of Gang Delinquency," *The Journal of Social Issues,* Vol. XIV, No. 3 (1958).

Chapter III. Notes on the "Feminization" of Society

1. Morton M. Hunt, *The Natural History of Love* (New York: Alfred A. Knopf, Inc., 1959), p. 382.

2. Claude C. Bowman, "Are Husbands Slaves to Women?" *Coronet* (April, 1950).

3. Philip Wylie, "The Womanization of America," *Playboy* (September, 1958).

4. *Ibid.*

5. Margaret Mead, *Male and Female* (New York: William Morrow & Co., 1949), p. 159 (also London: Penguin Books).

6. *Time* (March 20, 1964), p. 85.
7. Quoted by Thomas J. Fleming, "The World of Women at Work," *This Week Magazine* (February 9, 1964).
8. Garda Bowman, *The Image of a Promotable Person*. Unpublished dissertation. Ch. VI, pp. 231-240. September 1962. Listed in Diss. Ab. See also her "What Helps or Harms Promotability," *Harvard Business Review* (Jan.-Feb. 1964).
9. Mead, *Male and Female*, p. 314 f.
10. Quoted by John Lear, "Will Science Change Marriage," *Saturday Review* (December 5, 1964).
11. Ruth E. Hartley, "Children's Concepts of Male and Female Roles," *Merrill-Palmer Quarterly* (January, 1960).
12. Lois M. Stolz, "Effects of Maternal Employment on Children, Evidence From Research," *Child Development* (December, 1960).
13. Mirra Komarovsky, *Women in the Modern World* (Boston: Little, Brown & Co., 1953), p. 197.
14. *Playboy* (June 1962).
15. Russel V. Lee, "The Agony of Conforming: The Male Parent," *Man and Civilization: The Family's Search for Survival*, Farber and Wilson, editors (New York: McGraw-Hill Book Co., 1965), p. 133.
16. *Ibid.*, p. 133 f.
17. *Ibid.*, p. 134.
18. Wylie, *op. cit.*

Chapter IV. Back to the Good Old Days: The Patriarchal Myth

1. John E. Snell, Richard J. Rosenwald, and Ames Robey, "The Wifebeaters' Wife," *Archives of General Psychiatry* (August, 1964).
2. T. W. Adorno and others, *The Authoritarian Personality* (New York: Harper & Bros., 1950).
3. Ralph Linton, "Women In The Family," Johnson E. Fairchild, editor, *Women, Society and Sex* (New York: Sheridan House, 1952), p. 71.
4. Elena Padilla, *Up From Puerto Rico* (New York: Columbia University Press, 1958), p. 150 f.
5. Blood and Wolfe, *op. cit.*, p. 52.
6. Hylan Lewis and Camille Jeffers, "Poverty and the Behavior of Low Income Families," presented at the annual meeting of the American Orthopsychiatric Association, in Chicago, Illinois, March 19, 1964.

7. Michael Young and Peter Wilmott, *Family and Kinship in East London* (London: Routledge & Kegan Paul, 1957), p. 32.

8. Herbert J. Gans, *The Urban Villagers* (London: Collier-Macmillan, 1962), Ch. 3.

9. Pearl Buck, *Of Men and Women* (New York: The John Day Co., 1941), p. 4.

10. *Ibid.*, p. 24.

11. Mark Zborowski and Elizabeth Herzog, *Life Is With People* (New York: International Universities Press, 1952), Ch. IV.

12. Victor A. Christopherson, "An Investigation of Patriarchal Authority in the Mormon Family," *Marriage and Family Living* (November, 1956). Christopherson concluded that in the present generation of Mormons the family is still father-controlled but is less so than in previous generations. But it may well be that if the previous generations had come under direct sociological scrutiny, they too would have been seen to be less patriarchal than commonly supposed.

13. William J. Goode, *The Family* (Englewood Cliffs: Prentice-Hall, Inc., 1964), p. 75.

14. Gans, *op. cit.*, p. 48.

15. It's extremely difficult for participants—or outsiders in uncontrolled situations—to gauge how much influence is wielded by whom in the decision-making process. Iowa State sociologist William Kenkel illustrated this in a structured decision-making study involving married couples. Before tackling a specific decision-making problem under observation, each husband-and-wife team was asked to predict which of the two would wield the most influence in settling the problem. Only 10 percent of the respondents were accurate in their predictions. When the decision-making session was over, the participants were asked to identify their own and their mates' relative influence in settling the problem. Just 22 percent made the correct identification. William Kenkel, "Family Interaction in Decision-Making on Spending," *Household Decision Making*, Nelson N. Foote, editor (New York: New York University Press, 1961), p. 159.

16. Robert S. Lynd and Helen Merrell Lynd, *Middletown* (New York: Harcourt, Brace & Co., 1929), p. 118 (also London: Constable).

17. Eric Dingwall, *The American Woman* (New York: Rinehart & Co., Inc., 1956), Ch. 2 (also London: Duckworth).

18. Ray W. Pettengill, translator, *Letters From America 1776-1779* (New York: Houghton Mifflin Co., 1924), p. 118.

19. Erik H. Erikson, *Childhood and Society* (London: Hogarth, 1950), Ch. 8.

20. *Ibid.*, p. 291 f.

21. Phyllis McGinley, *Sixpence in Her Shoe* (New York: The Macmillan Co., 1964), p. 25.

22. Hunt, *The Natural History of Love*, p. 316.

23. Robert Sunley, "Early Nineteenth Century American Literature on Childrearing," *Childhood in Contemporary Cultures*, Mead and Wolfenstein, editors (Chicago: University of Chicago Press, 1955), p. 152.

24. Quoted by Dixon Wecter, *The Saga of American Society* (New York: Charles Scribner's Sons, 1937), p. 290.

25. *Ibid.*, p. 292.

26. *Ibid.*, p. 294 f.

27. Sunley, *op. cit.*, p. 152.

28. Geoffrey Gorer, *The American People* (New York: W. W. Norton & Co., Inc., 1964), p. 54.

Chapter V. The Paradox of the Contemporary American Father

1. Quoted by Sapirstein, *op. cit.*, p. 191.

2. Erich Fromm, *The Art of Loving* (London: George Allen & Unwin, 1957), pp. 39, 50.

3. Ashley Montagu, *The Natural Superiority of Women* (London: George Allen & Unwin, 1952), p. 142.

4. Quoted by Don Oakley, New York *World-Telegram* (June 25, 1964). Lest it be thought Judge Scott is biased in favor of men, he has also championed the rights of women—particularly mothers—in Ohio.

5. Irene M. Josselyn, "Cultural Forces, Motherliness and Fatherliness," *American Journal of Orthopsychiatry* (April, 1956). The traditional view holds that the father should be the sole disciplinarian and the sole provider of conditional love, because it's his exclusive job to instill conscience. Thus, Fromm states (*op. cit.*, p. 43) that "Father's love should be guided by principles and expectations," and although he insists that the father ought to be "patient and tolerant," rather than "threatening and authoritarian," the effect is nevertheless a distancing and lack of spontaneity between father and child.

6. Sapirstein, *op. cit.*, p. 176.

7. Donald E. Payne and Paul H. Mussen, "Parent Child Relations and Father Identification Among Adolescent Boys," *The Journal of Abnormal and Social Psychology* (May, 1956). Also, Paul Mussen and Luther Distler, "Masculinity, Identification and Father-Son Relationships," *The Journal of Abnormal and Social Psychology* (November, 1959). Also, Charlotte Himber, "So He Hates Baseball," *The New York Times Magazine* (August 29, 1965).

8. William Iversen, "Love, Death and the Hubby Image," *Playboy* (September, 1963).

9. A. M. Greenwood, "How to Get More Mileage out of Daddy," *Family Circle* (June, 1965).

10. Jhan and June Robbins, "Why Young Husbands Feel Trapped," *Redbook* (March, 1962).

11. William S. White, New York *Journal-American* (April 12, 1965).

12. Josselyn, *op. cit.*

13. Nathan W. Ackerman, *The Psychodynamics of Family Life* (New York: Basic Books, Inc., 1958), p. 172.

14. Hunt, *Her Infinite Variety*, p. 170.

15. Bruno Bettelheim, "The Problem of Generations," *Daedalus* (Winter, 1962).

16. Hartley, "Sex Role Pressures and the Socialization of the Male Child," *op. cit.*

17. *Ibid.*

18. Seeley, Simm, and Loosley, *op. cit.*, p. 201

19. Levy, *op. cit.*

20. Otto O. von Mering, "Forms of Fathering in Relation to Mother-Child Pairs," *The Significance of the Father* (New York: Family Service Association of America, 1959), p. 7.

21. *Newsweek* (November 30, 1964).

22. Quoted by Phyllis Battelle, New York *Journal-American* (March 25, 1965).

23. Hillel Black, *They Shall Not Pass* (New York: William Morrow & Co., 1963), p. 23. Also, John Keats, *The Sheepskin Psychosis* (New York: J. B. Lippincott Co., 1965).

24. Quoted by Joseph Lelyveld, "The Paradoxical Case of the Affluent Delinquent," *The New York Times Magazine* (October 4, 1964).

25. Gibson Winter, *Love and Conflict* (New York: Doubleday & Co., 1958), p. 73.

Q

Chapter VI. Potency and the Sexual Revolution

1. David Riesman, *The Lonely Crowd* (New Haven: Yale University Press, 1950), p. 174.

2. Quoted by Leonard W. Robinson, "English Secretaries Must Have 'Nous,'" *The New York Times Magazine* (December 20, 1964).

3. James S. Coleman, *The Adolescent Society* (London: Collier-Macmillan, 1961), p. 120 ff. Also Ira L. Reiss, *Premarital Sexual Standards in America* (London: Collier-Macmillan, 1960).

4. Among the explanations that Freud considered accounted for the virginity taboo were primitive man's dread of blood, his fear of the unknown, and his fear of "mysterious" woman herself—that she would take his strength from him, infect him with her femininity, and prove him weak: "The effect of coitus in discharging tensions and inducing flaccidity may be a prototype of what these fears represent. . . . There is nothing in all this which is extinct, which is not still alive in the heart of man today." Sigmund Freud, *Sexuality and the Psychology of Love* (New York: Collier Books, 1963), p. 70 ff. For other discussions of man's age-old sexual fear of and antagonism toward women, see Milton R. Sapirstein, *Paradoxes of Everyday Life* (New York: Random House, 1955), Ch. 1, and H. R. Hays, *The Dangerous Sex* (New York: G. P. Putnam's Sons, 1964).

5. Abram Kardiner, *Sex and Morality* (New York: The Bobbs-Merrill Co., Inc., 1954), Charter Books edition, p. 144 f.

6. For detailed accounts of this belief, see G. Rattray Taylor, *Sex in History* (London: Thames & Hudson, 1953), and Allen Edwards and R. E. L. Masters, *The Cradle of Erotica* (New York: The Julian Press, 1963).

7. Measuring one's sexual prowess against the Kinsey tables (or against that of other couples) is totally fallacious, however. Individuals vary widely in their sexual needs and sexual drives, as the two Kinsey reports made obvious. Furthermore, the Kinsey reports measure sexual adjustment and adequacy solely on the basis of one unit—the orgasm. But people do go to bed with each other for reasons that have nothing to do with racking up a high orgasmic score, and there's no correlation between high orgasmic frequency and sexual adequacy. Some of the men and women with the most orgasms to their credit are fundamentally among the most inadequate.

8. Komarovsky, *Blue-Collar Marriage,* p. 83.

9. Phyllis and Eberhard Kronhausen, *Sex Histories of American College Men* (New York: Ballantine Books, 1960), p. 152 f.

10. Gael Greene, *Sex and the College Girl* (London: Mayflower), Ch. 7.

11. *Playboy* (June, 1962).

12. Her instincts may, however, serve her well in terms of marital happiness. Studies show that marriages are happier when the wife, rather than the husband, is the more inhibited one. It seems that men would rather be sexually frustrated than continually face a reminder of their inadequacy.

13. Eduardes and Masters, *op. cit.*, p. 5.

14. Josselyn, *op. cit.*

15. Coleman, *op. cit.*, p. 121 f.

16. Grace and Fred Hechinger, *Teen-Age Tyranny* (London: Duckworth, 1964), Ch. 2.

17. Philip Wylie, *Generation of Vipers* (London: Muller, 1955), Ch. VI.

18. Komarovsky, *Blue-Collar Marriage,* p. 84 ff.

19. Joseph Stein, *Maturity in Sex and Marriage* (New York: Coward-McCann, Inc., 1963), p. 150.

20. *Ibid.*, p. 149.

21. John M. Murtagh and Sara Harris, *Cast the First Stone* (London: McGraw-Hill Book Co., 1963), Ch. 11.

Chapter VII. New Ways to Manliness

1. Leonard J. Duhl, "The American Character—Crisis, Change and Complexity," *The Journal of Nervous and Mental Disease,* Vol. 137, No. 2 (August, 1963).

2. Marya Mannes, "I, Mary, Take Thee, John, as . . . What?" *The New York Times Magazine* (November 14, 1965).

3. Robert Blauner, *Alienation and Freedom* (Chicago: University of Chicago Press, 1964), Ch. 2.

4. See, for instance, C. Wright Mills, *White Collar* (New York: Oxford University Press, 1953); Fred H. Blum, *Toward a Democratic Work Process* (New York: Harper & Bros., 1953); and Daniel Bell, *Work and Its Discontents* (Boston: Beacon Press, 1956). With job mobility becoming the mode for increasing numbers of Americans, even the emotional value of working with other men and of becoming a member of the team is lessened in contemporary times.

5. Vance Packard, *The Waste Makers* (New York: David McKay Co., Inc., 1960), p. 233 (also London: Longmans).

6. Harold L. Sheppard and others, *Too Old to Work—Too Young to Retire: A Case Study of a Permanent Plant Shutdown,* for the Special Committee on Unemployment Problems, 86th Congress, 1st Session (December 21, 1959).

7. Walter Buckingham, *Automation* (New York: Harper & Row, 1961), Mentor Executive Library edition, p. 63.

8. Vance Packard, *The Status Seekers* (London: Longmans, 1959), Ch. 8.

9. Ben B. Seligman, "Man, Work, and the Automated Feast," *Mass Society in Crisis,* Rosenberg, Gerver, and Howton, editors (London: Collier-Macmillan, 1964), pp. 468 ff.

10. Sheppard, *op. cit.*

11. Robert S. Lynd and Helen Merrell Lynd, *Middletown in Transition* (New York: Harcourt, Brace & Co., 1937), p. 178 (also London: Constable).

12. Paul Lazarsfeld, *Die Arbeitslosen von Marienthal* (Leipzig: Hirzel, 1933).

13. Mirra Komarovsky, *The Unemployed Man and His Family* (New York: Institute of Social Research, 1940), p. 74.

14. Donald E. Super, *The Psychology of Careers* (New York: Harper & Bros., 1957), p. 159.

15. *Ibid.,* p. 160.

16. M. Robert Gomberg, *Child Study* (Summer, 1957). It also helps if the parents don't reflect confusion in terms of what they expect of the child. But such confusion is often evident. In one study of an upper-middle-class group the following patterns were noted: (1) Mothers more often do the punishing; (2) both parents want both boys and girls to be bold and daring; (3) mothers more often than fathers prefer submissive boys; (4) fathers want their daughters to be traditionally feminine; (5) mothers prefer their daughters to be more masculine in behavior than the fathers do; and (6) the children see the mother, not the father, as the more influential figure in their lives. M. Radke, *The Relation of Parental Authority to Children's Behavior and Attitudes* (Minneapolis: University of Minnesota Press, 1946).

17. Private communication to the author.

18. Elizabeth Bott, "Conjugal Roles and Social Networks," *Family and Social Network* (London: Tavistock Publications, Ltd., 1957), Ch. 3.

19. *Ibid.*

20. Ernest W. Burgess and Leonard S. Cottrell Jr., *Predicting Success or Failure in Marriage* (New York: Prentice-Hall, Inc., 1939), p. 182 f. Although happiness is a rather tenuous quality to measure, several other studies do show a high correlation between marital happiness and equalitarianism in marriage. Dr. Paul Popenoe told me of one such study his organization made. The results: of the marriages where the wife was dominant, 47 percent were rated as happy; where the husband was dominant, 61 percent were so rated; of the equalitarian marriages, 87 percent were rated as happy.

21. But society would have to provide services to facilitate such an arrangement—for instance, day-care centers, educational institutions willing to provide part-time or discontinuous education to women, and part-time or half-day employment.

22. Dr. Emily Mudd sees many men who are "good cooks, and who love their gardens, and who are nurturing kinds of people" married to more competitive women. If they could reverse roles, she says, these couples "could be very happy," provided that society put no onus on this. Many experts would insist that such a drastic interchange of roles always produces identity problems for the children, if not for the adults. Problems invariably occur, of course, since at present society doesn't permit this kind of arrangement without considerable loss of status. It should be remembered, however, that identity problems also occur when the marriage partners play the traditional roles but are unsuited to and ineffectual in them. This whole area is rife for more intensive and unprejudiced socioscientific study than it has been getting. For one man's experiences in role reversal, see "Dilemmas of a Househusband," *Saturday Review* (January 2, 1965), p. 100.

23. Dr. Abraham H. Maslow's studies of self-actualizers—fully functioning individuals—relate to the traits I discuss here. See A. H. Maslow *Motivation and Personality* (New York: Harper & Bros., 1954) and his *Toward a Psychology of Being* (New York: D. Van Nostrand Co., Inc., 1962).

24. William James, *Essays on Faith and Morals* (Cleveland: The World Publishing Co., 1962).

25. Margaret Mead, "Must Our Children Fear the Future," *Redbook* (March, 1962).

26. Montagu, *op. cit.*, p. 141. Also, J. B. Priestley, "Women Don't Run the Country," *Saturday Evening Post* (December 5, 1964).

27. Reported by the New York *Herald Tribune* (March 12, 1965).

28. Erich Fromm, *The Sane Society* (New York: Holt, Rinehart, Winston, Inc., 1955), p. 339 (also London: Routledge).

29. Robert L. Heilbroner, *The Future as History* (New York: Harper & Bros., 1959), p. 74.

Index

GEORGE ALLEN & UNWIN LTD
London: 40 Museum Street, W.C.1

Auckland: P.O. Box 36013, Northcote Central, N.4
Bombay: 15 Graham Road, Ballard Estate, Bombay 1
Barbados: P.O. Box 222, Bridgetown
Buenos Aires: Escritorio 454-459, Florida 165
Calcutta: 17 Chittaranjan Avenue, Calcutta 13
Cape Town: 68 Shortmarket Street
Hong Kong: 105 Wing On Mansion, 26 Hancow Road, Kowloon
Ibadan: P.O. Box 62
Karachi: Karachi Chambers, McLeod Road
Madras: Mohan Mansions, 38c Mount Road, Madras 6
Mexico: Villalongin 32-10, Piso, Mexico 5, D.F.
Nairobi: P.O. Box 4536
New Delhi: 13-14 Asaf Ali Road, New Delhi 1
Ontario: 81 Curlew Drive, Don Mills
Rio de Janeiro: Caixa Postal 2537-Zc-00
São Paulo: Caxa Postal 8675
Singapore: 36c Prinsep Street, Singapore 7
Sydney, N.S.W.: Bradbury House, 55 York Street
Tokyo: P.O. Box 26, Kamata

SEXUAL LIFE AFTER SIXTY

ISADORE RUBIN

Demy 8vo

Sexual Life After Sixty is the first work to demolish the misconceptions that hinder a full, healthy and creative expression of sexuality in the later years.

Drawing on the most recent clinical and research data about sex functioning, needs, problems and interests in the years after sixty, it punctures myths surrounding frequency of intercourse, the years of sexual activity, menopause, masturbation, and the prevalence of psychological deviation in the sexuality of elderly men. It deals with the sexual changes that take place in ageing; reviews present and past attempts at rejuvenation and 'control' of ageing; and scrutinizes sex health frauds which have made older people their special victims.

Dr Rubin openly assesses 'the fear of failure' and other baseless anxieties; sex-hormone treatments; and the effects on sexual functioning of special health problems common in the later years, including heart disease, prostatic difficulty, hypertension and diabetes. He offers guidance to the post-menopausal woman; the person with inadequate sex response; and those who have had a hysterectomy, sex-organ surgery or other operation.

In a concluding section Dr Rubin outlines a strategy of living that dramatizes the need for society to recognize the normality of sex in this rapidly increasing sector of our population and the right of older people to express their sexuality freely and without guilt.

Dr Rubin has been Managing Editor of *Sexology* magazine since 1956. He is a Fellow of the Society for the Scientific Study of Sex; Treasurer of the Sex Information and Education Council of the United States and a member of the American Association of Marriage Counsellors, the National Council on Family Relations and the American Social Health Association.

LET'S GET WELL

ADELLE DAVIS

Demy 8vo

Adelle Davis is considered one of America's most highly regarded nutritionists, and her earlier books have been highly praised by leading experts in the field as well as by doctors and by patients who have benefited from her counsel.

Now Miss Davis has completed a book of even greater significance and practical value, a nutritional guide to aid in recovery from illness. In this remarkable book, she tells the millions who suffer from illness in which a lack of nutrients is a contributing cause, how proper diet can help restore health.

In simple non-technical terms, backed by medical references, Miss Davis reviews the scientific literature indicating that recuperation can be hastened by the proper selection of natural foods and the use of supplements.

Here are some recommended nutritional principles to aid recovery from such diseases as heart attacks, ulcers, diabetes, arthritis, gout and anaemia, Miss Davis also explains the function of nutrition in disease, related to the blood system, the digestive system, the liver, the gall bladder, the kidneys, the nervous system, the muscles, the skin, and in burns, accidents, surgery and sexual problems. Interesting case histories illustrate her points. The book includes a comprehensive index and tables of food composition.

BETTER SMOKING

MICHAEL SCHRODER

Cr. 8vo. Paper and cloth editions

NEW LIFE THROUGH BREATHING

WILLIAM P. KNOWLES

Cr. 8vo

Medical statisticians estimate that in Britain last year over 3,000,000 men, women and children suffered from serious disorders of the bronchial and respiratory system. Bronchitis is recognized as the most costly and deadly of all Britain's diseases: it costs annually over £20,000,000 for treatment and sickness benefits and accounts for the loss of some 30,000,000 working days at a cost to the economy estimated at over £150,000,000 or about 3 per cent of the national budget.

If we live in the United Kingdom, or in certain other countries where the expectation of life is long and the weather less than ideal, conventional medicine can do little save tell us that we must accept as an occupational hazard the strong possibility that we shall cough our way to the grave. William Knowles believes otherwise. For fifty years he has been practising and preaching a simple but fundamental discipline of exercises—in slow, deep breathing—with no mystical content, occupying only some ten minutes a day and developing rather than disorder the natural rhythm into a new habit or regime. These exercises aim to relieve the symptoms of even the most serious and chronic chest complaints; in many cases to lead to lasting cures, to build up in the healthy body resistance to respiratory ailments; to restore to the majority of those who spend much of their life bent over a desk, lathe or sink the benefits of breathing from a more natural posture and to effect a general toning-up of the system which would itself lead to increased resistance to fatigue, nervous disorders and perhaps more organic (but apparently unrelated) diseases —in short to promote better health through better breathing.

LONDON: GEORGE ALLEN AND UNWIN LTD